School Methods with Younger Children

A Handbook for Teachers in Africa

Margaret Grant, M.Ed.

Diploma in the Psychology of Childhood (University of Birmingham)

Evans Brothers Limited

Published by
Evans Brothers Limited
Montague House, Russell Square, London WC1B 5BX

Evans Brothers (Nigeria Publishers) Limited
PMB 5164, Jericho Road, Ibadan

First published 1960
Fourth impression 1964
Second edition 1968
Third impression 1971
Third edition 1972
Second impression 1973
Third impression 1974
Fourth edition 1978

Cover photograph
by James Ralton

Printed in Great Britain by T. and A. Constable Ltd., Hopetoun Street, Edinburgh

ISBN 0 237 50001 9   PRA 6313

Contents

I dedicate this book to the students of W. T. C. Ilesha, in gratitude for all they did to help me understand their country and traditions.

To The Reader

During the years when I helped to train teachers for Primary schools in West Africa, I felt the lack of students' reference books, written in simple English for that part of the world. That need prompted me to write this book. The methods you will find explained here have been well tried by me, by other teachers or by my students. I do not claim that my suggestions are original or that they are the only ones which can be used successfully. At the end of this book is a list of books which I have found helpful.

I have tried to fulfil the following aims:

1. To give students who are in training for Primary school teaching an introduction to the principles behind teaching methods, and to help them to gain some understanding of Primary school children.
2. To deal mainly with methods for the younger children, of about five to nine years old.
3. To make my suggestions as practical as possible.
4. To limit myself to the type of work which might be included in a teachers' certificate examination, yet to show that this is only a beginning and that a good teacher will continue to learn by observation, study and experience all his life.

I am greatly indebted to Miss N. Dalton for all her help especially, with the Infant methods; to my sister, Patricia Mitchell; to Mr W. Curr; and to Mr C. T. Quinn-Young for their careful scrutiny of the script and their helpful criticisns.

Recently there have been a number of advances in our understanding of how a child develops and learns. Some sections have been rewritten.

MARGARET GRANT

SUGGESTIONS FOR FURTHER READING

Ruth M. Beard   *An Outline of Piaget's Development Psychology for Students and Teachers*, Routledge & Kegan Paul

G. Cuisenaire and C. Gattengo   *Numbers in Colour*, William Heinemann Ltd.

M. O. A. Durojaiye   *A New Introduction to Educational Psychology*, Evans Brothers

F. G. French   *The Teaching of English Abroad, Parts 1 & 2*, Oxford University Press

W. R. Lee   *The Dolphin English Course, Teacher's Books 1 & 2*, Oxford University Press

M. S. Nielsen   *Biology and Hygiene for Tropical Schools, Books 1 & 2*, Evans Brothers

D. J. Williams   *English Teaching in the Primary School*, Evans Brothers

Part one   Education and the School

Chapter 1 The Aims of Education

When parents send a child to school, they expect the teachers to educate him. What do we as teachers mean by education? We mean our effort to train the child's whole being, helping his mind, body and personality to grow to the full. The aim of education is therefore to help the child to develop as well as possible intellectually, physically, morally, socially and emotionally.

We shall consider each one of these points separately.

Intellectual Development

In school we spend a great deal of our time teaching the child facts, which he has to remember, but a truly educated person should think for himself.

Encourage each child in your class to *think*. Do not always tell the child the answers to questions; ask him to find the answer by reading books or by making experiments. After the child has put some effort and thought into the question, ask him to tell you what he has discovered and then give him further help. For example, if you want the child to learn that two threes make six, instead of telling him, 'Two threes are six', give him some stones and ask him to count out six of them. Tell him to put three in one group and three in another group. 'How many groups of three have you?' 'Two groups of three.' 'Good.' 'How many stones altogether?' 'Six.' 'Two groups of three make six.'

Having found the answer by doing and thinking, the child will remember it much better. What is even more important, he will understand how the answer was obtained. As another example, to teach how a seed grows let the child plant it in a glass jar and watch it grow.

In this way not only have you taught the facts but the child has also had to think and observe for himself. If a child wants to know how far it is from Lagos to Accra and how the two ports trade, show him the kind of geography book, or reference book, perhaps even an encyclopaedia, which will help him and let him discover the answer for himself.

Language is most important for intellectual development. Too often children sit quietly in class copying exercises, when they should be talking to each other and to the teacher. Each child should be encouraged to express his thoughts clearly, and in an interesting manner. Try in each lesson to give all the children opportunities to think and to express their thoughts in words. This may mean more preparation for the teacher but it is very important, because each child should be helped to increase his intellectual capacity.

Physical Development

Physical education should not end with the Physical Education lesson. The teacher should help the child's body to grow strong and healthy. Hygiene and the correct diet are important. Teach each child to sit and stand properly, as continued bad posture will retard and spoil good growth. Make sure that the school meals, if these are provided, are nourishing and prepared under clean conditions.

If a child has a speech defect or has trouble with his ears or eyes, a good teacher will help him to get proper treatment. Watch for any illness in the class, and see that a sick child is given medical attention. The healthy children must be protected, so a child suffering from an infectious disease should be prevented from attending school until he is quite better.

Sleep is most important if the child is to grow well. Far too many children are unable to do their best work because they are tired; teachers should advise the children and their parents, so that at night each child has a really good rest in a well-ventilated room. A teacher who watches all these points will be helping each child to develop his best physical powers.

Moral Development

Children have to learn the difference between right and wrong. This is usually taught through religion, but it should be taught also any time during the school day when something happens to give the teacher an opportunity to explain what is right or what is wrong.

Suppose a child is honest and brings you a school pen he has found in the playground; praise him and tell the class they must all try to be honest. If a child is truthful even when it might bring him trouble, praise him for being brave enough to tell the truth. Tell a child who is weak at spelling or at doing sums to do his best without copying, for if he copies from the child next to him the teacher will not be able to tell how much he really knows, and will not be able to help him properly.

Though it may be necessary sometimes, try not to draw much attention to the wrong that children do. Always stress what is good and right. Stories of good men and women will encourage children to copy such people. Show each child how the wrong things he does make other people unhappy, while the good he does makes other people happy. The teacher's example is most important if children are to develop well morally. They will notice how the teacher behaves and will imitate him.

Social Development

Children must learn to live in harmony with other people. At school a child is a member of a bigger group than at home. He has to learn to live and work peacefully with children from other families.

When a child works in a group he will learn to take his turn and to share books, and things like paint or clay, with other children. If a child is in a team the teacher can let the team compete to collect the most marks, and each child will learn that if he does well the whole team will benefit, but if he does bad work the whole team will suffer and will lose marks. Encourage each child to consider and help others who are weaker than himself. Sick children can be sent cheerful letters, lame children can be treated kindly and small children can be taken safely home.

The social development of the child is most important, as it will help him to play his part as a good citizen of his country.

Emotional Development

Children must learn to control their anger if something does not please them. A child must try to be brave and not be fearful unnecessarily; he must learn to love and to be kind instead of hating or hurting others.

The teacher should help each child to use his emotions in the right way. He can be angry about evil things such as ignorance and injustice, and try to put these things right. Encourage the child to be brave, but help him to realize there are some things it is right to fear. He should fear playing with fire, for he may get burned, fear crossing the road without looking first, as he may get hurt; and fear making others unhappy through selfishness.

A child needs an outlet for his emotions, and plenty of hard work and creative work will help him to keep them under control. Let him express good emotions like love, by giving him opportunities to help other people. By imitating the good teacher a child will be greatly helped in his emotional development.

We must remember that the child should be the centre of all educational aims, and all we do will be to help him to develop to the best of his ability. Good examination results do not necessarily proclaim a well-educated person, whereas a conscientious worker, an honest thoughtful citizen, a helpful neighbour, an upright, kind husband or wife and a sensible parent do show that a man or woman is well educated.

Chapter 2   The School

What is a School?

First a piece of land and a building must be acquired; it is often necessary to erect a suitable building. Then the building has to be furnished and equipped. Before the children can be taught in the school, suitable teachers led by a headteacher must be appointed. The teachers must have the knowledge and ability to teach, and the head must be able to help and direct them. Finally, though it may seem obvious, there can be no school without children. The children are the most important part of the school, and for them everything should be planned. We shall consider, in turn, all the factors that make a school.

It is realized, of course, that many teachers who read this book may have little personal say in the site for a school or in the school building itself, though they should certainly have some say regarding equipment. The suggestions are included however in the hope that teachers will always use their influence with school authorities in order that the children can be taught under the best conditions.

The Compound for the School

A dry compound on slightly high ground should be chosen, because during the rainy season water will drain fairly quickly from high land, while it will remain longer on low land, thus making the ground damp and swampy. The compound should not be near a market, a railway station or any other noisy place. If possible it should not be on a main road, because the traffic will be disturbing, and during the dry season the cars and lorries driving past will make the school dusty. The site should be a reasonable walking distance from the homes of the children. Infant children particularly should not have to walk far to school, or they will be tired before they start their work. If possible pipes should be laid to bring water from the town supply; but if not, a good well should be dug, so that the children will have easy access to water. Hygiene cannot be taught without a reasonable supply of water.

The compound should be big enough to provide space for the following: (*a*) the school building; (*b*) a large field for Physical Education and games; (*c*) gardens and flower beds; (*d*) a school farm; (*e*) a rough space for digging and making models; (*f*) space for future building if the numbers in the school increase, as they probably will when more and more children desire to be educated.

When the compound is cleared a number of shady trees should be left, or new ones planted, so that the children may sit under them during outdoor lessons. The trees should not be too near the school or they may make the classrooms dark.

The Building

Single-storey schools are best for young children, as stairs may cause accidents. Each room should be big enough for the children to sit at desks when necessary, and yet leave a good space between desks, so that the teacher can easily reach each child to give individual help. There should be sufficient room for the arrangement of groups and for dramatics. The headteacher should have a separate room, where he can receive parents and visitors, and where he can keep his records and accounts. The teachers should have a staff room where they can sit at recess and lunch-time. A store room is necessary for keeping books, apparatus and extra equipment. There should be a latrine for every twenty-five or thirty children, and two for the staff.

A Suggested Plan for a Primary School Building

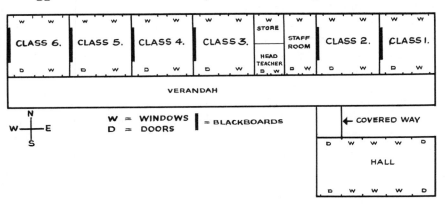

If there is not enough money to build a hall, it can be left until later Instead of a wall between classes 5 and 6 there can be a movable partition, which must, however, fit firmly, so that talking in one room cannot be heard in the next. If necessary, the two rooms can be cleared and used as a hall. All the floors should be concreted, so that they can easily be kept clean, and also to prevent white ants getting into the building. The walls should be colourwashed and kept in good repair. Round the walls there should be a number of wooden rails, so that pictures and charts can easily be hung up for the children to see; these rails should be at the children's

7

eye level. The shutters for the windows must hook on the outside walls when they are open, and strong bolts should be fitted to lock them at night. Each classroom should have a ceiling, to prevent noise travelling from one class to the next. If possible the outside woodwork should be painted; this looks more attractive and will preserve the wood.

This plan is simple, and should be fairly cool while providing plenty of light in the rooms. In the morning the sun will not shine into the classrooms to dazzle the children. When the sun reaches the south it will be high in the sky and will shine on the roof but not through the windows; a good ceiling will help to keep the classrooms cool. The windows should be as big as possible. An overhanging roof will help to keep the rooms cool in the hot season and will help to prevent the rain blowing in during the rainy season. If the roof is extended over the verandah it will shelter the children when passing from one room to the next. A large wall blackboard should be put in each room when the school is being built.

There are some new ideas in education and these require a different type of building. Teachers should study the new ideas carefully before making a decision about them.

The Integrated Day

The timetable is not one of lessons but of large blocks of time, for example all one morning may be given to Maths and Language, and all another morning may be given to creative activities. All subjects can be studied by different children in the same class during the morning. The idea is that each child should work at his own speed and interest. To a child all knowledge is one. It is we adults who split it up into subjects. For example, a child may be studying 'The Market'. He reads about it, writes about it (factual knowledge and imaginative stories), learns poems and songs about the market, and draws and paints it. He makes models (Craft); he works out a storekeeper's bills (Maths); he finds where the goods come from (Geography and Environmental Studies); he discovers how old it is, and how the market has changed with the years (History); he asks how the community uses it and how it can serve the neighbourhood (Civic Studies). Integrated days mean integrated studies. Learning in all subjects goes on side by side centred on the theme which the children are studying.

The Market, Buildings in Our Town, Farms in Our Area, Water, Transport, The Post Office, People Who Help Us, Growth, Happiness, A Local Building Site, are all themes within the children's experience. The teacher would try to expand this experience by helping the children to study the part of the theme, which is most interesting to them. When a child has done some good work he will tell the other children about it, and the class will discuss together. The children will help each other to learn. They will learn to co-operate. Sometimes a child will work alone, sometimes the whole class will work together. Plenty of space and equipment is needed and this will affect the design of the building.

An Open-Plan School
Because of the integrated day, some schools are built without definite classrooms, but have work areas instead: an art and craft area, a language area, a maths and science area, an environmental area, a music area, etc. There must be plenty of apparatus, books and materials. The children can move freely from one area to another. This means the teachers will probably decide to work together.

Team Teaching
The teachers will work as a team of two or three. Maybe in some schools all the teachers will be in the team. A teacher who is specially interested in maths will help in the maths area not only his own pupils but children from other classes as well. It is necessary for the teachers to like each other and be able to work together. One lazy teacher will spoil the team. In this sort of teaching system walls between the classrooms are unnecessary as the children should be free to move from one area to another. The school building will have to be designed in an open-plan way.

These are very brief descriptions of some new trends in education, and how they may affect buildings. The ideas may not suit your school, nor your area, but every teacher should be knowledgeable and able to discuss these ideas with inspectors and parents.

Equipment for the Classroom
1. There should be good blackboard space (one wall blackboard about three metres long, and one blackboard on an easel which can be moved).
2. A blackboard ruler, chalks and a duster.
3. Storage cupboards (as large as possible) with locks, and boxes with lids and locks for storing books and apparatus.
4. Movable tables or table desks and chairs with backs. All these should be light and easily moved. The size depends on the height of the children, whose feet should touch the floor, but whose legs should not be cramped.
5. Slates, chalks and slate-cleaners (for infants).
6. Tables for models, science displays, etc.
7. Textbooks and writing material.
8. Teacher's table, desk and chair.
9. Register, diary, record books and timetable.
10. Art and Craft equipment . . . paint, brushes, clay-boards, paste, scissors, sewing materials, raffia, cane for baskets (many of these things can be obtained from bush or scrap materials).

9

11. Various types of apparatus, depending on the age of the children, for Reading, Arithmetic, English, etc.
12. Cardboard, inks, pens and paints for making apparatus.
13. Books for a class library; book-shelves or a table.
14. A wastepaper basket.
15. A basin for clean water for washing.
16. Container for pure drinking water. Each child should have his own cup or calabash, as it is not hygienic for children to use the same cup.
17. A good clock. (This may be shared with other classes.)
18. Brushes and dusters for cleaning the classroom.

Equipment to be shared by all the Classes
1. Equipment for games and Physical Education.
2. Musical instruments.
3. A slide projector.
4. A gramophone and a radio.
5. A first-aid box.
6. Mats for sitting on the floor.

With a limited amount of money the most important equipment should of course be bought first.

The School and the Community
(i) *The Duty of the School to the Community*
1. To give the children in the community a good education.
2. To train the children to be good citizens, so that the community will benefit in the future.
3. To have Parent-Teacher meetings, so that the parents are kept informed of the progress of the children, and if necessary can be advised how best to care for their children.
4. To encourage parents and relations to visit the school, and see the children at their work.
5. To hold adult classes after school hours, when illiterate people in the community can be taught to read and write.
6. To help the people of the community to plan and build sufficient good schools, and keep them well equipped for the needs of the children.
7. To help to improve the standard of health, farming, housing, etc., through the education of the children.

(ii) *The Duty of the Community to the School*
1. To see that the school is properly equipped, so that the children can take full advantage of their education.

2. To co-operate with the teachers for the benefit of the children, by visiting the school when invited and by showing an interest in the work of the school.

3. To try to put into practice any advice the headteacher or teachers may give for the good of the children.

4. To see that the children go to school at the right age, attend punctually, and are neatly dressed.

5. To see that the school is supplied with the correct number of good, well-qualified teachers.

Chapter 3 The Staff

The Headteacher
The headteacher has a most important job to do, and on his or her ability depends the smooth running of the school. He or she has a number of responsibilities and we shall study each in turn.

The Headteacher's Responsibility to the Children
1. To make sure that the classrooms, furniture, compound, teaching equipment and health conditions are suitable and adequate for the children.
2. To teach by example good manners, kindness, punctuality, honesty and rules for health and good citizenship. To know all the children in the school by name, and to take at least one lesson per week in each class, so that he or she can judge how the children are progressing.
3. To see that children are admitted to the school at the correct age and time in the school year according to the regulations of the Ministry of Education. To see that the children are placed in the class most suitable to their age and ability.
4. If a class teacher is absent, to see that the children are kept busy and are well supervised. The headteacher should do this himself or herself as often as possible as two classes suffer if a class teacher is asked to supervise two classes at the same time.
5. To make sure that each class teacher helps every individual child to make reasonable progress, and that no child receives corporal punishment unless it is justified and the punishment book is signed.
6. To observe, help, direct and encourage classroom work and **really** know what is happening in the school. The headteacher should hardly ever be found in his or her room, but should be found involved with the children.

The Headteacher's Responsibility to the Teachers
1. To ensure the co-operation of the staff. To hold regular staff meetings at which the teachers can discuss their problems and give suggestions for the smooth running of the school. If possible these suggestions should be used so that the teachers feel that they are all working together for the good of the children. The headteacher should make sure that all the teachers know the rules and aims of the school.

2. To assist the teachers, giving them the benefit of his or her knowledge and experience, and so improve the standard of the school. Inexperienced and untrained teachers should be particularly guided and helped.
3. To draw up syllabuses suitable for each class, using as a guide any syllabus published by the Ministry of Education. To help the teachers make schemes of work and lesson notes.
4. To plan the timetable for the whole school, so that each teacher is guided to divide the time in school reasonably between the subjects in the syllabus.
5. To check registers and record books.
6. To see that there is an equal distribution of class and school duties among the teachers.

The Headteacher's Responsibility to the Parents

The headteacher should try to get the co-operation of the parents, so that the school and home will work together for the good of the children. He or she should form a Parent-Teacher Association, arrange for an Open Day occasionally and plan to have one afternoon per week when parents can come to discuss problems confidentially.

(I shall explain each of these functions and show how they help the parents to co-operate with the school.)

Parent-Teacher Association

Meetings are held once or twice a term and all the parents are invited. The parents can bring their problems and ideas for discussion, and the teachers can help. If they wish, the parents can see their children's work, and discuss the syllabuses.

The headteacher has a good opportunity for giving the parents a short talk about the aims and methods of Maths or Reading or Science or Hygiene or the needs of each child physically or socially. If a child is backward because he or she is always tired in school, or does not get sufficient nourishing food, and, therefore, has no energy to work, the teachers can encourage parents to correct these troubles. The teachers can do a great deal to advise the parents but they must beware of being proud and showing off their knowledge, or the parents may feel angry or ashamed and may not come to the next meeting. A good friendly relationship between the school and home will greatly benefit the children.

Open Days

These are held once, or at the most twice, a year. The school is open all day to the inspection of the parents and friends of the children. Exercise books, art, craft and needlework are all on show, and a short concert or demonstration lessons may be given. By showing the parents what happens in school their interest will be aroused, and when they find the teachers are real friends and guides to their children, the school may be sure of the parents' co-operation.

Visiting the School

Some parents have special problems that they wish to discuss with the headteacher. If the headteacher lets the parents know that there is one afternoon each week for them, they will not come and disturb the school routine at other times. A good head knows all the children and should be able to advise the parents, but if the class teacher can help, the head must see that the class is supervised when the teacher is busy with the parent. It is not good for the child to overhear such discussions.

The Headteacher's Responsibility to the Ministry of Education, the Proprietor and the Managers

1. To see that the school buildings are kept in good condition, and that faults are reported so that they can be repaired.
2. To carry out the policy of the Ministry of Education, and of the governing organization.
3. To see that school records and books are properly kept and checked.
4. The educational standard of the school, and the standard of discipline are the responsibility of the headteacher.

The Primary School Teacher

Teachers should never forget that their work is most important, and the state of the country in thirty or forty years will largely depend on how well the teachers of today have performed their duty. A teacher can have a great influence on a class, not only by what he says but also by his actions. Children notice everything their teacher does and they copy a great deal of it. It is no good telling children to speak the truth unless they always hear the teacher speaking the truth. It is no good telling them to be punctual and tidy unless the teacher is punctual and tidy himself. Below are listed a number of qualities which a teacher should have. For simplicity I shall refer to the teacher as 'he', but obviously the qualities apply equally to men and women.

1. The teacher should be a person worth copying.
2. He should be very interested in children, and should have endless patience with them.
3. The children should know they can rely on him and can trust his word. He should never make idle promises or threats.
4. He should guide the children in a friendly manner and they should never be afraid to come to him for help.

5. He must be interested in the things which interest children, and should listen with understanding to their news.

6. He should be enthusiastic and active in his work, so that he can pass on his enthusiasm and interest to the children.

7. He should have a knowledge of the needs of children, and of the best ways of teaching children at different stages.

8. He should have the ability to explain things in a simple and imaginative manner.

9. He should be a person who is interested in increasing his own general knowledge, and he should remember that a teacher will never know everything about teaching. He should continue to try to improve his methods by reading, attending vacation courses, and by experimenting.

10. He should be a happy and lively person whom the children and their parents can respect.

A good training is very necessary to help a teacher develop his interest and ability for teaching children. No one should enter or remain in the teaching profession unless he is determined to do his best for the children. Incalculable harm can be done by lazy or careless teachers.

Chapter 4   The Child

Because the most important person in our education system is the child, the teacher, if he is to do his job efficiently, must understand something about how a child develops. Psychology is the study of behaviour. Child Psychology is the study of the behaviour of children. The **psychology of child development** is the study of how children's behaviour develops and changes. The subject requires much study, and here I can only hope to awaken your interest so that you will read other books on the subject.

By a child most people mean a human being who has not yet reached adolescence. Sometimes, however, adolescence is included in the study of child development.

Approximate age divisions:

Newborn	o to 4 weeks
Baby	4 weeks to 1/2 years
Infant	1/2 years to 7/8 years
Middle childhood	7/8 years to 12/13 years
Adolescence	12/13 years to 16/18 years.

Development

By development we mean a change towards something that is better, more mature and independent, more complex. Usually people develop as they grow older. (But we do not talk of development when illness or old age bring decline.) The word develop also means 'to unfold'. It is the process of unfolding the inborn capacities, which are present in the newborn baby, but which need the correct environment for proper growth.

But development may be halted or seem to go backwards (called regression) due to illness or emotional upset. Here are some examples of regression. A boy who has been ill in bed for a long time forgets how to walk; because he has been unable to practise the skill, he needs to be taught how to walk again. A mother dies and her little daughter, who has been running about and talking, goes back to the baby stage, crawls and stops talking. (She needs a substitute mother to love and care for her and she will start developing again.) The parents of a little boy have a big quarrel and their child is very upset. He could read and write, but now he begins to hesitate and make mistakes. (Until there is harmony again in the home, he will be troubled.) When studying development, remember that most children progress fairly steadily, and those who do not, need special help.

Why a Knowledge of Child Development Helps the Teacher
Development and growth are often described as happening at a certain age. This is only for convenience and *age is merely a rough guide*. For example, most children start to say a few words by the time they are two years old, but some may start to talk at 12 months, and some not until they are about three. Yet all may be quite normal children.

It is more helpful to consider stages of development. A child must be helped to pass through each stage successfully, before he can do well at the next stage. So, if you try to teach a baby to run before he can walk, you are wasting your time and harming the baby. This seems obvious, but when teaching, stages may be missed unless the teacher is careful. A child needs plenty of practice with matching and grouping before he starts simple addition. He must be successful in all the pre-reading stages before he can confidently tackle a reading book. The steps between the stages are small and a good teacher makes them so small that a child does not notice them, but feels happy and successful in his work.

A good teacher should know the normal stages of development to be expected from children in his class, but he should also know what happens before and after those stages. **Help the child according to the stage he has reached,** not according to his age.

The more we study children, the more we can help them. Education is a two-way business. The children learn from us but we also learn from the children.

African Child Development
Much research and study about how children develop is taking place in Europe and the U.S.A. Be careful when you read books, because what is written may not apply to African children. Many African universities have research projects, so keep looking in modern teachers' journals for the results. Each teacher can do his own research by observing children carefully.

Two Important Warnings
1. Do not jump to conclusions. If you observe that most children do a certain thing by a particular age, do not conclude that a child who does not fit the pattern is unintelligent. There may be special reasons. If you can discover these reasons, you can help the child better. For example, most children can weigh accurately and work out simple weight sums between the ages of seven and eight. One boy cannot. What is the reason? Perhaps he is undernourished and cannot concentrate. Perhaps he came from

another area and lacks experience (no shop in his previous class, no sand or clay to weigh, no balance, no scales); maybe he has been ill and missed much of the early teaching; maybe he is afraid of failing, because his last teacher or his father has been too strict with him; perhaps he is ill and the fever makes his hand shake; maybe he is unhappy because of trouble at home.

2. Observing children carefully means that we find out many things which should be treated with confidence. Teachers must never gossip about children. The parents must know that anything we learn about their children is a secret, kept in our own heads. Our professional integrity (honesty) must be guarded by all teachers. If you want to discuss or write about your observations (and it is good to do these things) always use fictitious names so that no one can guess the identity of a particular child.

Rates of Development

Research shows that most growth is irregular with quick periods and slow periods. Physical development is very fast in the prenatal stage (before birth) and during the first two years of life. The rate is then much slower until puberty, when the boy or girl grows quickly again.

The rate of learning is irregular too. When starting to read the child may remember many words when the teacher plays the Flash card game. Then may follow a slow period, when he struggles with the reading book. If the teacher is helpful and encourages practice there will follow another period of rapid progress. It is during these periods of slow learning that the child may become frustrated, unhappy and stop trying. It is important for the teacher to recognize the different rates of development (and the rates will vary for each child), so that praise and encouragement will help the child to progress to the next stage.

Development of the Whole Child

Development goes on at the same time (but at different rates) in all areas. We see the *total* child, but it is a very complex picture and often we study one section at a time. Development can be looked at under different headings, but the following divisions are quite useful: physical, intellectual (including language), social, emotional and spiritual (including moral and aesthetic). Remember that one aspect of development affects all others.

Heredity and Environment

When a child is conceived, 23 chromosomes from the mother combine with 23 chromosomes from the father to make a new cell. The genes are carried on the chromosomes. The genes carry the *heredity* from both parents. From the new cell develops a completely unique being. (In the case of identical twins the cell splits into two, and two babies grow with the same heredity, but the environment will be slightly different for each). From the genes the child will inherit characteristics of the father and of the mother, and of the grandparents and the great-grandparents. Certain things are decided at conception, such as the colour of the eyes or hair, the height of the adult-to-be and the sex. It is also decided that certain things are possible for the new human being, and other things are impossible. But no one knows what these possibilities are.

The environment is all the factors outside the child affecting his development. The physical environment includes his home, the way he is fed, the toys he is given to interest him, and his experiences as he explores the world around him. The social environment includes the family, especially the parents. As the child grows older it also includes the people who live nearby, and most important, the teacher. The action of the environment on the genotype (decided by the genes) produces the phenotype, the person as he develops. If a child is removed from his home at birth, he will grow into a different person from the one he would have been if he had stayed at home. His environment will be different. Some children with good inherited characteristics may not develop well, because of a poor environment. For example, a baby may inherit the possibility of a tall, strong body, because both his parents are tall and strong, but if the child does not get the nourishment he requires he may get rickets and other malformations. Although his genes laid the foundations for tallness and strength, he will be short, misshapen and weak. The environment has hindered his development. Another child may have the genes of great intelligence, such as would make him a scientist, a writer or a great teacher, but because he is given no stimulation, no toys, no help with language, no interesting experiences, he will not develop well. The potential (possibility for good development) was there, but the environment was poor.

No one knows the potential of any one baby, so the environment must be the best possible to give all children the opportunity to develop properly. Remember that the womb is the first environment and if the mother lacks good food, or if she gets too tired, worried or anxious, this will adversely affect the baby even before he is born. (Although identical twins have the same heredity, they will not have exactly the same environment. They will sleep at different sides of the bed, one will be picked up before the other, one will be washed before the other, etc. These differences are small, but they are enough to show that even two children with the same heredity grow up with different personalities, because of environment.)

Child development is a very big subject and other books should be consulted. Remember it is the interaction of heredity and environment which produces the individual. He develops from within, following the stages of all human beings, but this development is helped or hindered depending on the environment.

Basic Needs of all Children
There are certain things, necessary for growth and development, which apply to all children (and adults too for that matter). Without these basic needs no one can develop properly.

Physical needs: Food, shelter, rest and sleep, exercise and play
A nourishing diet of proteins and vegetables as well as carbohydrates is necessary. Supervise any meals which are cooked at school. The buildings of home and school need to be kept in good repair. Advise the parents to send the children to school in suitable protective clothing. The child needs plenty of opportunity for movement, not only in P.E. lessons but also between lessons. Sometimes it is said that a change is as good as a rest, and careful planning of the school day will help give alternate quiet sitting times and active, moving about times. Sleep is most important, or the child will not be able to concentrate.

Emotional Needs: Love and security, success and a feeling of importance
For the development of a human being, love is necessary and without it no one can progress. A child should feel that whatever happens, his loving family will care for him. This love and care leads to a feeling of security. A secure child is usually a well-behaved child. Often a child misbehaves simply to find out if anyone cares enough to stop him. If the adult shows that he likes the child and cares to help him, the child will respond by trying to be good.

To help the child to feel secure in school, the teacher must be very regular in his behaviour. A teacher who punishes without warning, or who ignores something one day but punishes the child for the same thing the next day, will puzzle and confuse him. The child will then feel insecure. He will not be able to work well, because he will be wondering what the teacher will do next. There should be rules in the classroom, sensible rules for the good of all, and the child should understand them clearly. He will not then be surprised if the teacher is cross when a rule is broken. The regular daily routine of school helps a child to feel secure, because the same sort of thing happens each day and he knows what to expect.

A child wants to be himself; a person quite different from anyone else. Encourage each child to make the best of himself. What we think of ourselves is sometimes called a self-concept (a picture in our minds of ourselves). Each child needs to have a good self-concept, and to feel that he is a successful and important member of the class. Try to build up good self-concepts, by finding something every day to praise in each child. 'What lovely neat writing, Ali.' 'How hard you have tried with your sums today, Mary.' 'You have been thoughtful and kind today, Musa.' 'What an interesting specimen you found today, Anna.' Each child you speak to

THE CHILD

will not only feel successful, he will also feel important. He will be happy that all the other children look at him when he is praised, and he will try even harder to do well. Naughty children are often those the teacher has forgotten to praise and encourage. The teacher will call a naughty child's name and he will feel important, but not in a good way. He will have a bad self-concept.

Social and Moral Needs: Leading and following, being part of a group, an understanding of right and wrong

All children like to be a leader sometimes, as this makes them feel important. Try to give all the children in your class a turn at leading. They also need to be part of a group, and to take turns at following. Sometimes there is a child whom no group wants and he is pushed away (called an isolate). The teacher should watch for such a child, and help him to join in. We all need to be on our own sometimes, but in our society it is necessary to learn how to take our place in a group. This learning starts early in the Primary school.

Everyone needs to learn what his particular society considers right or wrong. Teach the child gently to behave in the right way, and to dislike wrong actions. Guide the child to understand the difference between imagination, dreams and real life (see page 23).

Emotional Needs: Expression of anger, fear, tenderness and happiness

Anger and fear are natural, but we need to help the child to express them in the correct way. Help him to control his anger, and to use the energy to improve poor conditions. Help him to realize that fear may help to protect him in dangerous situations, but he also needs to learn when it is necessary to be brave. (Clay and sand play, drama and story telling help children express safely, emotions like anger and fear.)

Tenderness also needs expression. No man is much use to his country if he selfishly tries to get everything for himself, without caring who is hurt or troubled. In an educated community the poor and weak are protected. Help each child to express tenderness and caring by helping any sick or weaker children, and by being kind to animals.

The classroom should be a happy place where children and teacher can have fun together. (But be careful never to laugh at a child, because great harm could be done to his self-concept.)

Intellectual Needs: Stimulation, opportunities to experiment and discover, opportunities to use language

For the mind to develop properly every child needs to be stimulated by adults. He needs things to see, hear, taste, touch, smell. He needs opportunities to discover interesting things. The more the child is stimulated to

21

experiment and find out, the more his interest and curiosity will grow. The child needs adults to help him have stimulating experiences.

At first the parents are the teachers. A tin to rattle will increase the child's listening ability, his physical co-ordination as he learns to hold it, his understanding of shape as he looks at it and feels it, his language as his parents tell him it is a rattle. This is only one small example of how parents can stimulate a baby. He needs many, many things to listen to, see, touch, taste and smell; things which bump, roll, bounce, float, sink, thread, fit one into another, can be put into groups, arranged in sizes, built one on top of the other, mixed together for food, looked at carefully, copied, etc. All the time the parents should be talking and explaining in words. With stimulation and *language* the child's intellectual needs will be met. *Language* is very, very important. As a child spends five or six years at home before he comes to school, **he needs language stimulation at home.** Parents should be told how important it is to spend some time each day talking to their children, telling them what is happening, asking questions, and encouraging the children to tell the adults about all they see and do together.

The teacher will build on the work started by the parents, helping the child to develop and use his language, so that he can express his thoughts clearly. The intellectual needs will then be met with more and more interesting lessons.

The Development of the Primary Child
Before the child comes to school he passes through a number of very important developmental stages, but space prevents them being discussed here. Parents and teachers, who are trying to give children a good start in life, should study books on pre-school development.

Usually a child starts school at about five or six years, and he is called an infant until he is about seven or eight. Then he is called a junior or a middle school child, until he is about 12 years old.

The Development of the Infant School Child
The child at five or six is well developed **physically**. He can run, skip and jump. His balance is good, and he can turn and change direction quite quickly. He can make large motor movements better than fine motor movements. He cannot sit still for long, and he needs plenty of bodily activity. If he has been sitting still for a while let him dance or play a short game, e.g. 'Who can stand as tall as a giant?' 'Who can make himself as small as a rat?' 'Be a drummer.' (Children beat the air and pretend to have drums.) 'Be a farmer digging the ground.'

Infant children should be encouraged to make big drawings and big letters with big paintbrushes and big pencils and crayons. This helps them to practise and develop the finer movements of the fingers and the wrist. Children should be shown big pictures and big printing, while they develop the fine co-ordination of the muscles of the eye. Sometimes co-ordination between hand and eye is poor, due to lack of experience (all the pre-reading activities will help); and sometimes it is because the small nerves have not finished growing. We can, and should, give children plenty of practice to develop co-ordination. But we must also wait for the inner growth, and never force a child, or he will be come frustrated and frightened.

Socially the child at five or six is ready to play and work side by side with other children, and he enjoys their company. But he does not really co-operate with others very well, nor for long. He can be taught to play reading, number and activity games in a group. It is good training to encourage a child to share with others in a group, and to wait for his turn. The group should be small, only two or three children. The teacher should not be surprised if the children do not agree together very well.

Adults are very important to the infant. In school the child considers his teacher the most important adult. He will copy your actions and speech patterns. He will work hard to get your praise. Try to help each child individually as often as possible, and make sure that each one knows you value him as a person.

This will also help him **emotionally**. He needs to feel he is important to the teacher. He cannot control his emotions much and is easily frightened or made miserable. Try to make your classroom a happy place, where the child can rely on your friendship and firm, kind help.

A young child has little idea of right or wrong. At home and at school he will gradually learn how his society expects him to behave. Remember that a small child who lies, may do so because he finds it difficult to tell the difference between what has actually happened and what he has imagined. In fact he is not telling lies in the adult sense at all. Never say to a young child, 'That is a lie.' Just say, 'Well I think you have made a mistake.' 'Go and look again.' or 'Think again about what happened.' Make as little fuss as possible. Give the child activities which will gradually help him to know the difference between reality and his imagination. Stealing is another problem with the young child. At home he will have started to learn about 'mine', 'yours' and 'ours', but his understanding will be poor. The teacher will help him to share, but also he needs to learn to respect other people's property and work. Sometimes a child takes something from another because he is jealous. Perhaps you have neglected him and he is trying to get your attention. Sometimes he may take things because he is unhappy, because his parents do not seem to care for him. Try to let the child know you like him, and help him to return what he has taken. Again make as little fuss as possible, because at this stage of **moral development** the child does not understand why it is wrong.

An infant child often seems to appreciate beautiful and wonderful things, and we must foster this aesthetic development. Try to have beautiful flowers, copies of famous pictures and examples of good local crafts in your room. Make attractive displays, and change them every fortnight. Display the children's own work neatly. Show them charts with careful, even printing. Encourage them to enjoy beautiful music and movement; invite local bands and dancers into the school, and help the children to make their own music and dances. Help them to enjoy the feel of things, rough, silky, spikey; and the smell of things, sweetly perfumed flowers, food cooking, refreshing rain. The classroom should be attractive and tidy, as well as being interesting.

Intellectually the child can be helped to develop his potential ability. Intelligence grows through understanding and experience. The primary class should be full of activities. An intelligent active mind is one which asks questions, and tries to solve problems, looks at the problems in as many ways as possible, considers relationships and all the possible answers to the questions or problems, and using experience chooses the answer which seems best. At the same time an intelligent mind realizes that with more experience a better answer may be found. The infant teacher can help to develop this kind of intelligent mind.

The infant child needs to do things for himself. He needs to see, hear, touch, explore, act, dance, paint, move, experiment, make things, take things apart and put them together again, and try to find things out for himself. In this way he will gradually understand more about the world, and through understanding he will think intelligently.

There should be little telling in the infant classes, but there should be a great deal of discussion about what the children are doing. Through language the child is helped to remember what he has done, think about what he is doing, and plan what he will do next, or what he will do later on in the day, or tomorrow, or next week. This thinking ahead is an important part of intelligent thought. The teacher should not tell the child much, but help him to think through asking the correct kind of question. (See notes on questioning.)

Many educationalists think that the early years are the most important in the child's whole life. If he is happy and likes school, he will continue to like the junior and the secondary schools. We know that if a child is not happy, he will learn little. If he is stimulated by the infant teacher and develops every side of his personality well, he will continue to be an interested, keen learner in later years. As a house cannot be built without good foundations, so junior and secondary teachers can only build on the good foundations laid by the infant teacher. An infant teacher's work is very, very important, and he should make a special study of child psychology to understand the development of the young child.

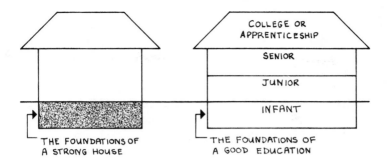

THE FOUNDATIONS OF
A STRONG HOUSE

THE FOUNDATIONS OF
A GOOD EDUCATION

The Development of the Junior School Child

A child does not suddenly change from an infant into a junior. It is a gradual development and some children are slower than others. For the first two or three years the junior school teacher needs a good understanding of the younger child, because the young junior needs to be treated and taught in a similar way to the infant.

The junior child has good **physical** control, and enjoys practising skills, sometimes of the most intricate movements. He can sit and concentrate for quite a long time if he is interested, but he still needs plenty of change and variety in his lessons. His hand and eye co-ordination is good, and his writing, painting, modelling, etc., should show satisfactory progress, as he becomes neater and attends more to detail. When reading he can see smaller print than the infant.

Socially the junior is ready to co-operate, take his turn and work in groups. His peers (children of his own age group) are very important and he will work hard for their respect and friendship. Adults are less important, but if he likes someone he will try to imitate that person. The adult may be so admired and copied, that we call it hero-worship. Teachers must make sure the children have good heroes to copy.

He is more stable **emotionally** than the infant. But he can still be frightened by an unkind adult, or become nervous in strange situations. He is learning to control his temper. He is beginning to understand that other people have feelings, and is ready to give friendship and kindness. The teacher should build up his courage, confidence and thoughtfulness for others, by praise and encouragement.

Morally he has quite a good idea of right and wrong. Sometimes he expects the teacher to act as judge, so be careful to be fair. He will notice how people behave and he needs good, honest, truthful adults to copy.

He will continue to appreciate beautiful displays, pictures, music, etc. It is the junior teacher's duty to foster and extend this understanding.

Intellectually the opportunities are enormous for extending the child's

25

mind. Help him to learn many interesting facts about the world. His memory is particularly keen and he likes repetition. It is a good time for learning tables, spelling, poetry, etc. But remembering without understanding is useless. He will gladly practise skills such as reading and writing of all kinds, and he needs step-by-step help. Although he is more ready than the infant to listen to the teacher talking, the emphasis must still be on **doing**. The child needs to solve his own problems with practical apparatus; **he needs to experiment and discover**. Most junior teachers talk too much. The child is the one who needs to develop his use of language. The teacher should use the questioning technique to encourage the child to think for himself.

The junior's interests are wider than those of the infant. He likes to know what happens in other areas, though visits in his local environment will provide most teaching topics. Machines and inventors catch his interest. He will read books of knowledge and adventure. The classroom still needs to be full of stimulating activities, practical apparatus, interest tables, displays of work, various kinds of books and opportunities for the child to use his imagination and creative talents.

How a Child Learns
Reasons for Learning (Motivation)
No child will learn unless he has a reason for doing so. The most usual reasons are: his own interest and curiosity; his wish to be like an adult; his wish to succeed; his desire for praise; his desire to please the teacher or his parents; his fear of failure or of punishment. A teacher must be very careful that a child does not become too anxious and fearful, for if this happens his fear prevents him from learning properly.

Imitation
A child learns a great deal by copying the example of grown-up people, and in school the teacher must try to set the child a good example in everything. A child will also imitate his friends, and the teacher should encourage him to imitate the good and hard-working children, by praising them.

Listening
A child learns by listening, but he soon tires of sitting still and just listening. Things which help to make listening more interesting, like gramophones and the radio, are called aural aids. (Aural means 'of the ear'.)

Seeing
A child learns by seeing. Anything which helps him to learn through his eyes is called a visual aid. Objects, pictures, charts and diagrams are all visual aids. (Visual means 'of the eye'.)

Doing

A child learns by doing. Though hearing and seeing help the child to learn, he must be active and do things for himself before he can master a subject. A child cannot concentrate for long if he is just listening. He can concentrate longer if he listens and watches, but **he can concentrate best when he is doing something himself**. A good teacher plans his lessons so that a child spends only a very short time sitting still and listening. He plans to use visual aids, but most of the lesson is taken up with the children being active.

Understanding

Without understanding there can be no proper learning. The teacher must make quite sure that all the children in the class understand the lesson. Each child should be encouraged and trained to ask questions when he does not understand. A teacher should never be cross or laugh at a child who does not honestly follow the lesson, and asks questions. Asking questions shows an interested, lively mind. All great men and women have questioning minds.

If only some of the children have understood a lesson, the teacher can give them a special activity, while he gives extra help to the others.

Habits

Good habits are very useful, as they save us a great deal of time and energy. In the first place a child has to learn a habit, but after it has been thoroughly learned he can do it almost without thinking.

The infant takes a long time to write because he has to think carefully how to form each letter. To write 'Pius' the child may think something like this. 'Pius. It has a big P. How do I make a big P? A straight line and a curve at the top. "i": It has a small straight line with a dot on top. "u": I must bring my pencil down, round, up and down again. "s": It looks like a curly snake.'

Watch a small child learning to write, and you can imagine him thinking like this as he slowly writes each letter. Then look at a child in the top class; how quickly and well he writes if he has been taught properly. He has learned a good habit of writing, and he can form the letters almost without thinking. Or watch a little girl learning to knit. How slow she is as she thinks where she should put her wool, but once she has mastered the skill of knitting and it has become a habit, she can do it very quickly and almost without thinking.

When learning to speak the child is very slow, but once the speech habits are formed, the child can speak quickly and easily. With reading habits the same thing applies, slow learning at first; then once the skill is mastered, quicker and quicker reading. Habits may take years to learn and they should be very carefully taught, so that they will help the child in his education. Bad habits are a waste of time, and they are very difficult to break or change. Teachers should watch very carefully that the child is only forming good habits.

Revision and Practice

Repetition (doing an action over and over again) forms a habit and this is one way of helping a child to learn. After a child has been taught something which the teacher has helped him to understand, it should be revised and practised often, so that the child will not forget it.

Attention and Inattention

It is important that the child attends to the lessons. Naturally he will not learn if he is not paying attention. This is rather a big point, so I emphasize it.

Causes of inattention in class:
1. Lack of interest.
2. Lack of materials.
3. The work is too easy or too hard, and the child does not attend either because he cannot understand or because he already knows the work.
4. Lack of variety.
5. The teacher does all the talking and the child has no activity.
6. The timetable is badly arranged; e.g. two very difficult lessons are put one after the other, and there are not enough breaks between lessons.
7. Bored and uninteresting teacher.
8. Teacher with weak discipline. One naughty child influencing others.
9. Outside distractions (e.g. noise from other classes, people passing by).
10. Lack of fresh air, sleep or food. Very hot or very cold weather.
11. Chairs too big or too little, making children uncomfortable.
12. Illness.

Check inattention and help attention by:
1. Interesting lessons and interesting subject matter.
2. Good introduction and sufficient apparatus.
3. Work suitable for the ability of the children. (Group work and well-prepared schemes.)
4. Plenty of variety.
5. Children doing most of the talking and activity, helped by the teacher.

6. Careful planning of the timetable.
7. Interesting and happy teacher, showing a liking for the children and the work.
8. Firm but reasonable discipline depending on the age of the children.
9. Letting the children look at whatever is distracting them, and then calling them back to the lesson (e.g. let the class look at the people passing by, then say, 'Now we have seen what is happening, we must carry on with our lesson').
10. Adequate fresh air by keeping windows open. Advise parents about sleep and food.
11. Seats of the correct size.
12. Help the sick child to get medical attention.

Memory

Learning depends to a great extent on memory. When we talk of a child's memory we mean his power to remember things. Some children seem to be born with better memories than others, but the teacher can help the child to remember by attending to all the points mentioned in this section: 'How a child learns'.

Chapter 5 The Child as an Individual

Individual Differences
Although we have been considering the development of an average child, it is important to remember that every child differs in some way from every other child in the class. While one child may find Maths easy, another may find it difficult; one may be very good at Reading, another may be very slow; one may be very upset by a cross word from the teacher, but another may have to be spoken to many times before he appears to hear. It is important to remember that each child in the class is an individual, and needs slightly different treatment from every other child.

Differences of Environment
Environment means the type of home and family from which the child comes. A teacher should find out as much as possible about each child's environment. One may come from a rich home, another from a poor home; one may come from a large family, another from a small family; one may be the youngest child in the family, another the oldest; one may have sensible parents who listen to advice, another may have foolish parents who continue to do foolish things (e.g. give the child a poor diet, refuse to take him to the hospital for treatment when he is ill, do not help him to practise the laws of hygiene). The following examples will give the reader some idea of what to observe.

One child comes from a humble home. The parents are illiterate, and although they have not much money they are sensible. They ask the teacher for advice about diet and cleanliness, and they feed their child as well as they can with their small amount of money. The mother takes her child to market, when she can, so that he can observe many things. When he asks questions about the things he sees, she explains as well as possible; she shows her child how to use money and count his change. She tells her child the house must be kept clean and free from germs, and the child must help her so that all the family will be healthy. The father talks to his child. If he hears anything interesting in the town he tells his child about it. When possible he takes his child out with him to the post office, the agricultural office or other public places. He takes the child to the farm not only to work, but also to learn the names of the plants, birds and insects that they see. In this way the child is learning all the time, he is getting ideas and his general knowledge is good. In school he is bright and interested in learning, because his parents have taught him to observe and think.

Consider another child from a foolish family; the rich mother is enjoying herself with her friends, and cannot be bothered to talk and play with her child. In this family, too, the father is away for weeks and even months, because he is very busy making money, and he sees his child only very occasionally. The child is left to the care of a servant, who may be quite good and kind, but a servant cannot train a child's mind nor form his character as a parent can. This child will appear dull in school because he has had no loving parent to awaken his mind. **School training can never take the place of a good sensible family life, and teachers can only build on the foundations started at home.** If, however, the teacher knows something about the type of home from which the child comes he can be more understanding towards the child. Remember that the child is not to blame for the foolishness of his parents, but as teachers we must help and guide the child and if possible through the Parent-Teacher Association advise and guide the parents as well.

I have only dealt with this subject very briefly, but the teacher will soon notice many different types of home environment and note the effect of environment on the children.

Differences of Ability
Every child is born with a different ability to learn and reason. We call this intelligence. If a child is born with a poor brain, nothing can be done to make it a very good intelligent brain, **but** the child can be helped to make the **very best use** of the brain he has. It is important to remember this.

A child with a poor intelligence may be doing his best, yet his work may not be up to the average standard of the class. The teacher must watch carefully and if the child is working hard he must be praised for trying. The teacher must help him very slowly, and step by step. A very clever child may find the work easy, and may not bother to work nearly as hard as the slow child. Often the bright child is given a great deal of praise when he has made very little effort. A child like this should be given more difficult work so that he also has to work hard to get good marks.

In Chapter 1, The Aims of Education, I said we were helping each child **develop to the best of his ability**. The clever, the average and the dull child are all part of our society, and all have an important job to do as citizens of their country. A lazy worker is no good in any position, and even if a man is very intelligent, he is no use to the community unless he works. A child with poor intelligence, who has been trained and helped to develop as well as he can, will find a job where he can serve his community well, and where people of real understanding will honour him for his conscientious work.

Physical Differences
It is easy to pick out the differences in the bodies of the children. Some are tall, some are short, some are fat, some are thin, some have good eyesight, some do not see very well and have to wear glasses, some are good at exercises in P.E., while others find this lesson difficult. Proper diet, rest and care during illness make a difference to the way a child grows, but children also take after their parents and grandparents, and if they are all small in stature we would not expect the child to grow tall, though he should be strong and healthy.

Moral, Social and Emotional Differences
The differences between the children's moral behaviour will depend on how they have been taught at home. The teacher must build on the home training and help each child to obey the laws of God and of his country.

Some children naturally like to play with a crowd of their fellows, while some prefer to be alone. The ones who like to be with others must be encouraged to be independent sometimes, while the ones who like to be alone must sometimes be encouraged to take part in group activities.

The teacher will soon notice the emotional differences between the children. One is calm and quiet, another is very excitable, another is easily upset and soon cries, while another loses his temper very quickly. The teacher must remember that emotions are good if used in a sensible way, and encourage the children to control them.

In conclusion we should be thankful that we are not all alike and equal, like beans out of the same pod. Life would be very uninteresting if we all resembled each other exactly in every way. Each child and adult with his own special individual differences has a part to play in the society where he lives. Children have different shapes and sizes mentally, physically and spiritually, and as teachers we must treat each one as an individual and help him to develop his own personality.

Children with Special Disabilities
Children who have special disabilities are those who are blind, deaf, dumb or have very weak brains. Teachers who teach these children need special training, and the children should attend special schools. There are few of these special schools in Africa, but as the educational systems grow, more schools will gradually be built. At present children with these serious defects are probably not sent to school at all, but the teachers in the ordinary school may get children who are slightly affected by these disabilities, and he should know how to help them.

Children who cannot See very well
The teacher can notice eye trouble when a child does very bad writing, or

copies incorrectly from the blackboard. Infant children often write letters back-to-front or upside down, but that is quite a natural stage in the training of their hand and eye co-ordination. If, however, a child continues to have difficulty writing after two or three years there may be something wrong with his eyes. Let the child sit in the front desk of the class, and be patient. There is no treatment the teacher can give. The eyes are very delicate organs and must be examined by a specialist. The teacher should do all he can to encourage the parents to take the child to the hospital.

A great deal can be done for these children nowadays, especially if they are sent to the hospital while they are quite young. Glasses can be fitted, but remember that only trained people in hospital can fit the correct glasses. The doctor can also give special exercises to help the eyes.

Children who cannot Hear very well

It is often more difficult to notice a child who does not hear very well. Quite often when such a child does not understand what the teacher is saying, he will just sit quietly and will be afraid to ask the teacher to explain again. If the teacher discovers there is a child who frequently misunderstands, or disobeys, the teacher should think before he gets cross, and consider the possibility that the child is slightly deaf. Watch the child carefully, and notice if he hears you when he is not looking at you. If he only hears when he is watching your lips move, he is probably a little deaf. Again the only help the teacher can give is to be patient and move him to the front of the class. Encourage the parents to take him to the hospital, as the earlier the treatment is started the more likely it is to succeed.

Children who cannot Speak very well

Sometimes the teacher will have a child in the class who cannot speak very well because of some trouble in the shape of his mouth. The teacher can only be patient and encourage the parents to take the child to the hospital as soon as possible, for a small operation may cure the trouble. More often the teacher will have children in the class who make mistakes in sounding certain letters. Do not make such a child uncomfortable by criticizing him in front of his friends, but help him by practising words with the sounds he finds difficult and correcting any mistakes quietly.

Another speech trouble is stuttering. This is when a child tries to say a word and repeats the first letter over and over again as he tries to say the word. 'P-p-please may I h-h-h-have a b-b-b-book?' This is usually due to a kind of nervousness and the teacher should be very kind and helpful. Try to ignore the stuttering as much as possible, praise the child when he does any good work and give him confidence. Try to make him feel a successful and useful member of the class and the stutter may disappear.

Children who have rather a Weak Brain

These children need to be treated most kindly and gently. They should be taught in a special group, and given an earlier stage of work than the rest of the class. They should be made to feel part of the class, however, by being given easy but important monitoring jobs, like cleaning the blackboard, watering the flowers or collecting the pencils. Children who are not clever often copy the work of brighter children sitting near by, because they are afraid of getting bad marks. This is not likely to happen if the teacher gives the children simple work to suit their ability. When they do their best they must be praised and encouraged, even if the result is not very good.

These children must be treated with understanding, and helped to realize they are part of the community, with a special job to do. If they are laughed at or treated unkindly, they will not understand why. Because their brains are weak, unkind treatment may even cause them to grow up to be thieves, wanting to hurt the community as the community has hurt them. The community has a big responsibility to these people, and those of us with good intelligence must use it to aid those of our brothers who are weak. The best way to help them is to see that they have a simple but necessary part to play in the life of the community.

Backwardness

If a child cannot keep up with the rest of the class and is always getting poor marks, we say he is backward. He needs special help and attention, but before the teacher can help him, he should try to discover the reason for the backwardness.

Reasons for Backwardness

1. *Cause:* The child may not have a very good brain and he just cannot do the work of the other children.

How to help: He should be given special work suitable to his ability. He should be given plenty of praise and encouragement when he tries, but he should not be expected to do the same work as the other children.

2. *Cause:* The child may have missed a great deal of school through illness, or because his parents do not send him regularly to school. If the child has been ill it is no one's fault, but if absence from school is the parents' fault, the teacher should talk to them and show them how they are preventing their child from learning.

How to help: These children should be given some extra help, in a group with other backward children or by themselves, during playtime or when the teacher has some other spare time. A good headteacher will arrange for these children to have some special help. Either he will have them in his room and help them himself, or he will take the class while the teacher gives them special help.

34

3. *Cause:* The child may have missed some schooling two or three years before and may never have caught up, or he may have had a lazy teacher, or a teacher who had poor discipline and allowed him to play about; thus he missed his work and did not attend, so he gradually became more and more backward.

How to help: Special help is again necessary, and the teacher should go back and explain the very simple beginnings which the child never learned. For example if a child cannot understand sums about metres and centimetres the teacher must go right back to the beginning and teach the child how to measure and use a ruler. Then he must explain the first simple sums, and give the child practice until he can do them. Gradually he will progress to harder sums.

4. *Cause:* The child may have a special disability (pages 32 and 33).
How to help: He usually needs special medical care.

A child may be quite good at most subjects and backward in only one. He then needs help in that one subject. It is easier to organize the class if all the backward children are put in a group, but the teacher must be careful he does not make them feel peculiar or different. Tell them they are in the special group so that they can be helped to catch up with the others, or because they are being given a little special work.

Chapter 6 The Teacher and the Child

The Teacher-Child Relationship

It is most important to have a friendly atmosphere in the classroom. The children should feel they can trust their teacher, and they should know by his attitude that he is ready to help and guide them. They should be able to speak to him if they are in any difficulties, knowing that he will listen sympathetically and will help if he can. It is terrible if the children are afraid to speak to their teacher for fear of a harsh word or a beating, and no real education can ever be accomplished by such a teacher.

A teacher must be friendly and kind, but this does not mean that the children are allowed to do as they please. They must be disciplined and trained to behave in a reasonable way. Always expect good behaviour and hard work, and, because the teacher is friendly and just, the children will try to please him.

Discipline

The simplest way of describing a teacher's discipline is to say, 'It is the way he helps his class to be well-behaved.' Order in the classroom is, however, often mistakenly called discipline. Here are two examples which will help to show the difference between order and good discipline.

In one classroom a very dull uninteresting lesson is being taken. The children are sitting quietly and they appear to be listening, but when the teacher asks questions, the children can only repeat in a muddled way what has been said by the teacher. The teacher is keeping order, because the children are afraid to move or talk, knowing that they will be punished if they do, and some are so bored that they are day-dreaming.

In another room there is a little noise, for the children are all busy working in groups as they arrange their Science specimens, and discuss what they will write about them. The teacher is visiting each group in turn, helping the children to write the names of the specimens and where they are found. There is not complete order and quiet in this room, but the children are learning as they discuss what they are doing; they are thinking for themselves as they decide what to write; they are learning to work together with other children in the group, and they are learning to control themselves as they keep their voices to a whisper so as not to disturb the other groups. The noise and movement is that of children working.

When the teacher wants the children's attention he asks the class to listen, and the children quickly put down their work to hear their teacher's words, which they know will help them in their work. These children like and respect their teacher, and they are very interested in the lesson.

In which of these two classes would you say that there is the good discipline which helps the children to learn?

A teacher should realise that he can expect different types of behaviour from different age groups. Obviously six-year-old children will not be so quiet or so well controlled as ten-year-old children, and the teacher must make allowances for the age of the children.

Good discipline trains a child to know what is good and reasonable behaviour, so that gradually the child learns to control himself, and behaves in a reasonable manner without continual reminders from the teacher.

Rules in the Classroom

Rules are usually connected with discipline. They are undoubtedly necessary, but there should be as few rules as possible. Children are really very sensible if treated properly, and if they are told the reason for a rule they are more likely to keep it. For example, 'We do not stand on the desks, as we may fall off and hurt ourselves'; 'We only talk very quietly in groups, because a noise will disturb the other group'; 'We sit still in our places when we are writing, because if we move about we might jog someone else who is trying hard, and we might spoil his work.'

The teacher must, however, remember that children cannot sit still for long and the lesson must have variety. If the teacher has sympathy and understanding for each child, he will be happy to do as the teacher asks, though of course no child is perfect and all are sometimes naughty. This brings up the consideration of punishments.

Punishments

The most common faults of children are:
1. Talking instead of working.
2. Doing untidy work.
3. Inattention.
4. Disobedience.
5. Dishonesty.
6. Unkindness to other children.

When giving punishments remember the following points:

(*a*) The aim of a punishment is to correct the child and educate him to do better.

(*b*) A good teacher does not give many punishments, because if they are given too often the children expect them and they become ineffective.

37

(*c*) 'The punishment should fit the crime.' This means that the punishment should suit the offence. For example, if a child cannot behave himself with others he can be made to sit by himself; he will feel ashamed and sorry because he has to sit away from his friends, and will try to improve. If he works well the teacher should (after a certain time) give him another chance to work properly with his classmates.

(*d*) A teacher must never punish a child in anger. He must wait until his anger has cooled and then think of a reasonable punishment.

Note well: A child may be punished for lazy or careless work, but **remember it is very wrong to punish a child who is not clever, for poor work.** If he has tried and done his best, he should be praised for trying, even if the result is not very good. It is not his fault if he has been born with rather a weak brain.

The Type of Punishment to Give (see also (*c*) above)

1. Speaking to a child is often sufficient. For example, 'Get on with your work, Sule'; 'That is not tidy enough, Toyin; do it again'; 'Mary can do her own work, Samuel; you make sure that yours is all correct.'

2. If the children are all supposed to be listening to the teacher, and one plays about or speaks to his friend, the teacher can stop what he is saying and just **look** quite fiercely at the child. Nothing is said at all, but there is a great silence in the room, except for the naughty child, who quickly looks at the teacher to see why he has stopped talking. If the teacher still says nothing but waits for the child to sit up ready to listen, the child feels very ashamed for stopping the lesson. This **silence and looking** are often much more effective than speaking.

3. Careless work must be done again, if the child is capable of doing better.

4. Naughty children can be deprived of a privilege, or not allowed to take part in a favourite activity. For example, 'As you have been disobedient all week, Joseph, and I have warned you many times, you cannot be the leader of your team any more. I shall choose a child who can help me by doing what he is told'; or 'We are having dramatics this afternoon, but as you only did one sum this morning, Grace, you cannot join us until you have done three more sums.' Do **not** use this kind of punishment often. If the child does not improve try a different form of punishment. Never make a child miss P.E. because he has been naughty, as he needs the physical exercise.

5. A good way to deal with a child who is often naughty is to keep him in at playtime and talk to him; try to discover the reason for his disobedience. Sometimes children are naughty because they are unhappy or unwell. If a child realizes that you are concerned he will probably try harder in future to please you.

6. Sometimes a child is naughty because he wants all the class to notice him. The teacher may have neglected the child and not given him sufficient praise to make him feel important (pages 20, 21 and 23). Try to give such a child a monitoring job and remember to praise him when he tries to do well.

7. Be careful about punishing a child who copies from the child who is sitting next to him. Always encourage a child to do his own work and rely on his own brains as much as possible, but make sure that the child has not been given work that is too difficult for him. Except during examinations and tests a child should be allowed to ask another for help if the teacher is busy helping other children in a different part of the class. Obviously the teacher cannot give individual help to every child at once. It is better for the child to get help from another child than to sit doing nothing waiting for the teacher. There is a difference between helping and copying, and the teacher can allow helping, if it is done quietly, and not too often.

It is, however, necessary for children to realize that it is dishonest to copy from others in tests or examinations.

8. Be careful also about punishing a child for lying, as it takes a child quite a long time to understand the difference between what he imagines and what is real. The teacher needs patience and kindness when dealing with children who appear to tell untruths. Another reason for lying is fear, and the teacher should make sure that no child in his class is frightened into this behaviour. By example and praise of truthful children, all the children will be encouraged to tell the truth.

9. Another form of dishonesty is stealing. The teacher must be very careful about punishing for this, as the child is probably very unhappy and insecure at home. He may steal to get attention, or because he is jealous of a child who seems to come from a happier home. Although the teacher must help the child to realize that such behaviour is wrong and cannot be allowed, by talking to him quietly but firmly, he should also try to be understanding, and help to make the child as secure and as happy as possible in school.

10. Corporal punishment should only be given very, very occasionally, and then only for continual disobedience or rudeness. The child should always be given sufficient warning and a chance to try to improve his ways. Corporal punishment must **never** be given for bad work, only for very bad behaviour, and the teacher should have tried all the other kinds of punishment first. **N.B.** The punishment book must be signed each time a child is given corporal punishment, and no man must ever give corporal punishment to a girl.

Rewards

1. The most usual reward in school and one the children love to receive

is praise. 'Uwa, that is lovely writing. You have tried hard.' 'Okeke got all his sums right today. Very good Okeke.'

2. Another reward is a star. This can just be drawn in the book by the teacher with a coloured crayon when a child has tried hard. Children are very pleased when they receive a star.

3. Remarks written in the work book are also good rewards. 'Good'; 'You have tried'; 'Better.'

4. Older children can be given marks: $\dfrac{10}{10}$ or $\dfrac{7}{10}$, for example, but **remarks are better.**

5. Team charts can be used with junior children. When a child does well or tries hard or is helpful he is given a mark for his team. At the end of each week the marks are added up to see which team has won. They can perhaps be given a small reward, such as five minutes extra play, or they may go to the headteacher for a special word of praise, but the fact that they have won is usually enough reward.

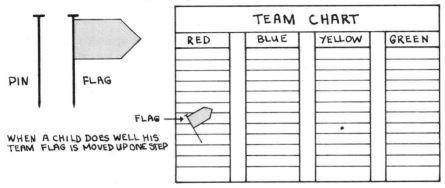

6. Some schools give prizes at the end of the term. These are not really necessary in a primary school, but if they are given do not just give them to the children who got top marks, but give them to those who worked hardest, were most helpful, most punctual, neat or well behaved. Instead of buying two or three expensive prizes, buy a number of cheaper ones, so that more children have a chance of winning one.

It must be remembered that prizes and rewards must not be used as a bribe, and the children must be trained to try hard even if they receive no reward at all.

The Preparation of Lesson Notes

The lesson notes are a guide to the teacher and he cannot expect to teach a good lesson unless it has been well prepared. Colleges teach different ways of planning lesson notes, and I do not recommend any particular one, but they should be kept fairly short. It is the mental thinking and the systematic planning that is important.

The **objectives** for the lesson should show what the teacher hopes to do in **one** lesson. He must think, 'Can I achieve this in **one** lesson?' If not the objectives are too big and must be reduced to what can be taught in one lesson. Sometimes it is better to have objectives for a week.

The teacher must decide on the best method for the lesson, class method, group method, etc., and must think if any special organization will be needed. Any change in the arrangement of the class, e.g. moving seats outside, must be planned. Any special apparatus which will aid the lesson should be written in the notes to remind the teacher what to take to school.

The actual procedure of the lesson is best planned in steps, and the teacher must have a clear picture in his mind of what will happen during each step.

The **introduction** should contain anything of special interest which will catch the children's attention, or something which will arouse their curiosity. It may be revision of previous work or a discussion and questions to discover how much the children already know about the subject of the lesson.

The **new teaching** is introduced in as interesting a way as possible, blackboard work, apparatus, demonstration, acting, etc. It is built on what the children already know, for they can only progress, with under-standing, step by step. If the children are not ready for new teaching the work must be revised in a **new** way. No lesson must ever be a repetition of another.

When the work has been taught it must be **consolidated** (made firm) in the children's minds. This is done through practice and activity, e.g. exercises, questions, re-writing the lesson in the children's own words, drawing, modelling, making a booklet, dramatization. This is a most important part of teaching, for we have not really taught anything until we have helped the children to learn it. (The work will of course have to be revised at regular intervals to prevent the children forgetting it.)

If groups are necessary they must be prepared very carefully, and the teacher must have a clear plan of the work of each group and where he himself will be at each stage of the lesson. If there are three groups it is really like planning work for three different classes.

The teacher must find out how much the children have understood and learnt of the lesson, by marking the work they have done, by question-ing or by noticing how the children manage to do the activity they have been given. The next lesson will be built on the children's ability to under-stand this lesson, so it is important that the teacher discovers what has been learnt. The **evaluation** of the lesson is most important.

Questioning. Questions are used to revise work, and they also make children think and reason (pages 141–2). When asking a question the teacher should wait until many children have thought and put up their hands, before he names a particular child to give the answer. If the teacher says one child's name, e.g. Samuel, and then asks the questions, the other children will think, 'This question is for Samuel, so we do not need to think about it.' By waiting until all the children have thought before calling a name, the teacher ensures that all the class attend. It also helps him to notice which children do not understand, for they will not put up their hands and the teacher will be able to explain any difficulties to them later. Sometimes ask a child who continually does not put up his hand, to see whether he is attending or not. Tell the children that though you cannot ask them all, you are watching to see who is working hard. Give praise when children do try. 'Grace has had her hand up for each question. Good. You have been working well.'

Working in groups. Older children often sit in rows, but the teacher of smaller children usually finds the organization of a lesson is easier if the desks are arranged in groups, and the children can sit in groups according to their ability. A child who is in one group for Maths may be in another group for Reading, so some changes may be necessary for this lesson.

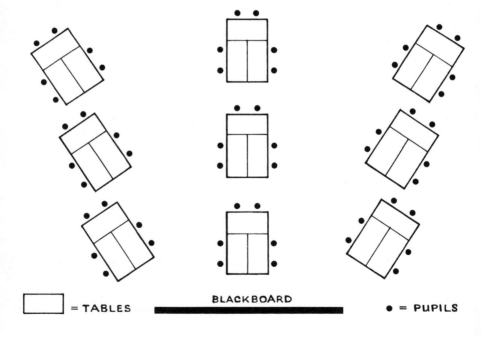

☐ = TABLES   **BLACKBOARD**   ● = PUPILS

The children quickly learn their groups and change over quietly; they can share apparatus in the group and help each other. The teacher must make sure that all the children have a fair share of the apparatus, and all are busy. More space for moving about and for dramatic work is available when the children sit in groups. The teacher must, however, make sure that all the children can see the blackboard when it is being used. If there are chairs these can be easily turned round, but with fixed seats special care is needed. Each child should see without twisting his neck much if the plan on page 42 is used.

Chapter 7   The School and the Child

Classification by Age

Children of the same age should be in a class together, because their interests and needs will be like those of others of their own age. If some children are very clever they should be put into a special group for certain subjects like Maths, Reading and English. They should not be put into a higher class with children two or three years older, because the older children will have developed far more, emotionally and socially. Similarly, backward children should be taught in a special group and not put into a lower class, unless the class teacher and headteacher feel a certain child would greatly benefit from being in a lower class.

Classification by Ability

Each child must be helped to progress at his own speed among children of the same age. Some children learn quickly, while some learn slowly, and when possible each should work individually. When individual work is not possible, the teacher should organize the class into groups. Three groups are usually sufficient, a quick group, an average group and a slow group, though the teacher may find that he has to make even more groups.

Streams. If the school is big, and there are two classes for each age group, the children can be 'streamed'. This means that all the slower children are put into one class, and all the quicker children are put into another. Instead of each teacher struggling with the difficult organization of a number of groups in the class, they will probably only need two groups.

The class with the slower children will be smaller than the other, because the children need more individual help from the teacher. He will be able to go at a slower pace, helping and encouraging his children to work to the best of their ability. The teacher with the quicker class will be able to keep all the children very busy. They can make good progress without having to wait for the slower children, because these will be in another class.

The streams are usually called **1a** and **1b**, **2a** and **2b** etc. If there are three classes in each age group, they will be called **1a** (the quick children), **1b** (the average children), and **1c** (the slow children). Sometimes teachers do not like children to know they are in the quick class, as they might become conceited, so instead of calling the class **1a**, they call it after the teacher's initial. For example, Mr Taiwo's class would be called '**1t**'. A slower class would be called '**1j**', if the teacher was called Mr Jimoh. Children, however, usually realize which class they are in. If you use this organization it is necessary that both classes understand that they must work as hard as possible, and that both quick and slow people have important work to do in the community.

Classes of mixed ability. A number of educationalists are, however, against streaming. As teachers we should educate a child's whole personality, not only his mind. If the classes are streamed, the minds of the bright children may be more fully developed, but they will lose a great deal of social training. The quicker children may think they are more important than the others, and this is bad for a democracy. Recent research in Europe has shown that children in b or c classes develop a poor self-concept. They picture themselves as slow, and stop trying. These children may have the potential to develop if the environment is improved (see pages 30 and 144). Remember that a child will not develop well unless we give him the best opportunities. Putting him in a slow class may mean his opportunities become limited. When quick and slow children are in the same class, they learn to understand and have patience with each other. Each learns to do his best and not to criticize his neighbour.

The Head must think carefully, and usually he will decide that mixed ability classes will benefit the children more.

Promotion. Children should usually be promoted with their own age group. If a child who is backward is one of the youngest in the class, and the teacher and the headteacher think that it would really benefit him to remain another year in the same class, he could be kept there, as he would only be a few months older than the new children.

Family Grouping
As families have children of different ages, so some teachers think we should have children of different ages in one class. Usually only two ages are combined. For example, if Mr P has 30 six-year-olds and Mrs T has 34 seven-year-olds, the classes could be reorganized by giving Mr P 17 seven-year-olds, from Mrs T's class, while she takes 15 of his children. (Sometimes three ages are combined in a similar way.) This organization is also called **vertical grouping,** and is usually found in schools which also operate an **integrated day.**

The Syllabus
Many Education departments publish a syllabus. This is a great help to the teacher, but he should remember that these syllabuses are suggestions

and each class is different. It is important to remember that the children should not be pushed to fit the syllabus, but **the syllabus should be changed to suit the children.**

Schemes of Work
Using the syllabus as a guide the teacher will prepare a scheme of work for each term. In it the teacher will put exactly what he hopes to teach during the term. Inexperienced teachers should be helped by the head-teacher to prepare their schemes.

Again, remember that the scheme is a guide. The teacher may find the children go very slowly and only half the scheme is taught, but **half a scheme well taught is better than a whole scheme badly taught** and not understood by the children. On the other hand, the children may learn very quickly and the teacher may have to add work to his scheme.

Always arrange the work to fit the children and remember that no two classes are alike. Never say 'I taught up to lesson 35 last year, so I must do it this year'. Each year will be different. When making a scheme, number the headings, 1, 2, 3, etc., but *never* put 1st week, 2nd week, 3rd week, etc., because no one can possibly tell exactly how much the children will learn in one week.

Timetables
Infant and Junior timetables should have different lengths for lessons. Because the Infant cannot concentrate for as long as the Junior his lessons should be twenty or twenty-five minutes long, and there should be more breaks, unless an integrated day is planned (see page 8). Usually the Infant child has half an hour a day less in school than the Junior child. (Remember, English is very difficult for the Infant, and fifteen minutes is quite long enough, if they must have half an hour per day, take fifteen minutes in the morning and fifteen minutes in the afternoon; the children will learn far more in this way than if they are given one half-hour lesson.) Infants need plenty of bodily activity, so they should have a P.E. lesson each day, as also should the younger Juniors if it can possibly be arranged. After a lesson needing a lot of mental concentration put an easier lesson. For example, after Reading, which is difficult for first-year Infants, put Drama or Hygiene, which are not so difficult.

Examinations
Examinations can be given to older Junior children twice a year, about June and then again before Christmas. It is only a waste of time to give examinations more often, but small tests can be useful when the teacher wishes to discover if the children have really understood a certain type of work. From the results of the tests the teacher can form the children into

groups; e.g. those children who did correct work can be shown the next stage, while those who made a number of mistakes can be taught again.

Examinations should be based on the work that has been done in the class, and should be neither too easy nor too difficult. If a number of children have full marks, then the examination has been too easy, and not a real test of the children's learning. If more than a quarter of the class get below 40 per cent the examination has been too difficult. The head-teacher should guide the teachers when making their examination papers, and should watch to see that the standard of work in the school is not falling, but is improving each year.

Examinations can be followed by a school report, which helps the parents to see how their child is progressing. On the report should be written not only the marks gained in the examination, but also **remarks** stating how the child has worked and behaved during the months before the examination. Remembering the children's different abilities the teacher must give praise for hard work and good conduct, even if the marks are not very good.

There should be no examinations for the Infant children nor for younger Junior children, but small tests can be given sometimes. Records of each child's progress should be kept by the teacher, and these are really more important than examinations.

Records of the Children's Progress
There are many different ways of keeping records of a child's progress. I mention a few that I have found useful.

A Record Book (with dates of observations, weekly or monthly).
A child's name is written at the top of each page and anything special that the teacher notices about the child is written underneath.

For example, Mary is the third child in a family of six children.

She missed school for eight weeks in January and February due to illness.

She is very good at Reading and Needlework.

She is weak at Maths and needs special help, but she tries very hard.

She is a friendly and helpful child. (Note made on 6 March).

If the headteacher or an Inspector want to know about Mary it is all written down, and these records can be a great help to the next teacher.

Maths Records
A chart can be made showing the different stages the teacher hopes to teach during the term, and a tick is given when a child has mastered the stage. An example of a Maths chart for an Infant class (children of six and a half to seven and a half years) is shown on page 48.

The recognition and understanding of the numbers to 20 would be learnt and practised often as an introduction, when later in the lesson the children would do addition or subtraction sums to 10. That is the reason why some children may be able to recognize numbers before they can do sums that are written before them on the list. This does not matter at all, as the sooner the children recognize and understand the written figures the better.

	ADDITION TO 10	SUBTRACTION FROM 10	ADDITION & SUBTRACTION MIXED TO 10	RECOGNITION OF NUMBERS TO 20	ADDITION TO 20	SUBTRACTION TO 20	ADDITION & SUBTRACTION MIXED TO 20	RECOGNITION OF NUMBERS TO 50	
JOSEPH	✓	✓	✓	✓					
PETER	✓								
PIUS	✓	✓	✓	✓				✓	
GRACE	✓	✓	✓	✓	✓				
MARY	✓	✓		✓					
etc									

Record of Tables (for juniors)

	2x	3x	4x	5x	6x	7x	8x	9x	10x	11x	12x	
John	✓	✓	✓	✓	✓				✓	✓		
Samuel	✓	✓		✓					✓			
Stella	✓			✓					✓			
etc.												

Record of Reading Groups
The record of reading groups is best kept in a record book, with a page for each group (page 49).

The teacher will continue in this way for as many groups as he has. Only the pages which the teacher actually hears the group read will be put in the record book. Sometimes the teacher will let the children read a page to the leader, and next time the teacher hears the children he will ask questions to see if they have understood the page. If a record is kept in this way the teacher knows exactly which page they have reached, and how often he has heard each group read in the month. This is also a great help to the headteacher if the teacher is ill and the class has to be taken by someone else.

GROUP I

Aina Sule Amadu etc.	May. Book I Pages 27, 28, 30, 31, 32, 34, 35, 36, 37, 39, 40, June 42, 43, 44, Book II 3, 5, 6,

GROUP 2

Peter Pius Teresa etc	May. Book I Pages 18, 20, 21, 22, 23, 24, 26, 27, 28, 30, 31, 32, June 33, 35, 36, 39, 40, 41,

Reading Records for Older Children
Once children can read they should be encouraged to read as much as possible, and each child should keep his own record of the books he has read from the school library and at home.

DATE	TITLE	REMARKS
14th JANUARY	The boy from the North	very interesting
22nd JANUARY	Our Village Customs	good explanations and pictures
2nd FEBRUARY	The children catch a thief	very exciting
9th FEBRUARY	The Eskimo Twins	difficult to understand

Records of Older Children's Marks

These records should be kept, as it helps the teacher to see at a glance how each child is progressing through the term.

Records can be kept like this of any subject where marks are given.

COMPOSITION	13th February Myself	20th February A visit to the market	27th February The story of a Yam
maximum mark	10	10	10
Sule	6	8	7
Musa	4	6	6
etc			

Chapter 8   The Teacher in the Classroom

Managing the Class

The following are suggestions to help the young teacher in managing his class.

1. When you have to stand in front of the class, stand well back from the children so that you can see them all.

2. Stand still in front of the class when asking questions, explaining new work or giving directions. It is distracting if the teacher wanders up and down, and some children may not be able to hear.

3. When going round the class correcting individual children's work, try to place yourself in such a position that you can still see most of the children. In this way no one will feel that you are not supervising him.

4. Sit down when telling a story, as this creates a more friendly atmosphere.

5. It is a waste of time speaking if **all** the children are not listening.
A word or two will call older ones to attention. 'John and Grace are sitting up ready to listen. Who else is ready?' All the children will sit up, as they wish to be praised also. If small infants are all chattering, it is not much use, in a large class, to shout above their noise. Try this: do some exercises or actions with your arms and fingers, and soon the children in the front row will copy you, then the ones behind will follow, until all the class is copying your exercises. When the children are all quiet, tell them what you want.

6. Giving out and collecting books can cause confusion if it is not properly organized. Always try to have monitors to give out books during recess or meal-times. If the children are too young to read the names on the books, give them out yourself during recess. The quickest way to collect books is to choose a child sitting in the last desk in each row; if you have four rows that will mean four monitors. When you want the books tell the children to put them at the side of the desk, ask the monitors to collect them, and it is all finished in less than a minute. If the children are sitting in groups one monitor is chosen from each group and the same result is obtained.

7. The children should be trained to enter and leave the room in an orderly fashion. This does not mean that they should look like little soldiers on parade, but they should walk quietly without pushing. Until the children

get used to what you expect, train them by sending out one row, or one group at a time, while you see if they walk well. After some weeks the children will know how you expect them to behave, and you can let them go out quietly when they have finished their work, because often children do not finish together, and it is poor training to leave a sum half done or a sentence half written.

Making the Classroom more Attractive

The teacher and the children should work together to make the classroom pleasant. Everyone can work better, and feel much happier, in attractive surroundings. The following are suggestions which you can try:

1. Keep the room clean and tidy. Choose monitors to be in charge of this.

2. Have flowers on the teacher's table and on any cupboards or spare tables. Take the labels off bottles before using them for vases.

3. Pin any interesting pictures on the wall, but remember to dust them, and do not leave them for more than a month before changing them for new ones.

4. Pin any of the children's best drawings and paintings on the wall. If the children have painted patterns use them to make a border round the room.

5. Pin up examples of the children's best writing and work.

6. Have a news sheet on which the children can pin any interesting news they have written themselves, or news which they have cut from a newspaper.

7. Have record charts and team charts hung on the wall.

8. Have Interest Tables, with stimulating objects for discussion and discovery.

9. Make a Home Corner, a Music area and an Activity area where children can work individually or in groups.

10. Have a book corner or a library table, from which the children can get books to increase their general knowledge.

11. Keep the blackboard clean when not in use, and when it is being used make sure that the writing is very good.

12. If possible have the walls whitewashed, and the doors and shutters painted in a bright colour.

The Use of Books in the Classroom

Books are most important to anyone who wishes to be educated, because we can learn such a great deal from them. Books should, therefore, be treated respectfully, and it is an important part of a child's training that he is shown how to use books. The pages should always be turned over carefully at the top. It is very wasteful to write or scribble in a book, and it should never be folded backwards in half, as that spoils the binding.

Books are expensive, but they are well worth the money. If they are treated carefully they can last for years and be used for a number of classes.

There should be a book corner in each classroom, and the children should be encouraged to read as much as possible.

The Use of Apparatus
Apparatus is the word used to describe anything which helps the teacher to make the lesson clear to the children, but **it must be remembered that though apparatus is useful it can never take the place of good teaching.** It is only an aid to teaching.

The most common piece of apparatus in the classroom is, of course, the blackboard, and if used properly it can be a great help to the teacher and to the children.

The Use of the Blackboard
1. All blackboard work must be clear and should set a good example for the children to copy.

2. There should be a good space between each word, but the letters in a word should be fairly close together.

The old man went to market.

3. When you wish to write on the blackboard and explain something to the class, there are three steps you should follow: (*a*) tell the children what you are going to do; (*b*) turn round and write or draw as quickly as you can while still doing neat work; (*c*) turn to the children again and discuss or explain what you have done. Never talk and look at the blackboard at the same time, for the children will not be able to hear you.

4. Always make use of your recesses to put any writing or sums on the blackboard, so that the children never sit wasting their time while you prepare the blackboard for the next lesson.

5. Always see that your blackboard is kept clean and black. It can be washed at least once a week, and blackened with blackboard ink when necessary. A grey blackboard makes it very difficult for the children to read what is on it.

6. Use your blackboard whenever possible to build up your teaching points.

7. Use coloured chalk to emphasize special words or diagrams. Blue and mauve chalk do not show up well and can be used for drawing lines. Orange and yellow are good for special words.

8. Draw lines in blue chalk, as they will keep your writing straight. The tidy clear blackboard which results is worth the little extra trouble.

Other Kinds of Apparatus

Apparatus also includes charts, pictures, diagrams, maps, flashcards and command cards, pre-number and pre-reading games, number and reading games, Interest Tables, individual cards with exercises which the children can do, clocks, weather charts, Nature charts, team charts, calendars and any other object which the teacher takes into the class to make his teaching plainer. If the teacher makes the apparatus it must be done most carefully, and any lettering or drawing must be as exact as possible.

Many of the pieces of apparatus are explained on other pages, but here are two suggestions for date charts.

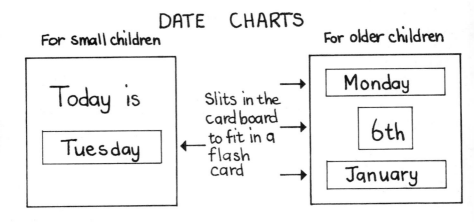

DATE CHARTS

Part two The Teaching of
Number and the
Beginnings of
Mathematics

Introduction

The world is becoming more technical and scientific every year, and people, who wish to keep in touch with new developments and inventions, need a wider and wider knowledge of the mathematics which lies behind science and technology. We shall not all become scientists, mathematicians nor technologists, but we should understand something of the work these people do.

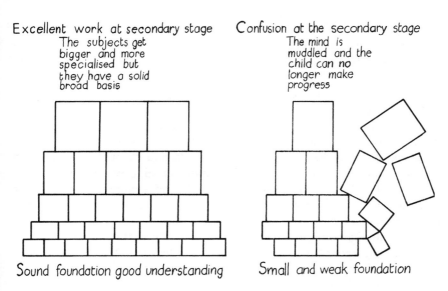

Excellent work at secondary stage
The subjects get bigger and more specialised but they have a solid broad basis

Confusion at the secondary stage
The mind is muddled and the child can no longer make progress

Sound foundation good understanding

Small and weak foundation

Many educationalists now call the Arithmetic lesson the Mathematics lesson (or 'Maths' lesson), to show they intend to give the child a **broad** grounding on which he can build later knowledge.

The following type of mechanical sums have been given too much attention in schools.

35		23		₦	k		m	cm		hrs	min		kg	g
26		+ 4		1	55		2	43		4	12			
+92		—		+	5		—	6		×	5		3 ⌐13	240
—		—		—			—			—				

Already there are machines which can work out this type of sum more quickly and accurately than the human brain. When our children grow up there will be even more of these machines, or computers. This does not mean that we no longer teach these sums, but we spend less time on them. We make sure they are not taught too early.

Understanding is more important than accuracy. The machine will get the correct answer in later life, if the man **understands** how to set the machine, because he **understands the principle** behind the machine.

It must be stressed that **the child must understand what he is doing.**

How do we Know the Child Understands?
This is an extremely difficult question, and cannot be answered completely at present, but every year new facts are discovered about the working of the brain. One recent, important discovery is that children in Infant classes do not really understand even what very simple numbers are. But you will say, 'My children understand numbers and can do many kinds of sums before they are seven.' Indeed they do, but they do not understand them in a mathematical way; they only understand them in a mechanical way, like a parrot. For technological development and scientific progress we must all understand in a mathematical way.

When children do begin to understand they develop slowly. This may have something to do with the way the brain grows. Just as a baby cannot walk before the legs are ready, so understanding cannot come before the brain has developed sufficiently. We can help and encourage the brain to develop, but we cannot force it. Full understanding will not be reached until the child is about twelve years old, and sometimes much later. Reference to other books is necessary for detailed explanation. Important points to remember are:

1. Understanding is the first aim of teaching Mathematics.
2. Spend more time on practical work, keeping numbers small.
3. Go slowly, very slowly until the children are eight years old.

(This depends, of course, on their intelligence, and may mean nine or ten years for some children.) Most syllabuses and textbooks progress far too quickly with mechanical sums.

Everyday Mathematics
It is necessary to help children to find the answers to everyday problems which occur in the home, at the market and, when they are older, at work. For example: counting yams for the market and working out how much money they will fetch; giving and receiving change; working out the cost of a journey; weighing cocoa; working out the time a certain job will take; weighing a baby and comparing it with the average weight of babies of that age; measuring a piece of cloth for a new dress.

Progress Comes with Confidence
As with other subjects, Mathematics should give children enjoyment and a feeling of success, as they discover and learn. When work is too hard the children become discouraged and frightened. Each child should feel happy and confident if he is to progress, and each brick of the foundation must be firm before building further.

Remember
1. Give the children as much **practical experience** as possible, using real objects which they can see and move about, to help them to **understand the meaning** behind the figures and the sums.
2. **Progress very slowly.** I have given various stages in the teaching of some processes, but only the teacher who knows the class can say when a child is ready for the next stage.
3. When a child is practising new work and later stages, **revise** previous work now and again, to keep it in the forefront of his mind.

The Vocabulary of Mathematics
We understand each other through words. When a child uses a word he does not always show that he understands what it means. It is through practising the use of the word, **in concrete situations, with help and correction from the teacher,** that the child gradually comes to know the true meaning of the word. Many Mathematical words are used in other lessons and outside school. They should be introduced and used at any suitable time.

The following words all express Mathematical ideas: many, not many; more, less; big, small, bigger, smaller, biggest, smallest; long, short, longer, shorter, longest, shortest; high, low; near, far; how long, how short, how near, how far; buying, selling, cost, price, profit, expensive, dear, cheap; wide, narrow; quick, slow; a long time, a short time; a large amount, a small amount; light, heavy, lighter, heavier, lightest, heaviest;

straight, curved; the whole, a part of, a fraction of, a half of, a quarter of; far, near; the points of the compass, North, South, East, West; above, below, in between; first, second, third, etc.; last, second from last, in the middle. There are many more. Make a list and use them often during lessons, and in conversations with the children. The more they are used, the sooner will the children begin to understand them. For example: a child who is ill may have visited the hospital.

'Is the hospital far from here, Yisau? How long did it take to walk there? Do you think the post office is nearer to our school than the hospital? How could we find out?'

Some of the older children may have brought oranges from the school farm.

'Did Class 5 pick many oranges? Did anyone count them? Was the basket heavy? Did you try to lift it, Ojo? Will the children sell the oranges? How much do you think they will cost? How much money will the children get?'

Some words used in the Mathematics lesson are not found often in everyday speech, and these need special attention. Such words are addition, subtraction, multiplication, division, square, rectangle, triangle, perimeter, area, circle, diameter, circumference, a cube, a sphere, a pyramid, decimal, average, scale, graph, angles, right angle, volume, ratio and cancelling. You will be able to think of many more. These special words will require special teaching. They will be introduced, revised and used many times during the Primary years.

I have used English words, but where there is a vernacular word use that. We are teaching Mathematical ideas at this stage and not English.

The teacher needs to study the background of the children. Town children will have had a different experience from village children. Children in a wet region will have a different experience from children in a dry region. With an understanding of the home life, the teacher will be able to build on what the children have learned at home.

Chapter 9   The Early Stages

The teaching of young children requires special techniques and is not just a simplified form of Senior teaching, as many people wrongly suppose.

The Child's Mind is different *from the Adult's Mind*
When children come to school they will have very little understanding of Number. They may be able to count, but they do not know what the numbers really represent. In Switzerland, Professor Jean Piaget has shown us something of the workings of the child's mind. It is not just a smaller mind than the adult's; it is often quite different altogether. With his clever and interesting experiments on Number, Piaget has discovered that the small child's mind cannot accept that numbers remain the same, when they **look** different. It is difficult for us to understand this, because it is a long time since we were children, and our minds have developed and changed over the years.

Try this experiment with a young child. Put 16 or 18 beads on his desk, and ask him to give the same amount to the teacher and to himself. 'One for me. One for the teacher. Another for me. Another for the teacher. Another for me. Another for the teacher,' and so on. Do not help the child to count. If he wants to count, let him, **but do not interfere.** Just make sure that every time he gives a bead to himself he also gives one to the teacher. The actual number you have does not matter, as long as the child is sure you **both have the same amount.**

'Have we both the same amount of beads, Amadu?' If the child agrees, the teacher should spread her beads out.

'Have we both the same amount now, Amadu?' If the child is of average intelligence and under seven years old, he will probably say they are no longer the same amount. 'Who has more, Amadu? You or I?' He may say the teacher has more beads because hers are spread out, or he may say the opposite; he has more beads because his are closer together. The important thing to note is that they do not **look** the same, therefore they are not the same to the child's mind. How can he understand that if he adds 5 and 3 it makes 8, if sometimes his 8 is more than your 8, and sometimes his 8 is less than your 8. If you give him this sum $5 + 3 = $, he works it out because the teacher tells him to. If he puts a certain answer the teacher marks the sum right, and says, 'Good boy.' The child is pleased because the teacher praises him, but he does not **understand** Number. It is all a mystery to him, but if the teacher is pleased, that is all the child worries about. We must not teach children to remember the correct answer, because we say it is correct. We must help children to **understand** what they are doing, and to work out the correct answer because their mathematical foundation is good, **because they know exactly what they are doing.**

Warning: If you try this experiment (or any other experiment) **do not** say anything about the child being right or wrong. You must be **pleased** with any answer, because you are getting a little look into the child's mind. By looking surprised or cross, you can quickly teach a child to say whatever words he thinks will please you. Then you will never know if he really understands or not.

The age at which a child understands **simple** Number is often between seven and eight, but this depends on many things: home background, intelligence, health, etc.; **some may understand earlier; others may not understand until about nine or ten.** It will take even longer for a child to understand tens, hundreds, thousands and bigger numbers. It is probably not until a child reaches 12 years of age or older that he begins to think like an adult. Always remember you are dealing with a mind that is rather different from your own. In Mathematics, perhaps more than any other Primary school lesson, this is an important consideration.

Other books should be read to give greater knowledge of the ways children look at the world. These new ideas are not well understood by all teachers yet, and each year new facts are learned about how children think. Try to go to book exhibitions, and refresher courses after your main training has finished.

I. Pre-number Experiences: Groups

Children require a great deal of practice sorting objects into groups. This may seem very simple to you, but it is an important foundation for understanding Number.

Suggestions for Class Work

Draw two large circles on the floor, and space the children around where they can see both circles. In fine weather this can be taken outside. 'All the girls are to stand in this circle and all the boys are to stand in that circle. Good. Now we have a group of girls here and a group of boys here. Stand outside the circles and we shall make some more groups. Stand well back so you can all see. Now in this circle we shall put books and in that circle we shall put pencils. Make the groups. Good. What is this a group of? Aina? Good, it is a group of pencils. What is this a group of? Sule? It is a group of books. Good.'

Make other groups. For example: chairs and benches; slates and chalks; rulers and sticks; flowers and fruit. If you put all the objects on the floor before you begin, the children will enjoy finding what you ask for, and putting the things into groups.

It is possible to have a group which is empty, and this should not be forgotten. 'Now we shall make some new groups. Here we shall put all the flowers, and here all the coconuts. Good. We have some flowers in this group. We have no coconuts, so this group of coconuts is empty. Pick up the flowers, please, Aina. Good. Pick up the coconuts, please, Amadu. You cannot pick up the coconuts. Why not? Because we have no coconuts. Correct. That group is empty.'

The children will enjoy playing these group games. Later draw circles for three groups and then for four groups.

Suggestions for Individual Work (or Small Groups)
Collect boxes into which you will put many groups of things, all mixed up together. For example, you might put one button, two pencils, three seeds, four stones, five sticks, six lids, seven pieces of wool (all about the same length), eight pieces of cloth (all about the same size) and nine pieces of string (all about the same length). In another box there might be five stones, five small pieces of chalk, five bottle-tops, five leaves, five flowers and five beads. Sometimes the groups in the boxes can be all the same amount; sometimes all the groups can be of a different amount. Vary the boxes to give the children experience of groups up to ten at first (later up to twenty). Remember you do not mention the actual numbers at this stage. When the children have arranged the groups they can draw them on their blackboards or paper, before getting another box to sort out.

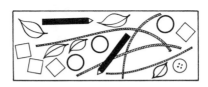

Numbers and counting are not introduced yet. **You are giving the children concrete experience of grouping.**

II. Matching Groups
The children need a great deal of practice in matching groups, and the teacher should collect as many things as possible for the children to match. **No numbers are used at this stage.**

Suggestions for Class Work
'All the girls stand up. Now each girl take a boy for a partner. There are as many boys as girls standing here. Each girl has a boy partner. Over there we have a few boys with no partners. Never mind. You may get a partner next time. All go back to your places. Good.

'Okeke, Ifi, Kurubo, Aina, Data, Musa and Chume sit on the floor here. In this game I want some children to stand behind these sitting children. One standing child to one sitting child.' (If you have a large class all the children cannot play each game, but they can all watch. Make sure that all the children have a turn as often as possible.)

'In this game all the children sitting on this side of the room will play. Try to stand behind a sitting child. Ready. Run. Good. Now there is one child standing behind each sitting child. Are there any extra? Yes, there are a few extra. They did not manage to get a partner. Never mind. You all tried hard. Sit down and we shall play the game again with different children.'

In this way children begin to see one group matching with another group; for example, a group of sitting children matched with a group of standing children. Other ideas for matching: a group of girls matched with a group of chairs; each girl must have a chair to sit on; a group of boys holding pencils matched with a group of boys holding books; a group of children holding flowers matched with a group of children holding jars to put the flowers in; a group with bowls to put food in, matched with a group with spoons to eat the food; a group with hoops matched with a group holding bean-bags to throw through the hoops. Try to think of as many ways as possible to play this matching game. **No numbers are used at this stage.** The teacher, of course, will make the groups of different sizes to give the children experience of groups from one to ten (later to twenty). There is no counting of groups by the children. **One is matched with one only.** One piece of chalk with one blackboard; another piece of chalk with another blackboard; another piece of chalk with another blackboard.

Suggestions for Individual Work (or Small Groups)
Give the child some leaves and ask him to put a seed beside each leaf. 'Have you the same amount of seeds as leaves? Good. Draw them on your blackboard.'

Actual numbers are not mentioned. **It is the matching which is important.** As the children become more skilful larger groups can be introduced. 'Here are some books. Put the same amount of pencils on the table, so that each book has a pencil.'

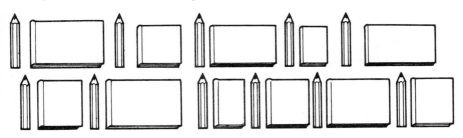

65

Other Ideas for Matching Individually or in Small Groups

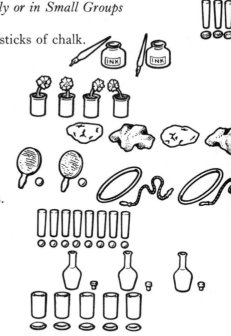

Kobo, or other coin, matched with sticks of chalk.

Ink bottles matched with pens.

Flowers matched with jars.

Stones matched with balls of clay.

Bats matched with balls.

Skipping ropes matched with hoops.

Skittles matched with balls.

Bottles matched with bottle tops.

Tins matched with tin lids.

Always have a few more objects in one group. The child will then have to match carefully, and **there will be a few extra to put on one side.** It is a good idea to have a table for this apparatus. Children can work by themselves or with a partner. They can match any group with any other group, but it will seem more sensible if there is some connection between the groups. It does not matter if the objects on the table get into a muddle, as it is a good exercise for the children to tidy the table and rearrange the objects into groups, all the bottles together, all the spoons together, all the lids together, etc.

Collect boxes of the same size for smaller apparatus, which can be matched on the desk. Give the children the objects mixed up and ask them to put the same amount in each box. 'Here are some buttons and some thread for sewing them on to a dress. Put some buttons in this box and a piece of thread for each button in this box. You may have some extra. Draw them on your blackboard, and then get some more boxes.'

  Buttons matched with thread or wool

Sticks matched with seeds

After the children have had plenty of practice using concrete objects you can use pictures. These are smaller and easier to deal with on the desks, but if a child has pictures today, make sure he has a turn with the actual objects tomorrow. The pictures are only second best, but they are useful for extra practice. If you are not very good at drawing, cut pictures from magazines and catalogues.

Suggestions for Pictures
Feet matched with sandals.

Fires matched with pots.

Goats matched with food.

Hens matched with eggs.

Shapes are Good for Matching
Squares matched with circles.

Triangles matched with rectangles.

Rectangles matched with squares.

Circles matched with semicircles.

Small triangles matched with large triangles.

Small squares matched with large squares.

Colours are also Good for Matching
Red sandals matched with green sandals.

Blue dresses matched with red dresses.

Green pentagons (five-sided figure) matched with black pentagon.

Brown hexagon (six-sided figure) matched with white hexagon.

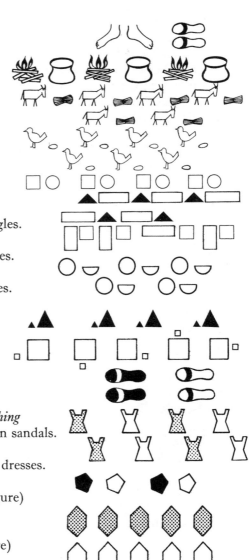

It is good for them to see as many different shapes as possible. You can make one shape carefully in strong cardboard, and draw round it to make more shapes quickly.

III. Arranging More than Two Groups
Now children can make three, four, five or more groups all having the same amount in each.

Suggestions for Class Work
Draw some circles or squares on the floor and ask children to put the same amount into each group. 'Put some leaves in this square, Sule. Aina, will you match Sule's group and put the same amount of flowers in this square, while Odibo puts the same amount of jars in this square and Data puts the same amount of mats in this square. Good. Put the jars on the mats, Musa. Do they match? Good. Put the flowers in the jars, Laide. Are there enough?' In this way help the children to check that all the groups match each other.

Individual Work
(*a*) Give boxes as before, but children will use more than two boxes each time.

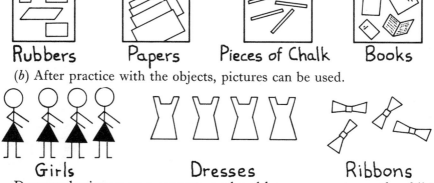

(*b*) After practice with the objects, pictures can be used.

Draw each picture on a separate card and have some extra so the child must match.

(*c*) Groups of similar objects but different colours. (It is not necessary for all the objects to be exactly alike, but they must be similar.) **Always give some extra** to make it necessary for the children to match one to one, another to another and so on.

(*d*) Pictures of similar articles but of different colours:

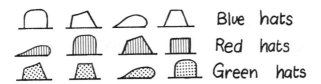

(*e*) Shapes in different colours:

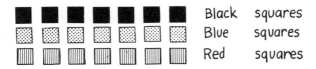

As the child progresses through these stages keep revising the earlier ones, especially those using concrete objects.

IV. Sequence

For number understanding it is important for children to recognize the pattern of numbers. Two is one more than one; three is one more than two; four is one more than three. Numbers progress in a definite pattern:

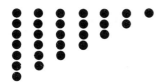

This is called number sequence.

(*a*) *Single Sequence*

Before learning number names children need a great deal of practice putting objects and shapes into sequence patterns.

'Here are some tins. You can see they are all different sizes. Can you arrange them so that the smallest is here, and they get larger and larger as we go along the line?' Do not start counting yet.

At first children may not be able to do this at all well.

Suggestions for Class Work
Use articles which will stand on the floor or the desk.

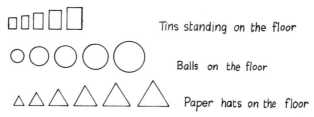

Tins standing on the floor

Balls on the floor

Paper hats on the floor

Put balls of different sizes on the floor. 'Can you pick out the smallest ball, Laide? Good. Put it on the floor here. Now look to see which is the next smallest. Who can pick it out? Yisau. Good. Put it by the smallest. Who can find the next one? Aina. Good. Put it by the others. Each ball is a little bigger than the one before.' Continue in this way until all the balls are arranged in sequence. Mix them up and start again, but this time begin by picking out the largest ball first, and then the next largest and so on until you come to the smallest. Play this game with as many objects as you can find. The children can also arrange themselves in order of height.

Suggestions for Individual and Group Work
Children can arrange big apparatus on the floor or smaller things on the desk; for example, buttons, clay, envelopes, books, bowls. (Do not use sticks, pencils or rulers at this stage.)

(b) Double Sequence
Teach this in the same way as the single sequence, but when you have arranged one pattern of objects arrange another sequence to match the first. 'Here we have some wooden dolls. Who can pick out the smallest? Aina. Good. Put it over here. Who can pick out the next smallest doll?', and so on. 'Now we have arranged these dolls, we shall arrange these bowls, giving the smallest bowl to the smallest doll, the next smallest doll will have the next smallest bowl and so on until we come to the largest doll, who will have the largest bowl.'

A good exercise is to give the children the dolls and ask them to make bowls, balls, hats, etc., in clay for the dolls. The largest doll must have the largest hat, the smallest doll has the smallest hat.

Suggestions for other double sequences:

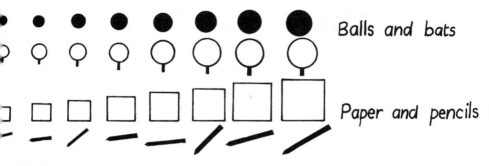

Balls and bats

Paper and pencils

(c) Sequence Using Strips

Make strips of cardboard so that each one is 3 cm longer than the last. Ask the children to put them into order from the smallest to the largest. Even though they have had practice with the large concrete objects, the strips may prove difficult. Before, the apparatus stood on the floor or on the desk, which were flat surfaces. The child only had to look at the top of the objects. Now he must look at both ends of the strip. At first he may be unable to concentrate on these two aspects of the strips, and you will find arrangements like this

He is making a sequence with one part of the strip, but is not considering the whole strip. This is quite normal, and the child should be encouraged to consider the complete length. The same kind of arrangement may be seen with other shapes of this type, such as pencils or sticks. This is why they should not be used in the first stage.

It may help the child to give him a ruler or a straight piece of wood, and suggest he puts one end of each strip against the ruler. Take the wood away when the sequence has been made.

71

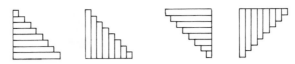

The first two arrangements can be called staircases. Give the child a cardboard doll, and let it walk up the staircase one step at a time. This helps to fix the progression in the child's mind. Mix the staircase up and make it again. 'Have you made your staircase? Good. Put the doll on the ground. Now put the doll on the first step. Let the doll walk up the staircase one step at a time. Which step is he on now, Ifi? Good, the top step. Let the doll walk down one step. Let him walk down one more step. Let him walk down another step,' and continue until the doll is at the bottom again. The child can draw the staircase on his blackboard. Once the child becomes quite skilful at the staircase give him one with 2 cm steps, and then 1 cm steps, so he has to look more closely, and compare the strips more carefully.

Chapter 10   Number Experiences

I. Counting

Counting should be introduced orally (speech only, no writing) whenever possible during the day, when there is occasion to count something; for example, count the number of children present for the register; count the pencils to be given out; count the flowers brought to school; count the pictures the children have painted. **But** do not count the pre-number apparatus at this stage. Introduce counting at different times during the day, and although the children will not understand what the numbers mean, they will begin to realize that counting is useful. The children may chant the numbers with you, and gradually learn the words. **Remember this does not show that they understand the mathematical meaning of what they are chanting.**

When you decide the children are ready for counting lessons always use concrete objects to count.

Suggestions for Class Work

At first count up to five only, using something big which all the children can see, rulers, balls, books, etc.

'I have one book. And another book makes . . . . Grace? Two books. Good; and another book makes . . . . John? Three books. Good; and another book makes . . . .' Continue up to five books. 'Who can show me five pencils? Jimoh. Good. Hold them so all the children can see. Let us help Jimoh count them. One, two, three, four, five. Good. Who can show me five slates?' Continue with a number of different objects.

Let children have small things, such as stones, beads, leaves, seeds, to count on the desks. 'Put one on the desk. And another stone. That makes . . . . Etim? Two stones. Put another stone on the desk. That makes . . . . Ibrahim? Three stones. Good.' Continue in this way.

Taking one away is just as important as building one on each time. Always reverse the process.

'We have five books. Good. If I take one away, how many books have I now? Uwa. Four books. Good. I shall take another one away. How many have I now?' Continue until there is one book left.

'I have one book. I shall take it away. How many books have I now? Chinua. None. Good. I have no books at all now.' It is very important to give experience of none, nothing and an empty group. Use all the apparatus you have for exercises like this. Adding one on each time, and then taking one off.

Suggestions for Individual Work (or Small Groups)
All the apparatus you collected for the pre-number experiences can be used again, only now the children may count.

'How many bowls have you? Three. Good. How many spoons will you need, so that each bowl has a spoon beside it? Three. Good. Count the bowls. Count the spoons. Good. Draw them on your blackboard.'

II. Counting and Arranging in Sequence
Let children arrange the apparatus to show that each row is one more than the next.

Help them to count backwards, noticing that each row is one less than the one before.

Collect boxes (e.g. matchboxes, sugar boxes) and the children can put one more object in each box.

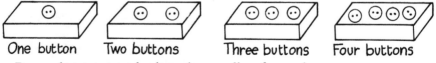

One button   Two buttons   Three buttons   Four buttons

Remember to count backwards as well as forwards.

III. Counting to Higher Numbers
Progress slowly as a good foundation is most important. This cannot be gained quickly. When you think the children are ready, introduce the next number. Use all the apparatus again, counting both forwards and backwards.

The children should have a good understanding of numbers up to 100 by the time they are in the third or fourth class, so you have plenty of time to go slowly. Numbers to 20 might be aimed at in the first year, but it is difficult to say this definitely. It depends on whether the children really understand.

Other Suggestions for Counting
   1. Count as many different objects as possible.
   2. Children skip or jump while they are counting.

3. The teacher calls one child to the front of the class, and he calls another and so on, while the rest of the class count.

4. Children throw bean-bags into a basket as they count.

5. Children clap while they count.

6. Children stand in a circle. They dance in one direction counting to ten, then turn round and count ten as they dance back.

Number Rhymes

These simple rhymes are quickly learnt by the children. They can be said or they can be sung to any suitable tune. Whenever possible the children should act them, but when this is not practical they can count their fingers or some seeds while they say the rhyme. These English examples will give you a few ideas, and you will soon make some up in the vernacular.

> One little, two little, three little, four little, five little African boys.
> Six little, seven little, eight little, nine little, ten little African boys.

As the children say the rhyme the teacher points to different children in turn, so that at the end of the rhyme ten children are standing up.

> The farmer picks his oranges one, two, three,
> The farmer picks his oranges four, five, six,
> The farmer picks his oranges seven, eight, nine,
> And then he picks another and that makes ten.

> One yam in the basket
> Knack, knackity noo.
> Two yams in the basket
> Knack, knackity noo.
> Three yams in the basket,
> etc.

> Old Mrs Blank,[1] she had one child,
> Old Mrs Blank, she had one child,
> Old Mrs Blank, she had one child.
> And he danced all around her.
> Old Mrs Blank, she had two children, (repeat twice)
> And they danced all around her.
> Old Mrs Blank, she had three children, etc. up to ten children.

> The old drummer beats his drum, one,
> The old drummer beats his drum, one, two,
> The old drummer beats his drum, one, two, three, etc.

(The children can beat the desk.)

---

[1] One child is old Mrs Blank and the children dance round her. The word 'dance' can be changed if the teacher wishes the children to walk, hop, crawl, skip, etc.

Some Apparatus to help Counting

All the pre-number apparatus is useful and good for giving practice in counting. The children need hundreds of experiences of grouping, matching and counting.

Bead frame: The child can move and count the beads. He can see at a glance that each line has one more bead than the line before.

How it is made:

The frame is made of wood about 2 cm wide and 1 cm thick. The beads are bought or made of wood or clay, and their diameter is about 1 cm. They are hung on wire or string pulled very tight. The beads should be painted bright colours to make the apparatus more attractive. Rough edges or pieces of wire must be smoothed off, to prevent the children hurting themselves. The measurements are for small desk frames.

Snap: The teacher draws dots on any suitable sized card, about 5 cm by 5 cm. Make about four cards for each number, four for group one, four for group two, four for group three, etc. Arrange the dots differently

for each card, thus making it necessary for the children to count. Two children play the game. They mix the cards up, and with the plain backs of the cards on top share them out equally. The first child turns over his top card, laying it on the desk. The second child turns one up, laying it beside the other one. Both look to see if the cards have the same number of dots. If not, the first child turns over another card, laying it on top of his first one. Both children again look to see if the cards match. If they do, the first child to say the number wins all the cards which are on the desk. He puts these cards at the bottom of his own pack. The game continues until one child has won all the cards.

Later when the figures have been taught, this game can be played using the number symbols.

Dominoes: This is a very old game, and the children will enjoy matching the dots.

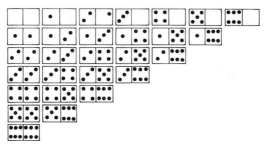

The dominoes are drawn on pieces of card measuring about 5 cm by 10 cm. There are 28 pieces altogether, and four children play, getting 7 pieces each. Each child looks at his own cards, but he does not show them to anyone else. The child with the double six puts it out first. The other children then take it in turn to match one of the groups on the desk. The first child to match all his cards wins.

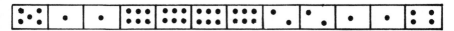

IV. Number Symbols
Suggestions for Class Work
'Now you are able to count so well, I shall show you how to write the names of the numbers. We can write them in words,

one   two   three   four   five

and we can write them using special shapes we call figures. Show me one skittle, Ojo. Good. I shall draw the skittle on the blackboard. Now I shall write the figure for number one. Here it is I, figure one. Show me two skittles, Mary. Good. I shall draw them on the blackboard. Now I shall draw the figure for number two. Here it is 2, figure two. Draw figure one in the air. Good. A lovely straight one. Draw figure two in the air. Good. A curved figure two. Draw the skittles and put the figure beside them. Try to find the reading word which means the same. When you have finished take some matching apparatus from this table.'

Take about a week to introduce the number symbols slowly up to 5 and let children practise using the figure shapes.

Suggestions for Individual Work (or Small Groups)
Cut cards about 5 cm by 8 cm in size and write the numbers neatly. You will need a large supply of these. All your pre-number apparatus will come in very useful again, as the children can place the symbols beside the group arrangements. The sequence apparatus should not be used, excepting the strips of card, which are described on page 82.

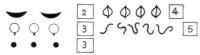

Some Apparatus for Practising Number Symbols; Individually or in Small Groups

Hanging bead frame: This piece of apparatus shows the figures and a group of beads representing each figure. The children can see the sequence at a glance. The children count the beads as they take them off, and again as they are put back on the hooks.

How it is made:

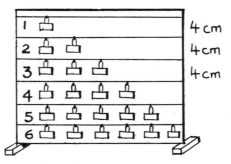

A piece of wood measuring about 30 cm by 30 cm is needed for the back. Hooks, either bought or made from scrap wire, are fitted at intervals of about 4 cm from each other. The square beads are made of wood or clay. At the top of each bead a loop of wire or strong string is fixed. The beads look brighter if painted. The numbers are written on paper and stuck on the left-hand side, or they can be painted on to the board.

Threading beads on to a string: The children thread figures on to string, and then thread the number of beads to match the figures. The teacher will be able to notice quickly any child who is confusing the number symbols, and give him help.

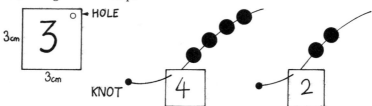

How it is made: Write the numbers neatly on pieces of card about 3 cm × 3 cm. Punch holes in one corner of each card. Put the cards, clay beads and pieces of string in a box. If the child has learned only to number six, then give him cards 1 to 6 and at least 22 beads. As he learns other figures increase the cards and beads in the box.

Self-correcting matching cards: The child matches the number symbol with a group of dots. As each card is cut in a different way, the figure and group will only fit properly if they are correct.

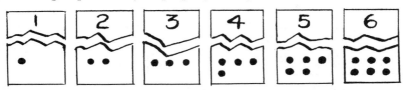

Keep each set of cards in an envelope. Increase the number of cards as the child learns more number symbols.

How they are made: Cardboard measuring about 12 cm by 8 cm is divided as in the diagram.

For dots draw round a small coin

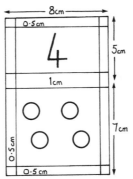

Who has the number? Write out the number symbols which you have taught on pieces of paper, so that each child in the group has one. Ask, 'Who has figure three?' All the children with figure 3 will come running out to the teacher. The teacher will then write figure 3 on the blackboard to remind all the children of its shape.

Jumping on a number: An oblong is drawn on the floor. A small group of children stand around. Do not let the children stand where the figures will appear upside down to them. 'Who can jump on figure six? Ifi.

1	3	6
5	4	2

Good. Which figure has Ifi jumped on to? Amadu. Six. Good. Who can jump on to figure three? Aina. Good. Can three children jump on to figure three? Good. Now there are three children standing on figure three.' etc.

Lotto: This game can be played in three stages as the children learn their figures: 1 to 10, 1 to 20 and 1 to 100.

Lotto 1 to 10: Four to six children play together. Each is given a card with figures on it.

3	6	2
5	9	4

7	3	8
10	5	1

A tin is needed, and in it are placed all the numbers from 1 to 10, written on small pieces of card. Each child has some plain pieces of card. The teacher takes the number symbol 4 out of the tin. She does not let the children see the symbol, but calls out, 'Four'. All the children who have 4 on their cards cover the 4 with a piece of plain card. The teacher will be able to check, and notice if anyone has forgotten the symbol.

She can then show her card ⟨4⟩ as a reminder. The teacher picks out another card, 'Nine!' All the children with 9 cover it. The winner is the child who covers all his cards first. Once the children know the game a leader can call out the numbers instead of the teacher.

Strips

When children come to do addition and subtraction, multiplication and division, we want them to have an idea of the whole number in their minds. Adding 3 and 4 should mean adding only two things, a complete 3 and a complete 4. Many children, and adults too, add in ones. They think of three, and add four, five, six, seven, using fingers, or something else, as an aid to this counting in ones. This used to be considered all right, but educationalists now think it slows the child up when he reaches the secondary level. The child progressed quickly and seemed to be learning quite hard sums at the lower primary level, but he began to fall back when he reached higher classes. It is now thought that children should be taught to think in blocks of numbers. *This means much slower progress in the younger classes, but the rewards and benefits will be seen later on.*

In all the work I have suggested so far, numbers have been considered in ones, though the groups have also been stressed; a group of five seeds, a group of nine balls, a group of six pencils, etc.

One of the best ways of giving the idea of a complete group is to use blocks or strips. You can buy very good apparatus for this. Cuisenaire,

Stern, Unifix and others make good number apparatus. Unfortunately they may prove to be rather expensive for you, but you can make strips of cardboard yourself.

For number one use a card measuring 3 cm²; two will be 3 cm × 6 cm; three will be 3 cm × 9 cm; four will be 3 cm × 12 cm and so on to ten, 3 cm × 30 cm.

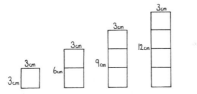

Some teachers make each number in a different coloured cardboard, and Cuisenaire's blocks have a special colour for each number.

Once you decide on a colour for a number, it should be the same throughout the school. Do not change the colours, as that would confuse the children. You may have to paint some of the cardboard, which should be as thick as possible, to stand much wear.

I suggest the following colours, which are based on the international colour coding used by the electronics industry. If the colour words are not used in the vernacular, teach the English words. In the earlier stages the children should have practised grouping in colours.

one	*brown*	five	*green*	nine	*white*
two	*red*	six	*blue*	ten	*black*
three	*orange*	seven	*violet*		
four	*yellow*	eight	*grey*		

Violet is the colour obtained when red and blue are mixed. There should be more red than blue in the mixture.

For each child you will need at least twenty ones, ten twos, ten threes, ten fours, ten fives, ten sixes, five sevens, five eights, five nines and thirty tens.

Using the Strips to Help Learn the Symbols
Until the children have learned the numbers we are calling each strip, they will have to continue to count in ones.

Suggestions for Class Work
All the children need some strips.

'Who can pick up the smallest strip? Aina. Good. What colour is it? Brown. Good. We shall call the smallest strip, number one. Who can remember how we write the figure one? Write it on the blackboard, Ojo. Good. Who can find the next size? Sule. The red; good. How many brown ones will fit on to the red. Try it and tell me. Uwa. Two brown ones will fit on to the red. Good. Who can write the figure two for us on the blackboard? Amadu. Good. Who can find the next size? The orange strip. Good. How many brown ones will fit on to the orange strip? Try it. Ifi. Three. Good.'

Continue in this way, asking the children to pick out the strips and arrange them in a staircase. Probably the first five strips will be sufficient for the introductory lesson. In the following lessons revise, and add new steps to the staircase when the children are ready, until you reach ten.

Suggestions for Individual Work (or Small Groups)
Give the children strips and the number symbols to make the sequence in as many ways as they can. The shapes can be drawn on blackboards or paper.

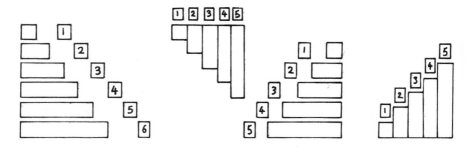

V. The Idea of Addition and Subtraction without Using Number Symbols

'Put a red strip on your desk with a yellow strip beside it. Who can find a strip which matches those two together? Try the other strips until you find one. Sule. The blue strip matches exactly.

'Put the blue strip on your desk. Cover part of it with yellow. What would fit into the space left? Try the strips to see. Aina The red. Good.'

Blue *take away* yellow *is the same* as red.

'Put blue out again. Cover it with the red this time. Which strip will fit the space that is left? Okeke. The yellow.'

Continue in this way using other strips. For individual work the children will make up as many of their own sums as they can.

Remember there are **four** patterns for each of three colours.

Example: Brown, violet and grey.

brown + violet = grey	*They can*	grey = brown + violet
violet + brown = grey	*also be*	grey = violet + brown
grey − brown = violet	*arranged*	violet = grey − brown
grey − violet = brown	*like this.*	brown = grey − violet

Teaching all these arrangements is important. At first children will be satisfied if they find only one, but always encourage them to find all eight.

Encourage the children to experiment, and soon they will be arranging much more complicated patterns with more than three colours.

Example: Matching the yellow strip.

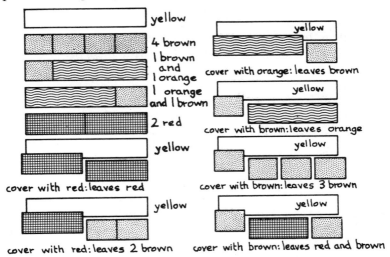

There is not room to draw all the arrangements, but this shows how the children can start.

VI. The Idea of Multiplication and Division with the Strips

'Put the blue strip on the desk. Can you make a pattern to match the blue strip, using only one other colour? Chume. You have two orange strips to match the blue. Good. Uwa. You have three red strips to match the blue. Good. Ifi. You have six brown strips to match the blue. Good.

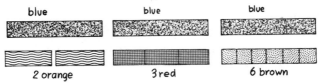

'Put the black strip on your desk. Can you make some patterns, using one colour at a time to match the black? Aina. You have found two green

83

strips to match the black. Good. Kurubo. You have found ten brown strips matched the black. Good. Musa. You found that five red matched the black. Good. You are all correct. Make all the patterns on your desk.'

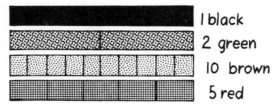

To write these patterns the children will use some number symbols, so take only oral work until the children have practised the symbols in other lessons. For individual work, the children can make as many patterns as possible; then draw them using coloured chalk or crayon.

When you think the children are ready to write these patterns show them like this:

2 green = black	(Two greens equals black.)
5 red = black	(Five red are the same as black.)
10 brown = black	(Ten browns match the black.)
Show also the reverse	black = 2 green
way of writing.	black = 5 red
	black = 10 brown

'How many green will cover the black strip? Uwa. Two green will cover the black strip. Good. Can you cover the black strip using only one colour? Sule. You used brown. Good. Ten brown will cover the black strip. Amadu. You found five red covered the black strip. Good.'

$$\frac{black}{green} = 2 \quad \text{(How many greens will cover the black?)}$$

$$\frac{black}{red} = 5 \quad \text{(How many reds will cover the black?)}$$

$$\frac{black}{brown} = 10 \quad \text{(How many browns will cover the black?)}$$

Children can also be told that green is half of black: green = $\frac{1}{2}$ black. Yellow is half of grey: yellow = $\frac{1}{2}$ grey. Other simple fractions can be taught using the strips:

red = $\frac{1}{4}$ grey; blue = $\frac{3}{4}$ grey; $\frac{1}{2}$ red = brown; brown = $\frac{1}{4}$ yellow.

You will notice what a good foundation this is, not only for harder sums but also for algebra later on.

VII. Addition and Subtraction using Figures

It may take six months or longer for the children to understand the idea of addition and subtraction using the coloured strips. Do not think you must rush on to the next stage. **Go slowly.** Let the children experiment. These ideas without numbers are excellent for leading the children towards an understanding of the processes. When, however, the children can make many patterns with all the strips they are ready for the next state, which uses number symbols.

Two or three times a week the children will have been practising the use of number symbols as described on pages 77 to 80. **If they cannot write and use these number symbols to 9, easily and quickly, the children are not ready for the next stage.**

Suggestions for Class Work
'Put the orange strip on the desk, with the red one beside it. Which strip will that pattern match? Aina. The green one. Good. Orange and red equals green. We can write this pattern down using the figures we know. How many brown ones is the orange worth? Musa. Three. Good. Who can write figure three on the blackboard? Okeke. Good. What is the red worth? Uwa. Two. Good. Can you write it on the blackboard? Good. Together they stand for the same amount as the green. What is the green worth? Ifi. Five. Good. Who can write five on the blackboard? Sule. Good. $3+2=5$. Three plus two is the same as five. Find another pattern to make five. Ojo. Yellow and brown. Good. Who can write that using figures? $4+1=5$. Good. Four plus one equals five. Who can find another pattern? Red and brown and red. Good. $2+1+2=5$. Make as many patterns as you can for five, and write them on your papers.'

Explain + means 'and', 'plus' and 'add'. − means 'less', 'take away' and 'subtract'. = means 'equal' and 'the same as'. Give practice with the different words.

Suggestions for Individual Work
Choose a strip and ask the children to make as many patterns as they can. For example, the yellow strip represents four.

$3+1=4$	They can all be	$4=3+1$
$1+3=4$	written in the	$4=1+3$
$2+2=4$	reverse order	$4=2+2$
$1+2+1=4$		$4=1+2+1$
$2+1+1=4$		$4=2+1+1$
$1+1+2=4$		$4=1+1+2$
$1+1+1+1=4$		$4=1+1+1+1$
$4-3=1$		$1=4-3$
$4-1=3$		$3=4-1$
$4-2=2$		$2=4-2$
$4-1-2=1$		$1=4-1-2$
$4-2-1=1$		$1=4-2-1$
$4-1-1=2$		$2=4-1-1$
$4-1-1-1=1$		$1=4-1-1-1$

None, Nothing and Zero

Children often find the idea of nothing rather difficult to understand, and this needs careful teaching. They will have had experience of empty groups, which will help them towards understanding. The following teaching suggestions should be introduced gradually over some months.

'Put out the yellow strip. Match it with another yellow. What else do we need to make the strips equal to each other? Nothing else. Good. Yellow and nothing else matches yellow. What is the yellow worth? Four. Good. Four and what else matches four? Four and nothing else matches four. Good. We write it like this. $4 + o = 4$.'

Show the other patterns for the same idea.

$o + 4 = 4$ Nothing added to four is the same as four.

$4 = o + 4$ Four is the same as nothing plus four.

$4 = 4 + o$ Four equals four with nothing added to it.

'Cover the yellow with another yellow. What space have we left to fill? We have no space left to fill. Good. What is yellow worth? Four. Good. Cover four with four. How much space is left to cover? There is no space left. Good. We write the difference between four and four equals nothing. $4 - 4 = o$.'

The idea of taking away can also be shown.

'Put out a four strip. Take four away. Pick it up and take it away from the desk. What is left on the desk? Nothing. Good. Are there any strips left when we have four and we take away four? No, none left. Good. We write it like this: $4 - 4 = o$. Four take away four leaves nothing, or four subtract four equals nothing.

'Put the four strip on your desk. Take nothing away. What is on the desk? Four is still there. Four take away nothing is the same as four. $4 - o = 4$.'

Sometimes call 'o' zero, as it means no number or no amount.

VIII. Multiplication and Division

As with addition and subtraction, make patterns which the children now know well, and show them how to write the patterns using number symbols.

$$4 \text{ red} = \text{grey}$$
$$4 \times 2 = 8$$

Explain that '×' stands for 'multiples'. Perhaps the easiest way for small children to understand is to call × 'of'. Four *of* the red strip is the same as the grey. Four *of* the two strip is the same as the eight strip: $4 \times 2 = 8$. And the reverse. Two of the four strip equals the eight strip: $2 \times 4 = 8$.

How many reds will cover the yellow? Two.

$$\frac{\text{yellow}}{\text{red}} = 2$$

When we use figures we say, 'How many of the twos will cover the four? Two.' $\frac{4}{2} = 2$.

It can also be written thus: $4 \div 2 = 2$. Cover the four with the two; two times.

Cover the six with the two; three times: $6 \div 2 = 3$

Cover the six with the three; two times: $6 \div 3 = 2$

Remember to encourage the children to write the sum down in as many different ways as they can. All the ideas will be introduced very gradually.

Larger Numbers

All the suggestions so far have been for numbers up to ten, but if you give the children plenty of practice and allow them to make up their own patterns, soon the brighter children will begin to experiment with larger numbers. For example, a child may put a ten and a two together to make twelve, or a seven and a five to make twelve, and experiment with patterns to match twelve.

This is good, because the child knows himself when he understands and is ready to make more complicated patterns. Encourage the children, but do not force the slower ones to go more quickly.

Other Concrete Experiences of the Four Rules of Number

By the four rules of number we mean addition, subtraction, multiplication and division.

All your pre-number apparatus can be useful again, and should be used two or three times each week. Although the children will count the objects in ones instead of in blocks of numbers, this is unavoidable in the early stages. Our aim is to progress to considering numbers in complete blocks or groups, but this takes time to learn.

The apparatus will require some reorganizing. The children will use groups of things which are alike. A group of three buttons and a group of five buttons will be the same as a group of eight buttons.

$$3 + 5 = 8$$

A group of six leaves and a group of one leaf equals a group of seven leaves.

$$6 + 1 = 7$$

From a group of five triangles take a group of two triangles. A group of three triangles is left.

87

 $5 - 2 = 3$

Three groups of two pencils is the same as a group of six.

 $3 \times 2 = 6$

How many groups of three can I make out of a group of nine? Three groups of three.

$9 \div 3 = 3$

The groups can be made on the desk. It is a good idea to have boxes for the children to put the groups into, to prevent one group getting mixed with another.

Warning: For the sake of understanding it is not wise at this stage to mix different kinds of apparatus together. Adding three sticks to four books to get seven does not make sense to the child. It is not something one would do in everyday life. When practising the four rules keep the apparatus separate. For example, use beads, and when the child has finished, put the beads away, before getting skittles to use. When he has finished with the skittles put them away, before getting lids.

IX. More Formal Work on the Four Rules of Number

When the children have followed all the stages mentioned, and have **revised and practised them a great many times,** they will require some more directed work on the combinations to 10. To ensure that each child practises all the combinations (sometimes these are called number bonds) write them down, ticking off each one as you write it on a work card.

Addition combinations to 10

1	2	3	4	5	6	7	8	9	10
1+1	1+2	1+3	1+4	1+5	1+6	1+7	1+8	1+9
	2+1	3+1	4+1	5+1	6+1	7+1	8+1	9+1
		2+2	2+3	2+4	2+5	2+6	2+7	2+8
			3+2	4+2	5+2	6+2	7+2	8+2
				3+3	3+4	3+5	3+6	3+7
					4+3	5+3	6+3	7+3
						4+4	5+4	4+6
							5+4	6+4
								5+5
1+0	2+0	3+0	4+0	5+0	6+0	7+0	8+0	9+0	10+0
0+1	0+2	0+3	0+4	0+5	0+6	0+7	0+8	0+9	0+10

88

Subtraction combinations to 10

1	2	3	4	5	6	7	8	9
10−9	10−8	10−7	10−6	10−5	10−4	10−3	10−2	10−1
9−8	9−7	9−6	9−5	9−4	9−3	9−2	9−1	
8−7	8−6	8−5	8−4	8−3	8−2	8−1		
7−6	7−5	7−4	7−3	7−2	7−1			
6−5	6−4	6−3	6−2	6−1				
5−4	5−3	5−2	5−1					
4−3	4−2	4−1						
3−2	3−1							
2−1								
1−1	6−6	1−0	6−0					
2−2	7−7	2−0	7−0					
3−3	8−8	3−0	8−0					
4−4	9−9	4−0	9−0					
5−5	10−10	5−0	10−0					

Each sum should be written at least twice on your set of cards, and the harder combinations three or four times. For example, if you make twenty cards 5 + 3 might appear on Card 2, Card 9, Card 13 and Card 17. Measure the cards carefully, spacing the sums neatly. Your writing is to be a good example for the children.

Stage 1a. *Addition cards:* Horizontal addition

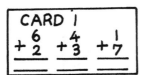

Stage 1b. Vertical addition

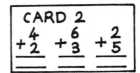

The children should experience both methods of writing. Remember the zero, or nothing, needs plenty of practice.

Stage 2a. *Subtraction cards:* Horizontal subtraction

CARD 1
$7 - 4 =$
$5 - 5 =$
$4 - 3 =$
$6 - 6 =$
$9 - 7 =$

CARD 2
$8 - 3 =$
$7 - 0 =$
$5 - 2 =$
$4 - 4 =$
$2 - 0 =$

Stage 2b.   Vertical subtraction

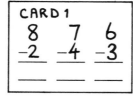

Stage 3. *Mixed addition and subtraction:*

CARD 3
$6 + 2 =$
$7 - 3 =$
$8 + 2 =$
$6 - 0 =$
$4 + 5 =$
$8 - 8 =$

CARD 5

6	2	4	8
+3	−2	+2	−7
—	—	—	—
3	8	5	4
−2	+1	−3	+4
—	—	—	—

These suggestions are only for two combinations. You will need to make work cards for three and four and more combinations.

Stage 4.

CARD 6
$1 + 4 + 3 =$
$2 + 6 + 0 =$
$4 + 1 + 3 + 1 =$
$1 + 0 + 2 + 2 =$
$5 + 2 + 2 =$
$2 + 4 + 3 =$

CARD 10
$6 - 4 - 1 =$
$8 - 3 - 2 =$
$9 - 1 - 3 - 2 =$
$7 - 5 - 0 =$
$6 - 3 - 3 =$
$4 - 1 - 1 - 1 =$

Remember to make lists of the combinations, and mark each one as you put it on a card, to make sure that none is missed.

The children can work through the cards in any order as long as they keep within the stage. Each stage can be written on a different coloured cardboard. Write the children's names on a sheet to hang on the wall. When a child takes a card he can tick the space by his name. In this way both the teacher and the child know how many cards he has worked.

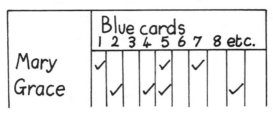

Although the teacher will mark and check the cards whenever possible, train the children to check their own work by using apparatus. The strips are especially useful for this.

If the child has written this sum: $4 + 2 = 6$, he will lay the yellow strip beside the red strip and match them with the blue strip. When he sees he is correct he can tick the sum. If he finds he is incorrect he can use the strips to help him discover the correct answer. **Whenever a child is puzzled, he should be allowed to use any apparatus to help him find the answer.**

Our aim is for the child to learn the combinations so well that he can answer immediately any sum he is asked, without pausing to count in ones 'in his head'. (At this stage up to 10, and later up to 20.)

Test by asking the combinations orally, 'Three and five.'

If there is any pause for working out the answer, encourage him by saying he is doing well, but needs some more practice. If they have been given enough preliminary work, the children will understand what they are doing at this stage, as long as the numbers remain small. Now the aim is speed and accuracy.

When the children can read give little problems on the four rules, keeping the numbers under 10 at this stage.

4 balls and 5 balls = 9 balls
7 buttons take away 4 buttons = 3 buttons left
2 girls each with 3 pencils = 6 pencils altogether

Some Game Suggestions for practising Number Combinations
Threading Beads and Adding

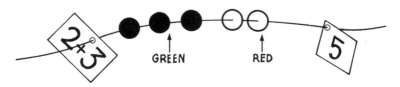

The beads must be painted in different colours. The child threads a card with a sum on to the string, e.g. $2 + 3$. He then threads on two green beads and three red beads. Lastly he threads on the answer.

How to make it: In a box put a number of sums written on cardboard measuring about 3 cm by 6 cm, $2 + 3$ a number of beads painted in at least two different colours, and numbers for the answers on card measuring 3 cm by 3 cm, 5 Some long pieces of string, knotted at one end, are needed for threading the sums. Holes must be punched in the cardboards.

The Way Home

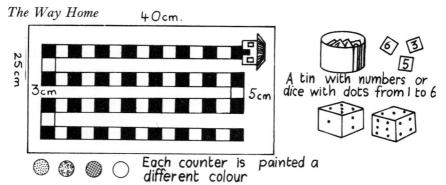

A tin with numbers or dice with dots from 1 to 6

Each counter is painted a different colour

The children play in a group of four. One throws two dice or picks two numbers from a tin, and adds the numbers together. He then moves a counter forward the number of spaces that he gets for his answer, e.g. $4 + 3 = 7$, the child moves 7 spaces. Each child has a turn to throw, and gradually works his way along the road until he gets home. The first one home is the winner.

How to make it: On a piece of card measuring 40 cm by 25 cm, draw a road so that each square is 3 cm by 3 cm. Leave margins as in the diagram. The dice is made of a little block of wood measuring 3 cm by 3 cm by 3 cm. The dice is of no use if it keeps falling on the same number. A tin containing little cards, on which are written the numbers, can be used instead of a dice. The counters are made of circles of cardboard 1·5 cm in diameter, and each one is painted a different colour.

This game can be played when the children are practising counting if only one number or one dice is used. The child counts the numbers which he throws on the dice, e.g. if he throws 4, he counts and moves his counter 1, 2, 3, 4.

Picture Puzzle

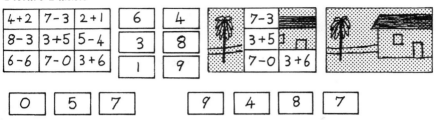

The child matches the answer to the sum so making the picture. He knows if he is wrong with any sum for the picture will not be correct. This is an interesting game and helps the child to enjoy doing sums. Any kind of sum can be written depending on the stage the child has reached.

3cm	4+2	7-3	2+1
3cm	8-3	3+5	5-4
3cm	6-6	7-0	3+6

5cm   5cm   5c.m

3	4	6
1	8	5
9	7	0

A picture is pasted on the other side

How to make the puzzle. Two pieces of card 15 cm by 9 cm are needed. Thick crayon lines are drawn as in the diagram. The picture is stuck on the plain side (i.e. the side without the crayon lines) of one of the cards. Sums are written on the other card. When the picture is firmly stuck, the card is cut along the lines. (The picture will be in nine pieces.) Place the cut-up pieces of the picture on the other card, then pick up one piece at a time, look at the sum and write the answer. If this is not done very carefully the answers will be on the wrong piece of picture.

Skittles

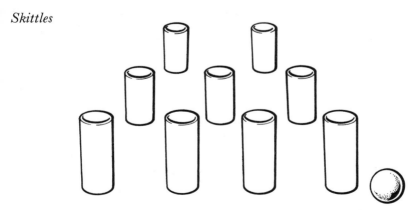

The skittles are made from bamboo or painted, long, empty tins. The nine skittles are placed on the floor. The child stands a little way from

93

them, and rolls a soft ball along the floor. He writes on his blackboard the number of skittles he has knocked down. He rolls the ball again, and adds the second score to the first, thus making an addition sum. $4+2 = 6$, $3+0 = 3$.

If the children are only at the stage of adding to 6, only six skittles would be used.

(More skittles can be used when the children are adding to 20 (Chapter 11), and to give further practice three scores can be added together, e.g. $2+4+3 = 9$, $6+2+5 = 13$, $3+0+4 = 7$.)

For subtraction, the number knocked down can be taken away from the number of skittles altogether. The answer can be checked by counting the number of skittles still standing, e.g. $9-3 = 6$.

Skittles are best played in small groups.

X. Some Other Mathematical Experiences

During each mathematics lesson two or three groups should be allowed to experiment with other concrete apparatus.

Sand: Have a tray or pile of sand. Making roads, heaps and shapes are all useful experiences. Children learn much through playing. Have many different-shaped boxes, bottles and tins for the children to fill. (Make sure the tins have no sharp edges.) Suggest they make a pile of sand and guess which tin it will fill. Choose a smaller tin and ask them to guess how many times the same sand will fill that. After guessing the children will fill the tins to check if they are correct, or to see if they guessed too much or too little. Two children can make a pile of sand each, and guess which is the greater. They can check by filling a box or tin. If the sand is kept slightly damp it is easier to use. Very dry sand can be put in bottles. Children can make patterns with shells, and watch the sand run through mosquito netting. When the children use money they can play at markets and sell tins of sand. When you introduce weighing, the sand again provides useful experiences.

Water: This can be messy and is best taken outside. A number of buckets or an old bath can hold the water. Again children learn much by playing. Give bottles and tins for filling. Ask them to discover how many times the small bottle has to be filled with water, and poured into the big bottle, before the big bottle is full. If the big tin is full, how many times will it fill the little tin? Again children guess first and then check. Funnels and rubber tubes also give useful experiences.

A children's playhouse: In one corner a frame of wood is covered with cloth to make a little house. Inside boxes are used for tables and chairs. These can be painted by the children. Old cups and plates can also be kept in the house, or clay cups can be made. This house is useful for a small group of children. Two can pretend to be mother and father; some can be children; some can be visitors. It provides opportunities for good speech practice and social practice as well as mathematical experiences. How many visitors have come today? How many plates do we need? Mother has to buy dinner for four children. How much money will she need? The children get experience of space. How can we arrange the chairs to make it comfortable for all the family? Where should we put the table? The children can also pretend the house is a hospital or shop, or anything they like.

A shop: In another corner have a shop or market-stall. At first the children will only spend kobos, or whatever the smallest local coin is. One child can be the shopkeeper, while two or three come to spend their money. When the children can, they will write down bills.

$$\begin{array}{ll} \text{A pencil} & 3k \\ \text{A comb} & 6k \\ \hline \\ 9k & \text{change from 10k is 1k.} \end{array}$$

A discovery table: This might be called science apparatus rather than mathematics apparatus, but as science and mathematics are very closely linked, it is mentioned now. On this table put anything interesting for the children to touch and examine. If possible allow children to take things to pieces, to discover how they work. The teacher will always be looking out for old things which are broken and not much use to anyone; for example, an old clock, an old wireless, an old lamp, old electric plugs and fittings, bits of wood, screws and screwdrivers, an old bicycle pump, old taps, old fountain pens, old locks and keys, springs, hinges, door handles, wheels, in fact anything with which the children can experiment, or can use, to discover how it works. Always make sure, of course, that the articles are safe, and there is nothing in them which could harm the children. Magnets are very interesting, as children discover what they attract. A good clock is useful for watching, and for timing experiments or lessons. Nails knocked in wood can be used with rubber bands to make interesting shapes, and help with the teaching of area.

nails at corners

3cm squares

Pairs of compasses, set squares and protractors help the child to draw interesting shapes. **What is discovered is remembered better than**

what the teacher tells the children. In the older classes the children will bring many unusual pieces of equipment for the discovery table.

Other useful apparatus: Some of these are expensive, but can be bought gradually: clock, thermometer, magnifying glass, calendar, compass for finding north, south, east and west, a set of weighing scales, metre rulers.

Chapter 11   The Ten to Twenty Stage

This is the stage most often taught badly or neglected altogether. Some teachers think that once children can add to ten, they can add tens and

units. Sums are written like this $\dfrac{\begin{array}{r}16\\3\end{array}}{19}$. The children add $6+3=9$.

They write 9 in one column, and then put the one in the next column. It appears to be a one and a nine. They have no understanding of nineteen being the same amount as sixteen and three. They mechanically obey what the teacher tells them, but there is no mathematical understanding. For many children the ten to twenty stage is the hardest one, and should be taught slowly and carefully.

While the children have been experiencing and practising number and sums to 10, counting exercises will be introduced to 20 and even further; for example, counting the register, counting the pencils, counting flowers.

Grouping and Matching up to 20
All the pre-number apparatus can be used again for experiences of numbers to twenty.

'Let us count eleven girls. One, two, three, etc. Each of these girls will come here and bring a chair. How many chairs have we here? Eleven. Good. How many girls have we? Eleven. Good. Has each girl a chair to sit on? Yes. Good. Now let us count twelve balls. One, two, three, etc. How many balls have we here? Twelve. We want to match each ball with a bat. How many bats shall we need? Twelve. Good.'

Continue as before with class and individual work. The children can draw the group in their books. **Later** when the symbols have been taught, give children cards with figures written on them. They can put the figure beside the group.

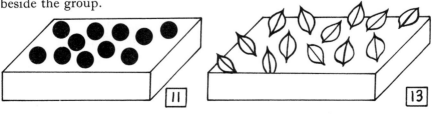

I. Number Sequence and Number Symbols to 20
Numbers to 20 Using Strips
Ask the children to make the staircase to ten. Let them make a little doll out of paper. The doll can walk up the steps until it reaches the top.

'Who can tell me the next step? Eleven. Good. How can we make eleven?' The children may have many ideas. Listen and encourage those who try to discover a way on their own. **It is better to think about a problem and get an incorrect answer than not to think at all.** Praise for effort. After a while someone may suggest using a ten strip and a one strip.

'Good. Ten and one more will make eleven. Let us make the new step that way. Put the little doll on the eleventh step. What would the next step be called?' Do not worry if the children call it twelve (instead of the twelfth) step at this stage. Eleventh, twelfth, thirteenth, fourteenth etc., can be taught later.

'How can we make step twelve? Good, a ten strip and a two strip. What is ten and one more? Eleven. What is ten and two more? Twelve. Make the step and put the doll on it. We can write the figures now. Eleven is one ten strip and one more: **11**. Twelve is one ten strip and two more: **12**. What would the next step be? Thirteen. Good. How can we make it? Twelve and one more. Yes, but can you think of another way? Ten and three more. **Both are correct,** but we shall use the ten and three more because it will help us to remember how to write the figures; the ten strip and three more: **13**.

Continue in this way building up the staircase (it will not be done all at once) until nineteen is reached. The staircase continues to give an understanding of sequence. Each step, and therefore each number, is one more than the one before, and one less than the one after. As each step is made, show the children how we write one ten strip with the unit number beside it. When we reach twenty we have two ten strips and no units: **20**.

Much practice will be needed to ensure that children really understand how to build up the numbers to twenty. The combinations with ten are most often used, and as many countries have adopted the decimal system for money and length, an understanding of the combinations with ten becomes more and more important. The English names we give to the numbers even mention the ten, thirteen *threeten*, fourteen *fourten*, fifteen *fiveten*, twenty **two** *tens*, thirty **three** *tens*. Eleven and twelve should really be called one-ten and two-ten by this system, but for historical reasons the English words are quite different, and may need to be practised more often. Another thing to notice is that though we say four-ten (fourteen) we write ten-four, 14. We say six-ten (sixteen), but write ten-six, 16. Point this out to the children, and help them to remember the difference between speaking and writing. There is no logical reason for the words being composed the wrong way round; perhaps some of the vernaculars have a more sensible way of building up the word names for the numbers.

Practice with the Staircase
Play games with the staircase, to develop an understanding of sequence.

'Put the doll on the tenth step. What is the next step? What is the step before? Let the doll climb up three more steps. Which step is it on now? What is the step before? What is two steps down? What is the next step? What is the step two higher called? If the doll stood on step sixteen, how many steps would it have to climb to reach the top? Put the doll on step fifteen. How many steps backwards must it go to reach step number twelve? Try it if you like. Put the doll on the top step. Count backwards until the doll reaches the ground . . . . three, two, one, zero. Zero stands for no number or the starting-point for our counting. When the doll is ready to climb it stands on the ground ready to start. We have no step number. It is zero. We start counting as the doll goes on the first step, one, the next step, two, and so on. If the doll is on zero (on the ground) how many steps must it tread on to get to step six? to get to step nine?' etc.

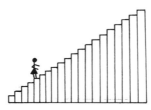

Further Practice with Symbols
Children will write the figure for the step the doll stands on. The pre-number apparatus should be used with symbols (see page 64).

Practice to 20 with Sticks
Sticks tied into bundles also help the children to understand the idea of a

ten. Give children a number of sticks, and something (elastic bands or raffia) with which to tie them.

'Let us all count ten sticks and put them on the desk, one, two, etc. Tie up the ten sticks into a bundle. We have one bundle of ten. Who remembers how we write ten? Good. One bundle and no single ones: ▓▓▓ 10. Lay one stick beside the bundle. How many sticks have we now? Eleven. Good. Who can remember how we write eleven? Good. One bundle and one single: ▓▓▓ | 11. Lay another stick by your eleven. How many bundles of ten do you have? One bundle of ten. Good. How many singles? Two singles. Good. One ten and two makes . . . .? Twelve. Good. Write twelve on the blackboard. Good. One ten and two ones: ▓▓▓ || 12. Lay another stick on the desk. How many bundles do we have? One bundle of ten. Good. How many singles or how many ones have we? Three ones. Good. How many altogether? Thirteen. If you listen carefully you can hear three and ten, thir-teen. How do we write thirteen? Good.

Remember we write it ten-three: ▓▓▓ ||| 13.'

Continue in this way, though of course you will not take all the numbers to nineteen in one lesson. When 20 is reached it is taught as two bundles of ten, and written 2 tens and no ones. Later 21 is shown as two tens and one single, twenty-two as two tens and two ones, and so on to thirty, which is shown as three bundles of ten and no singles.

▓▓ ▓▓ 20.   ▓▓ ▓▓ | 21.   ▓▓ ▓▓ || 22.   ▓▓ ▓▓ ▓▓ 30.

When the higher numbers are taught, the use of bundles of ten helps the children to understand what they are doing, and gives concrete experience of the actual numbers. **Do not, however, introduce the higher numbers until the children have a good understanding of the numbers to 20.**

Individual Work

Give children cards with the numbers written on them. The child uses sticks to show the number, remembering to tie the tens into a bundle.

Practising Recognition of the Symbols

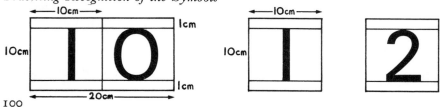

This piece of apparatus is useful for practising recognition of the number symbols, **after the concrete experiences.**

Hold up the flash-card of 10. 'What is this number? Ten. Good.' Hold up the card with 1 written on it. 'What is this number? One. Good.' Place the 1 over the 0 on the big card, making 11. 'Ten and one more make . . . . Eleven. Good!' Lay down the card with 1 written on it, and hold up the flash-card for 10 again. 'Here is ten.' Hold up the card with 2 written on it. 'What is this number? Two. Good.' Place the two over the zero on the large card. 'What number have we now? Twelve. Good. Ten and two more make . . . . Twelve. Good.'

Gradually, all the numbers to 19 are revised and practised in this way. Although the children must learn the figures in sequence, they should also be able to 'read' the figures in any order. Sometimes mix them up, for example 13, 15, 11, 19, 16.

A new large card is necessary to show 20. Later when the children are ready for the symbols over twenty, the units can be placed over the zero, to make 21, 22, 23, etc. Large cards can also be made for 30, 40, 50, etc.

II. Addition and Subtraction to 20

Using the Strips

The children are accustomed to using the strips for addition and subtraction to ten, and they should also have had much individual practice making as many patterns and sums as they can with all the numbers to twenty. (Follow the same teaching plan as suggested before on pages 82-86.) Give a number, for example, twelve, one black and one red, and make as many patterns to match as possible.

'Put the five strip on your desk, with the six strip beside it. Can you find a strip to match this pattern? No, none of the strips is long enough. What can we do? We can use two or three or four strips. Good. Let us use just two strips. Which two can we use? Nine and two. Yes, any others? Four and seven. Yes, and others? Ten and one. Yes, you are all correct, because all these patterns match and make eleven. We write eleven, ten and one, 11. Which pattern will be most useful to us? The ten and one pattern. Good. Everyone makes the ten and one pattern to match the five and six pattern. How can we write this down? Show us Mary. Good. $6 + 5 = 11$. Six and five is the same as eleven. Put the eight strip and seven strip on your desk. Who can find another pattern to match? The ten and five pattern. Good. This is useful, because it tells us how to write the figures, one ten and five more, 15. Can you show me the pattern for fifteen minus eight? $15 - 8$. Which strip will match fifteen less eight? The seven strip. Good. Come and write the answer on the blackboard. $15 - 8 = 7$. Make the pattern fifteen take away seven. Which strip matches the amount that is left? The eight strip. Good. Write it on the blackboard. Good. $15 - 7 = 8$.'

Individual Work

Children can make up their own sums, making use of the ten strip each time and writing the eight patterns for each combination.

$7+9 = 16$	$16 = 7+9$
$9+7 = 16$	$16 = 9+7$
$16-9 = 7$	$7 = 16-9$
$16-7 = 9$	$9 = 16-7$

Using the Sticks

'Put out eight sticks and five sticks. We want to add them together. Take some sticks from the five to make the eight into a bundle of ten. It is easy to see our answer now, one bundle of ten and three singles, 13. $8+5 = 13$. Can you turn the sum round? $5+8 = 13$. Good. Do it with the sticks to check the answer. You have ten and three, 13 sticks. Take away eight. $13-8$. You will have to undo the bundle of ten. What have you left? Five. Good. Write it down. $13-8 = 5$. Who can tell me what 13 minus 5 equals? Eight. Good. Check it by using the sticks.'

Give practice like this. Children can make up their own sums. Tying the sticks into bundles of ten for addition, and untying for subtraction, helps with the understanding of a very important idea in our number system. It does mean the children count in ones, but the idea of ten being a new thing (a bundle in this case), is important. Give children variety. Sometimes use strips and sometimes use sticks.

Using other Apparatus

The children need many different experiences. Sometimes use the pre-number apparatus for addition and subtraction to 20. Have boxes with the symbol of 10 on them.

'Five and nine. Put ten in the box. Now we have one box of ten and how many ones? Joseph. One box of ten and four ones. Good. Write it $5+9 = 14$. Can you tell me what nine added to five will give us? Fourteen. Good. Put out nine and five and check the answer using the ten box.'

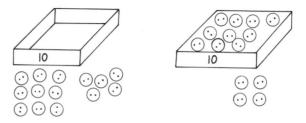

'You have fourteen leaves. One ten box and four singles. Take nine away. You will have to take the leaves out of the ten box. How many have we left? Five. Good. There are not enough for the ten box. It is empty now. We have five single leaves on the desk. Write it, $14 - 9 = 5$. Who can tell me what fourteen minus five will equal? Nine. Good. Check it with the apparatus.'

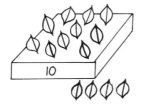 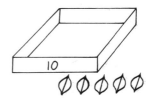

Remember when using various types of apparatus, not to mix two articles at this stage, beads should be used only with beads; shells with shells; circles with circles, etc.

Further Practice of Addition and Subtraction to 20

Cards can be made and records kept, as with the combinations to 10 (page 91). Write out all the combinations when making the cards, to ensure that none are missed.

A large space would be needed to write them all, but here are a few, and you can write the remainder yourself.

10		11		12	
10 + 0	0 + 10	11 + 0	0 + 11	12 + 0	0 + 12
9 + 1	1 + 9	10 + 1	1 + 10	11 + 1	1 + 11
8 + 2	2 + 8	9 + 2	2 + 9	10 + 2	2 + 10
7 + 3	3 + 7	8 + 3	3 + 8	9 + 3	3 + 9
6 + 4	4 + 6	7 + 4	4 + 7	8 + 4	4 + 8
5 + 5		6 + 5	5 + 6	7 + 5	5 + 7
				6 + 6	

1	2	3	4	5	6	7
20 − 19	20 − 18	20 − 17	20 − 16	20 − 15	20 − 14	20 − 13
19 − 18	19 − 17	19 − 16	19 − 15	19 − 14	19 − 13	19 − 12
18 − 17	18 − 16	18 − 15	18 − 14	18 − 13	18 − 12	18 − 11
17 − 16	17 − 15	17 − 14	17 − 13	17 − 12	17 − 11	17 − 10
16 − 15	16 − 14	16 − 13	16 − 12	16 − 11	16 − 10	16 − 9
15 − 14	15 − 13	15 − 12	15 − 11	15 − 10	15 − 9	15 − 8
14 − 13	14 − 12	14 − 11	14 − 10	14 − 9	14 − 8	14 − 7
13 − 12	13 − 11	13 − 10	13 − 9	13 − 8	13 − 7	13 − 6
12 − 11	12 − 10	12 − 9	12 − 8	12 − 7	12 − 6	12 − 5
11 − 10	11 − 9	11 − 8	11 − 7	11 − 6	11 − 5	11 − 4

8	9	10	11	12	13
20 − 12	20 − 11	20 − 10	20 − 9	20 − 8	20 − 7
19 − 11	19 − 10	19 − 9	19 − 8	19 − 7	19 − 6
18 − 10	18 − 9	18 − 8	18 − 7	18 − 6	18 − 5
17 − 9	17 − 8	17 − 7	17 − 6	17 − 5	17 − 4
16 − 8	16 − 7	16 − 6	16 − 5	16 − 4	16 − 3
15 − 7	15 − 6	15 − 5	15 − 4	15 − 3	15 − 2
14 − 6	14 − 5	14 − 4	14 − 3	14 − 2	14 − 1
13 − 5	13 − 4	13 − 3	13 − 2	13 − 1	13 − 0
12 − 4	12 − 3	12 − 2	12 − 1	12 − 0	
11 − 3	11 − 2	11 − 1	11 − 0		

Always encourage the children to write down the eight combinations which can be learned together. The children learn eight sums for the effort of one, for example, $4+9 = 13$. Once this is remembered the rest follows.

$$9+4 = 13 \qquad\qquad 13 = 4+9$$
$$13-9 = 4 \qquad\qquad 13 = 9+4$$
$$13-4 = 9 \qquad\qquad 4 = 13-9$$
$$9 = 13-4$$

Addition card   Subtraction card

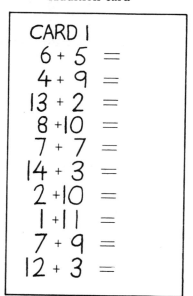

Give practice too in adding and subtracting more than two figures.

CARD I

$$4 + 2 + 6 =$$
$$5 + 6 + 4 =$$
$$8 + 7 + 1 =$$
$$3 + 8 + 3 =$$
$$6 + 1 + 2 =$$
$$9 + 7 + 2 =$$
$$1 + 4 + 5 =$$
$$7 + 3 + 7 =$$
$$2 + 8 + 4 =$$
$$5 + 4 + 2 =$$

The Continued Use of Apparatus

Always allow children to use apparatus to help them find the answer. Quicker children will stop using the apparatus of their own accord. This will show they have passed the stage of needing it. Suggest they use the apparatus (strips or sticks) to check their work, and mark their own answers. **After a further time of practice, they will not even need to check, because they are so sure they are correct.** Now they are ready for another stage.

Slower children will continue to need apparatus. Encourage them to use it. You can help them towards understanding, but you cannot force them. If you make them feel ashamed of using the strips they will start using their fingers. This begins a bad habit, which will hinder them in higher classes.

A few children, however, may need the suggestion that they drop the apparatus. 'Try to do the work card today without using apparatus, but remember the strips are there if you need them.'

When the children reach the age of eight to eight and a half, and still need apparatus to help them find the answer for sums to 20, they need some help to remember the combinations. If they have been given plenty of practical experiences, only the very backward child will not understand what he is doing by this age. (Of course this backward child needs special help and encouragement, with the continual use of apparatus.)

The other children now need practice in speed and in recalling the answers they understand, but have not learned completely.

Some Suggestions for Speeding the Memory of the Combinations

Team games: These sometimes encourage children to make the effort to remember, in order to help their team to win. Each child can have twenty pieces of paper with the numbers 1 to 20 written on them. Write a sum on the blackboard, or call it out. The first child to hold up the correct answer wins a point for his team. Another time the teams can sit on the floor. When the teacher writes the sum on the blackboard the children put the answer on slates, and stand up. The first team to have every child standing wins. Of course the answers must be checked, and if any are incorrect the next team would get the point. Another time the teacher could call out a sum, for example, $5 + 7$ and twelve children in each team would stand up; $6 + 8$ and fourteen children would stand up. The first team to have the correct number standing would gain a point. If there are not enough children in the team they could hold up their hands, for example, seven children would hold up fourteen hands. You will be able to think of other team games.

Lotto: This game is explained on page 80. Print the numbers 1 to 20 on the cards. Print combinations to 20 on the small cards, for example,

$8+7$. All the children with 15 cover the figure. $12-4$. All the children with 8 cover the figure.

Snap: This game is explained on page 76. Print the symbols 1 to 20 on the cards. Choose a combination you want the children to practise, for example, 15. The first child to notice two cards make fifteen wins the cards.

Picture puzzles: These are described on page 93 and can be made for combinations to 20.

Quick tests: These show the teacher which children cannot remember the combinations. Ask the questions speedily. Many children become very clever at using their fingers behind their backs or under the desk. Say nothing, but observe, as this is a secret way for you to discover when a child is not sure of the combinations to 20. He requires more practice. The child needs plenty of good experiences to help understanding. **Memorizing without understanding confuses the child.**

III. Multiplication and Division to 20

Continue with experiences such as those suggested on pages 86–87 using numbers up to 20.

'Make a long strip with a black and a blue. Using only one colour at a time, can you make some patterns to match this? John. You have two greys. Good. Grace. You have sixteen brown. Good. Thomas. You have four yellow. Good. Samuel. You have eight red. Good. Make all these patterns on your desks. Now we shall write these patterns with figures. Two of the grey strip. What is the grey worth? Eight. Good. Two of the eight strip equals . . . . Mary. The sixteen strip. Good. $2 \times 8 = 16$. What other sum can we make from these figures? Anna. Eight twos are the same as sixteen. Good. $8 \times 2 = 16$. Which strips show this pattern? Eight of the red. Good. Is there any other way we could write this? Sixteen equals eight twos and sixteen is the same as two of the eights. Good. $16 = 8 \times 2$, $16 = 2 \times 8$.'

Continue in this way giving children time to try out different patterns using one colour at a time.

Use the pre-number apparatus again to put into groups.

'Make a group of three shells. One group of three shells equals . . . . How many shells? Three. Good. We shall write it $1 \times 3 = 3$. Make another group of three shells. How many groups have we now? Two groups. Good.

Two groups of three shells is the same as . . . . Is the same as six shells.
Good. $2 \times 3 = 6$.

'Make another group of three shells. Three groups of three shells
equals . . . . How many shells? Nine shells. Good. $3 \times 3 = 9$.'

Continue in this way up to $3 \times 6 = 18$. Other tables can be practised in
the same way, but keep under 20 at this stage. Let the children draw
circles or use boxes to put in the groups of articles. If they are just lying
about the desk, it is not very easy for the child to see the groups.

   $3 \times 3 = 9$

Practise also the empty group. 'No groups of three shells is the same as
nothing. $0 \times 3 = 0$.'

'Make a long strip with the black and the blue. Cover it with only one
colour. Tell me what patterns you have made. Data. You have covered
it with two greys. Good. What does black and blue stand for? Sixteen.
Good. What does grey stand for? Eight. Good. How can we write this
down? How many eights will cover sixteen? Two. Good. $\frac{16}{8} = 2$. Can we
write it another way? Cover sixteen with the eight; two times. Good.
$16 \div 8 = 2$.' (This shows the opposite of $2 \times 8 = 16$. Sometimes revise
the opposites, multiplication and division together.)

'Can you think of another sum using the same figures? How many twos
will cover sixteen? Eight. Good. $\frac{16}{2} = 8$. Can we write this another way?
Cover sixteen with two; eight times. $16 \div 2 = 8$. Good. What is the
opposite of this? Eight of the two strips is the same as sixteen. Good.
$8 \times 2 = 16$.'

The idea of division as sharing can be shown using the pre-number
apparatus.

'Put sixteen buttons on your desk. We want to share them with two
children. Draw two circles. Put the buttons for one child in the first circle
and for the other child in the second circle. Make sure they both have the
same. How many buttons for each child? Eight. Good. If we share sixteen
between two children, what does each get? Eight. Good. We write it in
the same way as we have learned already. $16 \div 2 = 8$. Put the sixteen
buttons out again. Now we want to share them with eight children. Get
eight boxes to put them in. Each box must have the same amount. If we
share sixteen between eight children, how much does each get? Two

each. Good. $16 \div 8 = 2$. Could we write it another way? Two equals sixteen shared by eight. $2 = 16 \div 8$.'

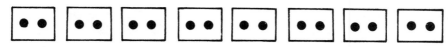

Remember to teach the empty group.

'We have no buttons to share with eight children. How many will each get? Put out eight boxes. How many buttons can you put in each, if you have no buttons? None at all. Good. $0 \div 8 = 0$.'

Problems

Once children show some quickness in understanding the numbers to 20, do not rush on to bigger numbers. **Reinforce your teaching by giving problems, keeping the numbers under 20.** Use anything in school to help the children to use numbers. You may be able to buy simple books of problems, but you can also make cards. Most of the children should be able to read by the time they reach this stage. Keep the words simple. Problems can be on anything the children have experienced. With the discovery table, the shop and the house, you will have gradually introduced ideas of money, weight, measurement, time, etc. (See pages 109–115.)

Suggestions for Cards

Number: Write the numbers to 20 starting at 2 and adding 2 on each time.
  Start at 1 and add on 2 each time till you come to 19.
  Start at 3 and add on 3 each time till you come to 18.
  Start at 2 and add on 3 each time till you come to 17.
  Start at one and add on 3 each time till you come to 19.
  Make up some of your own. Try to do some backwards.
  Number ($+ - \times \div$): I have six yams. I dig up seven more. How many have I now?
  Mother has eight bowls, and she breaks one. How many are left?
  There are four children. Each is given two socks. How many socks altogether?
  Six children want to share eighteen coconuts. How many will each get?
  Money: I have 5k and my father gives me 4k. How much have I now?
  Mary has 16k. She buys a book for 6k. How much has she left?
  The shopkeeper has pencils for 3k each. He sells five pencils. How much money will he get?
  John, David and Samuel earn 18k for helping on the farm. If they share it equally, how much will each get?
  Measurement: If I need a piece of wood 6 cm long and another piece 10 cm long, how much do I need altogether?

I cut 2 cm off a piece of ribbon 20 cm long. How much is left?

Thomas needs 5 pieces of wire. Each piece must be 3 cm long. How much wire does he need?

Mother has some cloth 18 cm long. If it is cut in half, how much will each piece be?

Weight: I have a kilo of oranges, a kilo of nuts and five kilos of yams. How heavy is my bag?

A bag of cocoa has 12 kilos of cocoa in it. The shopkeeper sells 4 kilos weight. How much is left?

Seven children collect 14 kilos of beans. How many kilos can each have if they share it equally?

Four children each have 4 kilos of bananas. How much is that altogether?

Time: The Mathematics lesson lasts for half an hour, and the Craft lesson for an hour and a half. How much is that altogether?

John thought it would take 20 minutes to sweep the yard, but it only took 14 minutes. How much time did he save?

It takes me five minutes to sew on one button. How long will it take to sew on three buttons?

One man digs a hole in twenty minutes. How long should it take if another man helps him?

As long as the numbers are kept small, the more varied the type of problem, the better.

Encourage the children to use apparatus or draw pictures to help them find the answer. The Mathematics book can be full of pictures; e.g. a banana costs 5k. What would 3 bananas cost?

Four children want to share 12 oranges. How many will each get? The child could use stones and share them out, or draw the oranges.

= 3 oranges each

Money, Measurement, Weight, Capacity and Time
These must all be dealt with **practically.** Each child in the class must be

given practice with the apparatus. Watching someone else is not sufficient. The lessons are usually introduced to the class with a teacher's demonstration and explanation, and then the children must do practical work. These lessons need very careful preparation, as the teacher must know exactly what each child will be doing. Use local money, measurements, etc., if they are different from the ones described here. The methods will be the same.

Money

This should be introduced through a class shop or a class market-stall. At first articles are introduced using the first standard coin, a real one if possible. If cardboard coins are used show the children real coins and explain, 'I have not enough real money to spare, so I have made these cardboard coins. You can all have one, and we shall have an interesting lesson pretending to buy from the class shop.'

Individual children will spend their money at the shop. The teacher will draw the articles on the blackboard, and show the class how to write

one kobo. **Ik** Write the vernacular word beside the article to give reading

practice.

two dates   Ik

a rubber   Ik

a piece of ginger   Ik

The children will copy from the blackboard.

After the first lesson let the children shop in groups of three. One child will be shopkeeper, and the other two will buy from him. The two shoppers will draw on their boards what they have bought. The shopkeeper will draw what he sells. When they have finished, three more children will have a turn at shopping. Meanwhile, the rest of the class will be practising whatever stage of addition or subtraction they have reached. In this way all will be busy, while waiting for a turn to shop.

When the teacher feels that each child has had sufficient practice in using a kobo, he can take a class lesson to introduce articles costing 2k and 3k.

Write labels for the articles. In the lessons which follow, groups of children will do practical work. Gradually articles costing up to 10k are introduced. Then the children will buy two things or three things and add the money, but in the early stages of using money the answer should not be greater than 10k. Introduce other small coins, and help the shopkeeper to give change—e.g. a comb costs 4k; the child gives the shopkeeper a 5k-piece, so he must get 1k change. Introduce a 10-kobo piece and show the children that it is worth 10 separate kobos. Give practice in buying things up to 10k and also give practice with change from 10k.

All the above will be introduced only one at a time, and the teacher must decide how soon the children are ready for the next step. When explaining something new the teacher will be the shopkeeper, but then as many children as possible must be given turns at shopping and selling. Remember that while a group is shopping the rest of the class should be kept busy with practising their addition and subtraction sums or with money cards, or some other activity depending on the stage they have reached. If the teacher can organize two or three shops, the children will not have to wait so long for a turn, and they will benefit from the extra practical experience.

Suggestions for money cards

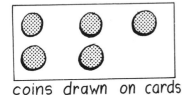

coins drawn on cards

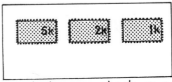

used stamps stuck on card

The children add together the money represented on the cards.

a book 6k

a comb 4k

The children write the sum in their books. 6k + 4k = 10k. Later these cards can be used for subtraction, if the teacher tells the children that they have a 10k-piece and must find the change for each article.

$$10k - 6k = 4k$$
$$10k - 4k = 6k$$

These money sums will be practised alongside other activities with the numbers up to 10. When the 10 to 20 stage is introduced in the number games, money sums can also be given up to 20k. This will help to reinforce the 10 to 20 bonds in an interesting way, as well as giving the child practical help with money.

Measurement

Introduce measurement by using parts of the body. Tell the children that in the olden days when people wanted to measure some land before building a house they might use their feet. Measure the length of the classroom by asking one of the children to use his feet; the heel of one foot must touch the toe of the other. Write down the measurement, e.g.

The classroom is 20 of Ali's feet long

Explain the difference of 'long' and 'wide', but probably it will be clearer for the children if you only measure the length of things at first, introducing the width in another lesson.

Before the lesson the teacher will have written a list on the blackboard, e.g.

The path is   long

The garden is   long

The model is   long

The Headteacher's room is   long

The teacher will read the list and then divide the children into pairs, telling them what they will measure. 'Sule and Aina will measure the path. First Sule will measure carefully with his feet while Aina helps him to count. Then Aina will measure the same path, while Sule helps her count.' The pairs of children must be well spaced throughout the compound, so that they do not get in the way of other groups. Children who finish quickly can return to the classroom and copy the list from the blackboard, writing in their own measurement. The teacher will go round helping children with their measuring. When all the children are back, the teacher can ask for the measurements.

The teacher will draw attention to the fact that different children counted different measurements with their feet. 'When Aina measured the path, it was 14 of her feet long, but when Sule measured the path it was 19 of his feet long. That is very interesting. Let us find out how we measured the other things on our list.' Do not tell the children why the measurements for the same things are different, but draw their attention to the fact that usually the measurements are not the same. 'Why do you think that Aina and Sule measured differently? Yes, perhaps they did not always remember to touch their toes with the heel of the second foot. Can you think of any other reason? Yes, perhaps they made a mistake in counting. Can you think of any other reason? Yes, perhaps their feet are not the same size. Let us find out.' Draw round Aina's foot with chalk, and ask Sule to put his foot on the outline. Draw round his foot. Compare the two outlines. All the children can compare their feet lengths with their partners in this way, or they can draw round their feet on newspaper and cut them out. The lengths can easily be compared then. 'Because our feet are all slightly different we do not measure the path in the same way. What do you think would happen if I, the teacher, measured with my feet?'

During the next lesson use the hand for measuring.

My desk is   long

The blackboard is   long

My chair is   long

The book is   long

Question the children as before to discover if they realize why the measurements are different. In following lessons other parts of the body can be used, the distance from the elbow to the end of the fingers, the last joint of the thumb, etc. Pieces of string can be knotted to represent the length of the foot, hand, distance from elbow to finger-tip, etc., and many things in the classroom and compound can be measured. You are helping the children to understand the idea of measuring, and at the same time they will begin to realize that parts of the body vary according to the size of the person. 'If in the market a piece of cloth measuring 10 hands long cost 40k, would you buy from a trader with big hands, or one with little hands?'

Gradually the children will realize that we need a standard measure, that everyone agrees about, and which the government fixes at a set length. 'In this country we use the metre. This is a metre stick. Let us measure the length of the class with the metre stick.'

After the demonstration help the children to measure many things in the classroom and compound as before, but this time all the measurements should be the same. (As the children are young they will always be slightly inaccurate. This does not matter very much as long as the children realize that if they were very, very careful they would get the same measurement each time.)

To introduce centimetre, paint a metre stick in 10 colours (or in two colours alternately). Show the class that 100 centimetres make a metre, and demonstrate how to count in tens, 10, 20, 30, 40, 50, 60, 70, 80, 90, 100. (If the children have not yet reached the stage in their number work of counting to 100, just explain the relationship between the centimetre and the metre, and give them practical work with centimetres using numbers up to 10 and later up to 20. When the children have some understanding of 100, probably by Standard 3, they can be given exercises measuring 30, 40, 50, etc., centimetres.)

Again have a list on the blackboard and let the children measure in pairs. Sticks 20 or 30 centimetres long (depending on the stage) and marked in centimetres will be given to each pair of children.

My pencil is 12 centimetres long

My foot is 14 centimetres long

At this stage explain that we have a short way of writing centimetre: cm and metre: m.

Further practice in measuring can be given by preparing pieces of paper, string, twigs, stalks, etc., for the children to measure. Work cards can be made with lines to measure.

Card 1
Measure these lines and draw them in your book

Later children can measure two pieces of paper or two sticks or two stalks and put them together to make a new length. (This introduces

THE TEN TO TWENTY STAGE

adding, but keep the numbers small. There is no value in using large numbers. It is the idea of adding lengths which is important.)

$$5 \text{ cm} \qquad\qquad 3 \text{ cm}$$

$$5 \text{ cm} \quad + \quad 3 \text{ cm} \quad = \quad 8 \text{ cm}$$

To introduce subtraction, the child can measure paper, string, etc., and cut some off, measuring the remainder. For example, measure this string. It is 9 cm long. Cut off 4 cm. There are 5 cm left.

$$9 \text{cm} - 4 \text{cm} = 5 \text{cm}$$

Weight and Capacity

Local weights and measures should be used, and connected with the price of articles in the class shop. Help the children to learn the difference between 'light' and 'heavy', by holding various things and feeling the weight. Help them to notice that some bottles and tins hold a lot, and some only hold a little. By showing them differently shaped tins, pots and bottles which all hold the same amount of water, demonstrate that shape has nothing to do with the amount they hold.

It is muddling to the small child to introduce metric weights and liquid measures, if he neither sees nor uses them. He may be taught them later in the junior classes, but by then he will have a larger experience, and may have visited shops where these measurements are used.

The Teaching of Time

Usually the days of the week are taught first, using a date chart, and by writing the day on the blackboard each day. (The day not the date, e.g. Monday, Wednesday.) Later the date can be introduced, and written each day, so helping the children to learn the names of the months, e.g. 6th June and later 21st November 1978. The date should not be written like this 21 · 11 · 78 until the children are much older.

Telling the Time by Reading a Clock

During the second year in school the children can be taught how to tell the time, using a clock. The teacher needs a large classroom clock with movable hands, one of which must be clearly bigger than the other.

Be careful when making the clock that all the figures are written upright.

How to make a child's clock: Each child should make his own small clock. The teacher must see that each child is provided with a circular piece of cardboard (about 8 cm in diameter), two pieces of cardboard for hands one 5 cm long and the other 3 cm long, a small nail and a matchbox.

The teacher shows how to write the figures by blackboard demonstration. The 12, 6, 9 and 3 divide the clock into quarters. The other figures are fitted into the spaces, using the teacher's clock as a copy. It is good for the children to try to place the figures, but most of them will find it difficult and the teacher *must correct* each clock carefully with coloured crayon. The teacher must mark the middles of the clocks before giving them to the children, so it will be fairly easy for them to fit on the hands, the long one on top of the short one. Each child holds a matchbox under his clock and pushes the nail through the hands, the cardboard of the clock and the top of the matchbox. The nail allows the hands to move easily, and its sharp end is in the matchbox and cannot hurt the child.

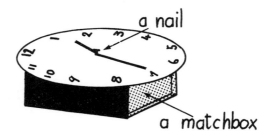

a nail

a matchbox

Stages of Teaching the Clock

1. *'O'clock':* Tell the children that when the big hand points to 12 it says 'o'clock'. The little hand tells us 'what' o'clock.

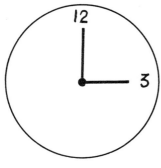

Three o'clock   Eight o'clock

Let individual children move the class clock, and then each child can move his own, checking it by the class clock. Connect the hours with times the children know. We come to school at 8 o'clock. Who can put the hand to 8 o'clock? Good. Everyone put his own clock to 8 o'clock. We have a break at 10 o'clock, etc.

2. *'Half-past'*: Revise the 'o'clock' times. Show that from 1 o'clock to 2 o'clock the little hand just moves from 1 to 2, but the big hand moves all the way round from 12, back to 12 again. Show that from 2 o'clock to 3 o'clock the big hand again moves all the way round, etc.

Show that when it gets as far as 6, the big hand has moved half of the way round, and we call it 'half-past'. From 3 o'clock move the big hand to 6. 'It is half-past 3.' From 7 o'clock move the big hand to 6. 'It is half-past 7', etc. Give the children plenty of practice on the class clock and their own clocks. Connect the 'half-past' with the times they know. We go home at half-past 1, etc.

3. *'A quarter-past and a quarter to'*: Draw a clock on the blackboard and show the quarters. Write 'past' on the right, and 'to' on the left. Demonstrate with the class clock. 'It is 2 o'clock.' The big hand moves a quarter of the way round. 'It is a quarter-**past** 2.' It moves another quarter. 'We know this time. Who can tell me what the clock says? Good.

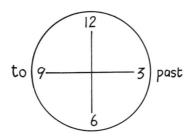

Half-past 2.' The big hand begins to move towards the next o'clock. 'Which o'clock comes after 2 o'clock? 3 o'clock. Good.' The big hand moves a quarter of the way to 3 o'clock, and it says: 'A quarter **to** 3.' While the big hand has gone all the way round the little hand has moved from 2 to 3. Give the children plenty of practice with the quarters.

4. '5 *past and* 10 *past*. 5 *to and* 10 *to*': Tell the children that it takes 5 minutes for the big hand to move from one number to the next. The class can count in fives round the clock, 5, 10, 15, 20, 25, etc., making 60 minutes in an hour. Draw the clock on the blackboard showing the quarters again. Write 'past' and 'to'. Then continue as in the diagram below.

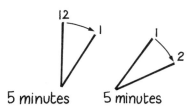

5 minutes   5 minutes

'It is 6 o'clock. The big hand moves to the 1. It is 5 minutes **past** 6 o'clock. It moves to the 2. It has moved for ten minutes. It is 10 minutes **past** 6. The big hand moves to the 3. What time is it now? We shall not learn these other numbers today, but we know what the time is when the big hand points to 6, and then to 9. Now it moves to 10. It is ten more minutes to the next o'clock. 7 o'clock. It is 10 minutes **to** 7. The big hand moves to 11. Now it is only five minutes to 7 o'clock. It is 5 minutes to 7.'

5. '20 *past and* 25 *past*. 25 *to and* 20 *to*': These are taught in a similar way to stage 4.

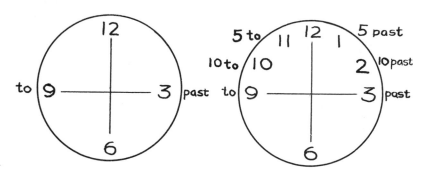

Always remember to give the children plenty of practice, and connect the teaching with times they know.

When the children can tell the time, give them simple oral problems, e.g. I left home at 20 minutes to 8, and I arrived at school at 5 minutes to 8. How long did it take me to walk to school? It took John 20 minutes to walk to the market. He left home at a quarter-past 3. What time was it when he reached the market? The children can move their clocks to find the answer.

Chapter 12   Bigger Numbers

The bigger the numbers become, the more apparatus is needed to experience them concretely. This can become difficult in a small classroom. Show the children big amounts when possible, because they need hundreds of experiences. Look around for examples. All the children at assembly may give the idea of three hundred children. This does not mean that the children will now understand what three hundred trees look like, or three hundred stars, or three hundred coins, or three hundred sheep, or three hundred shells. Even less will they have an understanding of three hundred as an idea in itself.

As numbers get larger they are more difficult to experience, and therefore more difficult to understand. Can you think of a thousand people and how much space would be needed for them all to sit down? Or ten thousand people and where they could all sit? Or what size car park would you need for two thousand cars? Or how big a store place is necessary for a hundred thousand bags of groundnuts? What size of store would six thousand books need? What would a million notes of money look like? How long is a thousand metres? How long is a million seconds? What kind of thing would weigh six thousand kilograms? Unless you have actually seen or worked with these things, it is unlikely that you can imagine such large amounts. You have an idea of a smaller amount, say a hundred, and you multiply your idea intelligently to make the new idea. But a young child cannot do this. Until he is about twelve years old and well educated, ideas are only understandable if he can experience them practically. The real study of large numbers must be left until children are older. They can be prepared and given as much experience as possible, but there is no virtue in working out long complicated mechanical sums, which machines can do better anyway, and which the children do not understand. **Aim at keeping work well within the children's experience; give plenty of problems and help the children to think and experiment.**

Suggestions for Giving Experience of Larger Numbers
Use the pre-number apparatus again to give experience of numbers up to 99, but more of everything will have to be supplied. Small desks may become rather crowded. If the floors are swept, children will usually work quite happily on the floor where there is more space.

Boxes labelled with the tens can be filled.

All the numbers to 99 can be experienced using different objects. The children pick out cards on which symbols are written, and then count out the number. Use only one type of article for each box.

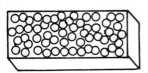 

Cards can be picked again and the number laid out using the coloured strips.

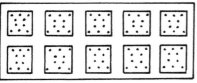

5 black and one grey [58]   Two black and one violet [27]

Continue counting registers, pencils, paint-brushes, etc. Count the flowers in the garden, the trees in the compound, the animals on the farm, the cars which pass the school, the people walking to market, the number of seeds in a bag of guinea corn, the number of nuts in a tin. This should lead to finding quicker ways of counting. Counting in twos, even numbers 2, 4, 6, 8, etc., and odd numbers 1, 3, 5, 7, etc. Counting in threes, in fours, in fives, in tens. Sometimes the numbers may be over a hundred. This does not matter, but introduce larger amounts very gradually. The time it takes to count very large amounts will probably prevent this happening very often. Children can, however, be given experience of a large number; **for example, a thousand groundnuts or grains of rice.** Let each child count ten, and by putting ten tens together in a box make a hundred. Repeat this ten times and the children have a thousand.

Ten in each small box = a hundred in the big box

Many, many experiences are necessary, and this takes years. Between the ages of eight and eleven gradually build up a good foundation of experience and understanding of large numbers.

I. Place Value

Work with numbers depends on the ability to understand the idea behind the word spoken for the numbers, and on understanding the written symbols for the numbers. The methods of writing numbers in most countries today is based on ten symbols: 0, 1, 2, 3, 4, 5, 6, 7, 8, 9. The place the symbol holds is very important, and allows the same symbol to be used over and over again. For example, 2 can stand for two things, or if it is moved one place to the left, **20** for twenty things, or if it is moved two places to the left, **200** for two hundred things, or if it is moved three places to the left, **2000** for two thousand things, and so on. The 2 stands for different things, depending on its place. The zeros hold the **2** in position, and show which place the **2** is in. This idea of place value is extremely valuable, as you will realize if you have tried to work out sums using Roman or old Egyptian symbols. The place idea took man thousands of years to invent, and we cannot expect a small child to understand this marvellous idea quickly. (Of course they can be taught to perform sums like a parrot doing tricks, but this is not understanding.) I should not start any serious or formal work using place symbols until the children have been in school three or four years, though preliminary experiences and oral problem work should be given. You will not find many other books which agree with me, but my reason for this recommendation is that if more time is spent giving a very good grounding the children will be confident and happy. They will understand what Mathematics is all about. Later they will pass in skill and understanding, those children who were forced to work with bigger numbers, before they were ready.

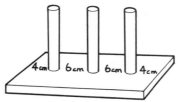

The Abacus. A board measuring about 20 cm by 8 cm has three holes about 6 cm apart. Three sticks are put in the holes. Each stick must be just long enough to hold 9 beads. This is an old counting frame and is very useful for showing the idea of place. If each stick can only hold nine beads it can be used for hundreds, tens and units, but it can also be adapted for other types of sums.

'The first stick holds the units or ones. How many ones will it hold? Nine. Good. If we want to show ten we must all agree that one bead on

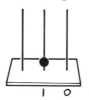

the second stick is equal to ten ones. One bead on the second column (or stick) and no beads on the first column (or stick) shows that it stands for ten. How can we show two tens? Two beads on the ten column. Good. How can we show twenty-three? Three beads on the unit column, and two on the tens column. Good.'

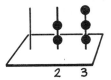 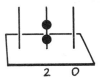

Make some frames, but the children can also practise by drawing the abacus.

Later hundreds can also be shown by agreeing that one bead on the third column stands for ten of the tens. Ten units are shown by one ten on the second column, and ten tens are shown by one on the third column.

The abacus can also be drawn as columns and dots.

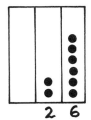 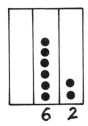 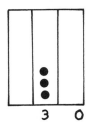

The strips: The children know that ten ones are equal to one ten strip. Practice in recognizing the symbols can also be given using the 'ten' strips and the units. Always place the tens to the left of the units.

3 black and 1 orange   5 black and 1 blue   8 black and 1 violet

To introduce the idea of a hundred when using the strips, place ten strips together. The children should be able to count easily in tens before this is taught.

'Let us count how many "ones" we have here. Ten in the first strip and ten more and ten more. Count them . . . . ten, twenty, thirty, etc. What do you notice about the shape we have made?'

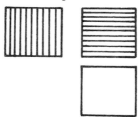

From other experiences the children should be able to recognize the square shape. 'A square shape. Good. Here is a square shape exactly the same size, but it is not divided up into ten strips. How many ten strips would fit on this square? Ten tens. Good. How many "ones" would fit on this square? A hundred ones. Good. Here are some squares I have cut for you. They are all the same size as the square we made with the ten "ten" strips. Divide your square up to show the hundred "ones".'

The children can draw round the 'ten' pieces and divide each again into ten, or they can draw round the 'one' pieces. Let them experiment on their own to show a hundred 'ones' on the hundred square. Question them to find out if they realize that the 'one' is also a square shape, and the 'ten' is a rectangle. Number symbols can be shown using these shapes.

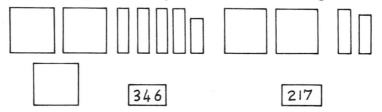

II. Addition and Subtraction of Number

When the children have grasped the idea of place value they can be introduced to sums using larger figures, and written down in the manner most of us learned in our childhood. **Of course they will have been using numbers over twenty orally and practically for problems.** For example, 'Uwa picked seventeen flowers and Musa picked sixteen. How many flowers have we all together. We gave out thirty-seven brushes and we have only thirty-one here? How many must we find?'

Introduce with sums the children are familiar with.

'You can all tell me the answer to this sum, 6 + 17. Anna. 23. Good.

We can write it more ways. $17+6 = 23$, $23 = 17+6$, $23 = 6+17$. We could also write it this way $\begin{smallmatrix}6\\1\overset{}{7}\end{smallmatrix}$ and this way $\begin{smallmatrix}17\\\overset{}{6}\end{smallmatrix}$. The answer will go in the box. This is a useful way to write the sum, when the answer is too big for us to do in our heads. We can work out the units column first, and then work out the tens column. Remember your abacus work. Which is the unit column? The column on the right. Good. Which figures are in the units column? A six and a seven. What do they equal when added together? Thirteen. Good. What do we call the next column? The "tens" column. Good. How can we break up the thirteen to make it useful for the next column? A three and one ten. We put the three in the units column and give one, the one ten, to the "tens" column. If you think you might forget it, write a tiny one in the "tens" column.

$$\begin{array}{r} 6 \\ + 1{,}7 \\ \hline \end{array} \qquad \begin{array}{r} 17 \\ + {,}6 \\ \hline \end{array}$$

Now we have . . . . how many tens? Two tens. Good. Six and seventeen equals twenty-three. The other sum, seventeen and six equals . . . Twenty-three also. Good.' (Always read the whole sum and especially the whole answer. The children must not think it is a two and a three, **but two tens and three units, twenty-three**.)

'Can we write some subtraction sums using these figures? Twenty-three minus seventeen equals six, and twenty-three minus six equals seventeen. Good.'

$$\begin{array}{r} 2\,3 \\ -1\,7 \\ \hline 6 \end{array} \qquad \begin{array}{r} 2\,3 \\ -\ \ 6 \\ \hline 1\,7 \end{array}$$

Do not work out the subtraction sums at this stage. The children know the answers from their previous experiences with patterns and number. The opposite of addition is subtraction.

Give the children plenty of practice with simple addition sums like this. Keep the figures to amounts they can work out fairly easily in their heads, but ask them to work with the column method also to check the answers. Each time the children should write the addition sum in two ways, and the figures should then be changed round to make two subtraction sums. No mechanical method of working subtraction has yet been shown. Note that the signs $+$ and $-$ should always be well to the left of the sum, and not mixed up with the figures $\begin{array}{r} 3\,2 \\ +1{,}8 \\ \hline 5\,0 \end{array}$. Gradually introduce larger number symbols, and give practice with carrying more than one ten. (Changing to subtraction will not be expected for these sums.) Remember to practise the zero. Keep the symbols and the answers under 99.

When the idea of carrying is well grounded, subtraction can be introduced.

There are a number of methods, but the equal addition method is considered by many teachers to be the most speedy one, for work in the secondary school. If it is taught when the children are about nine it should not prove difficult. If the children are younger it may seem like magic, and that is bad for understanding Mathematics. Other methods can be shown to younger children, but what is the sense of teaching one method at eight and another at nine or ten? The children will only be confused.

The Equal Addition Method of Subtraction
First write many easy examples on the blackboard and ask different children for the answers. Add ten to each number and write it near the first sum. 'Seven and ten equals seventeen. Three and ten equals thirteen. What is the difference between seventeen and thirteen? Four. Good. What is the difference between seven and three? Four also. When we add ten to each of the numbers the difference stays the same. Let us try it with other sums to see if the same thing happens.'

$$7 - 3 = 4 \qquad 17 - 13 = 4$$
$$6 - 5 = 1 \qquad 16 - 15 = 1$$
$$8 - 4 = 4 \qquad 18 - 14 = 4$$
$$9 - 6 = 3 \qquad 19 - 16 = 3$$
$$10 - 4 = 6 \qquad 20 - 14 = 6$$
$$13 - 7 = 6 \qquad 23 - 17 = 6$$

'What has happened when we have added ten to each of the figures? The difference has stayed the same. Good. Now I shall show you how we can write sums which might be too big for you to do in your head. Thirty-four subtract sixteen $-\dfrac{3\,'4}{1,6}$. We can look at the two columns separately.

What is this column called? Units. Good. And this column? Tens. Good. We shall work the units column first. Four take away six we cannot. We shall give a ten to the top "unit" number and a ten to the bottom "ten" number. The difference will stay the same, but now we can work out the units column. Fourteen subtract six equals . . . . Eight. Good. Put eight units in the units column. Now we shall work the tens column. Three tens subtract . . . . This is not one ten any more. How many tens are here now? Two tens. Good. Three tens take away two tens . . . . One ten. Good. We write the one ten in the answer. What is thirty-four take away sixteen? Eighteen. Good.'

$$\begin{array}{r} 3\,'4 \\ -1,6 \\ \hline 1\,8 \end{array}$$

Always read the sum with the complete answer. The children should not think of the sum as being in two little bits. Notice the importance of a firm grounding in the ten to twenty stage here. Encourage the children to write the sum in other ways too.

34	34	18	16	34 − 16 = 18	18 = 34 − 16
− 16	− 18	+ 16	+ 18	34 − 18 = 16	16 = 34 − 18
18	16	34	34	18 + 16 = 34	34 = 18 + 16
				16 + 18 = 34	34 = 16 + 18

III. Multiplication and Division

All the tables will gradually be built up using apparatus at first. Help the children to realize that multiplication is a quick method of adding the same number.

Example of Building up a Table

'If we have no groups of two we have nothing. One group of two is two.

$$0 \times 2 = 0$$
$$1 \times 2 = 2 \quad \cdot\cdot$$
$$2 \times 2 = 4 \quad \cdot\cdot$$
$$3 \times 2 = \quad \cdot\cdot$$

I shall draw another group on the board. Now we have two groups. How many in each group? Two. How many altogether? Four. Two groups of two equals four. We shall make another group of two. Three groups of two equals . . . . Six. Good.' Continue in this way. As each group is added the children will use stones, seeds, etc., to build the table on the desks. If the children have had a good grounding with simple multiplication they should soon be able to build up any table they wish.

Teach the division table at the same time as the multiplication table. It is easier to learn them together.

'How many groups of two are there if we have nothing? No groups. Good. How many groups of two are there if we have two? One group.

$$0 \div 2 = 0$$
$$\cdot\cdot \; 2 \div 2 = 1$$
$$\cdot\cdot \; 4 \div 2 = 2$$
$$\cdot\cdot \; 6 \div 2 =$$

Good. How many groups of two are there if we have four? Two groups. Good. How many groups of two are there if we have six? Three groups of two. Good.'

Continue in this way, with the children using stones to work out the answers practically. Give plenty of practice and revision, until the children really understand how to build up and break down the tables. Usually the tables of two, three, five, ten, eleven and four are considered the easiest and are taught first.

$$0 \times 5 = 0 \qquad\qquad 0 \div 5 = 0$$
$$1 \times 5 = 5 \qquad \boxed{\cdots} \qquad 5 \div 5 = 1$$
$$2 \times 5 = 10 \qquad \boxed{\vdots} \qquad 10 \div 5 = 2$$
$$3 \times 5 = 15 \qquad \boxed{\vdots} \qquad 15 \div 5 = 3$$
$$4 \times 5 = 20 \qquad \boxed{\vdots} \qquad 20 \div 5 = 4$$
$$5 \times 5 = 25 \qquad \boxed{\vdots} \qquad 25 \div 5 = 5$$

A table book is useful. Each table can be written down, once it has been built up practically. The children try to remember the tables, but can look in their table book when necessary.

Suggestions for Teaching Harder Multiplication Sums

'When we want to multiply numbers which are quite large it would take a long time to keep building up the table. A quicker way is to break the number into units and tens. We multiply the units first and then we multiply the tens. Twenty-eight multiplied by three. How many units?

$$\begin{array}{r} 28 \\ \times 3 \\ \hline 84 \end{array}$$

Eight. Good. We shall multiply three times eight first. Who

remembers three times eight or eight times three? Twenty-four. Good. Can you break twenty-four into tens and units? Four units and two tens. Good. We write the units in the answer and carry the two tens to the tens column, just like we did with adding sums. Now we multiply the tens column. Three twos equal . . . . Six, and we add on the two we carried to this column . . . . Eight. Good. We write the eight tens in the tens column. What is the answer to twenty-eight multiplied by three? Eighty-four. Good. We can also write this sum: $28 \times 3 = 84$. Can anyone turn these numbers into another sum? Three times twenty-eight equals eighty-four. Good. Eighty-four divided by three equals twenty-eight. Eighty-four divided by twenty-eight is the same as three. Good. We shall write these down in as many ways as we can.'

$$\begin{array}{r} 3 \\ \times 28 \\ \hline 84 \end{array} \qquad 3 \times 28 = 84 \qquad 3\overline{)84}^{28} \qquad \frac{84}{3} = 28 \qquad 28\overline{)84}^{3}$$

$$84 \div 3 = 28$$

After the first sum there is no working out. The children should know the answers from their understanding of the first sum.

'You remember that multiplication is a quick way of adding. We shall write twenty-eight, three times and add. Eight and eight equals sixteen and another eight equals . . . . Twenty-four. Good. Put the four units in the answer and carry the two tens. Two tens and two tens and two tens and two tens equals . . . . Eight tens. Good. What is the answer to twenty-eight added three times? Eighty-four. Good. It is the same answer as before, so we have checked our multiplication sum.'

Children will need plenty of practice with multiplication sums. Encourage them to learn the tables, so they do not have to waste time looking in the table book. Always encourage the children to write the sums in as many ways as possible, and to check multiplication by addition. Keep the answers to tens and units for some time. Later answers can include hundreds, but do not introduce multiplying hundreds yet.

Suggestions for Teaching Harder Division Sums
'How many groups of five can we take from seventy-five? To help us we can break 75 into tens and units. Seven tens and five units. How many groups of five can we take from seven? One group of five and two left over. Good. Remember it was seven tens, so the one is **one ten,** and must be written in the tens column. We have two left over. Two what? Two tens. Good. If we put the two tens with the five units, how much have we? Twenty-five. Good. How many groups of five can we take from twenty-five? You know this from your tables. Five groups of five. Good. We have been working in the units column, so this is five units. How many groups of five can we take from seventy-five? Fifteen. Good. We can also write this sum $75 \div 5 = 15$; $\frac{75}{5} = 15$. What other sums can you make with these numbers? Five groups of fifteen can be taken from seventy-five. Good. We can write this in three ways. Who can write them on the blackboard? Good.

$$15\overline{)75} \qquad 75 \div 15 = 5 \qquad \frac{75}{15} = 5$$

Can you make any more sums with these numbers? Five multiplied by fifteen equals seventy-five. Good. Fifteen multiplied by five is the same as seventy-five. Good. Who can write them on the blackboard in different ways? Good.

$$\begin{array}{r} 5 \\ \times 15 \\ \hline 75 \end{array} \qquad 5 \times 15 = 75 \qquad \begin{array}{r} 15 \\ \times 5 \\ \hline 75 \end{array} \qquad 15 \times 5 = 75 \qquad \begin{array}{l} 75 = 15 \times 5 \\ 75 = 5 \times 15 \end{array}$$

Again children need a great deal of practice. Keep to tens and units only at this stage.
'You remember that division is a quick way of taking away the same group over and over again. We can check our division sums by subtraction. From seventy-five we shall take away a group of five, as many times as possible. We shall draw a circle round each five we take away, as they will be easier to count when we have finished. Seventy-five take away five equals . . . . seventy. Good. Seventy take away five equals . . . . sixty-five. Good. Sixty-five take away five is the same as . . . . sixty. Good.' and so on to, 'Ten take away five equals . . . . five. Good. Five take away five equals . . . . nothing. Good.'

$$75 - \text{⑤} = 70 - \text{⑤} = 65 - \text{⑤} = 60 - \text{⑤} = 55 - \text{⑤} = 50$$
$$50 - \text{⑤} = 45 - \text{⑤} = 40 - \text{⑤} = 35 - \text{⑤} = 30 - \text{⑤} = 25$$
$$25 - \text{⑤} = 20 - \text{⑤} = 15 - \text{⑤} = 10 - \text{⑤} = 5 - \text{⑤} = 0$$

15 groups of five have been taken away

'Let us count how many groups of five we have taken away. Fifteen. Good. That is the same number as we worked out in the division sum. We have checked our answer and know we did it correctly.'

In every lesson help the children to *understand* the numbers, and also to learn ways of *checking* if their own answers are correct.

Problems: As soon as the children have some ability with these methods, give problems where these new methods can be used. Help the children to realize there is some reason for learning how to do these sums, learn tables, etc. When the children have a problem to work out, these methods provide a quick means of finding the correct answer. Make sure the problems **make sense to the children**, and are not adult problems.

IV. Money, Measurement, Capacity, Weight

These will still be dealt with practically. Shopping sums will deal with larger amounts of money, through making bills for traders and shop-keepers. Subtraction will be practised through the giving of change from paper notes, and by working out profits.

A trader bought a bicycle for ₦60 and sold it for ₦65.50. How much profit did he make?

The children should work this out practically with 'pretend' money and then be shown how to write the sum.

$$
\begin{array}{ll}
\text{₦} 65.50 & \text{selling price} \\
\text{₦} 60.00 & \text{buying price} \\
\hline
\text{₦} \;\; 5.50 & \text{profit}
\end{array}
$$

Multiplication can be introduced.

If my profit was ₦5.50 on one bike, how much will I make if I sell 7 bikes?

$$
\begin{array}{r}
\text{₦} \;\; 5.50 \\
7 \\
\hline
\text{₦}38.50
\end{array}
$$

Division is more difficult and probably should be left until much later, though a certain amount can be understood practically through the sharing idea.

If Father shares ₦4 between 5 children, how much does each get?

With 'pretend' money the children can work this type of problem out correctly.

Measurement should be continued as on page 114, giving children as much experience as possible using larger numbers. The difference between **length** and **width** and **height** should be explained and used. Metre sticks can be cut and the children helped to divide them into 100 centimetres, painting or scratching on the divisions. The ideas of longer, shorter, estimates and approximations should be introduced and used. The blackboard is longer than the table. The pencil is shorter than the book. It is very useful to be able to estimate a distance, because we do not carry metre rulers round with us very often. Always ask children to **estimate** a measurement before they measure it, and later to find out their error (this gives practice in subtraction).

Object	Estimate	Actual measurement	Error
the wall	40 m	37 m 30 cm	2 m 70 cm

Most of the time we do not need to worry if our measurements are not completely accurate, so introduce the idea of **approximation.** The wall is approximately 37 m long.

There is not much to be gained from multiplying or dividing metres and centimetres, but if you do decide to give practice, do it practically with paper, string, stalks, etc.

If I need seven pieces of cloth all 60 cm long, how much material will I need to buy?

If I want to divide a piece of string 2 m 40 cm long into 8 pieces, how long will each piece measure?

Capacity should be dealt with practically. The children should have poured water into many types of containers. **More than, less than** should be considered carefully and recorded.

'The bowl holds more than the milk tin.'

'The milk tin holds less than the bowl.'

Estimates should be encouraged, and recorded.

'I think the cup will hold more than the syrup tin.'

'I measured by pouring water from the syrup tin into the cup, and discovered that the syrup tin holds more than the cup.'

Now the children can be shown the standard container, the litre, because if we are buying or selling it is necessary to know exactly how much we are paying for. By pouring water the children can discover how many litres fill the bucket, the large tin, the big bowl, etc. By pouring water they can discover how many cups full of water are needed to fill the litre measure, how many small tins of water are needed to fill the litre measure, etc. At this stage the discoveries should be recorded carefully.

'The tin holds less water than a litre.'

'The bucket holds more water than the litre.'

'I filled the litre measure with $3\frac{1}{2}$ tins of water.'

'I poured water from the litre measure 6 times to fill the red bowl.'

Take the children to the nearest petrol pump (having made arrangements with the attendant beforehand) to watch the cars and lorries being filled with petrol. Help them to discover how much the petrol tanks hold, and compare the different cars and lorries. Friendly drivers will help you with this. Help the children discover the price of one litre, two litres, three litres, etc. Ask the drivers how far their cars or lorries will travel on 10 litres. This will bring in **kilometres, comparison of engine sizes** and **cost.** All this interesting knowledge can be discussed when you return to school and then the children can record what they discovered. Addition will be necessary to discover how much was sold while you watched. Subtraction may be used if you know how much petrol was in the tank, and the children can be helped to work out how much is left. Multiplication and division can be left until the children are older, but if you want to give practice **be practical.**

'If 5 cars all take 12 litres each, how much petrol is sold?'

'If a ten litre tin of oil is to be shared between five men, how much will each get?'

Weight will have been experienced practically, and comparison of **light** and **heavy, lighter, heavier** should be continued. Introduce large things which are light, e.g. balls of wool, polystyrene blocks, bags of feathers, and small things which are heavy, e.g. metal weights, lead piping, a heavy but small stone. It will be more difficult for the children to say which is lighter and which is heavier just by looking at them. They will be deceived by their eyes. It is good to help them to realize that weight may have nothing much to do with size. After looking and estimating which are light and which are heavy, let the children feel the objects, and then let them put them on a balance.

Introduce the standard measurement of kilogram. This is interesting if you do it in connection with weighing the children. We all like to know how heavy we are. If you can borrow scales, or go to a cocoa centre, the children can weigh many objects. Most of the weights will be approximate, because grams are not introduced until there has been plenty of practice with kilograms. When grams are introduced, scales are necessary again. (Maybe the secondary school will lend you some, if you have none.) For practical purposes grams are very small and it is better to weigh things of 50 g, 100 g, 200 g, etc. The children can add up the weights of things their mothers buy at market to discover how much she has to carry. If Ali carries the bag of rice, how much lighter will mother's load be? This type of question will require subtraction. If you want to give practice in multiplication and division, do it through practical examples of loads to carry, or amounts to sell, and keep the numbers simple and uncomplicated.

Whenever anything new is introduced show something the children know well and lead on from there, **one step** at a time. The teacher should think carefully about any new sum, to make sure that only one new idea is being introduced. **Go no further** until that one idea is well understood and mastered. Remember that our main aim for teaching Mathematics is to help the children to **understand** the scientific and technological world in which we live.

Part three   Language

Why the Vernacular is Taught

When further education is taught in English it could be argued that more time should be spent on English and less on the vernacular, but for the following reasons it is most important to teach the vernacular carefully.

1. The child's ideas and thoughts are in his own language, and will be long after he is speaking quite good English. If the child is to be encouraged to think for himself, as stated in our aims of education, he must first be helped to think in his own language.

2. The vernacular is the child's contact with his home, family and village, and education should give him better understanding and contact with the home and village.

3. The culture of his people is found in the child's own language, and the language should be taught at its purest and best, so the child can appreciate the literature, stories, songs and poems of his country and perhaps add his own contribution to them when he grows older.

Chapter 13   Spoken Vernacular for the Younger Children

There are always four things to be considered when we talk about a language: speaking, listening, reading and writing.

Speaking: The child should be proud of his own language and learn to use it correctly. Encourage him to pronounce words clearly, and use them in the accepted grammatical order. Teach the child to use greetings and terms of respect, and help him to practise the behaviour that goes with them.

Listening: There can be no conversation nor communication unless we all take a turn at listening. Small children find it difficult to listen carefully, because they are so full of their own thoughts. Help the child to concentrate on what the teacher says, by making all the spoken lessons very interesting. Local stories, poems and songs encourage careful listening.

Reading: Unfortunately there is little for the child to read in his own language once he has left school, except vernacular letters and newspapers. Teachers and educationalists should try to collect the literature of their people and get it published.

Writing: A foreign language hinders ideas from flowing from the child's mind. All the time the child is trying to remember **how** to write the words, so he has no time to think of interesting ideas or for using his imagination. As the child's thoughts are in his own vernacular he must be helped to express himself well in that language.

The Teaching of Language
The teaching of language in the Primary school can be divided into two parts.

Part 1: Extensive practice in the use of spoken language, careful listening, and the beginning of reading and writing skills.

Part 2: (*a*) Extended help with spoken language, encouraging fluency, the expression of logical thought and the use of the imagination.

(*b*) Opportunities for listening and interpreting what is said. (We should not believe all we hear. We should consider carefully and make intelligent judgements.)

(*c*) Encouragement to read as much as possible, to try to understand the author's meaning and evaluate his words. (Again we should not believe everything we read, just because it is in a printed book. Children need a great deal of help to consider and think carefully about their reading.)

(*d*) Encouragement to use his imagination and to express his own ideas in writing.

Spoken Language in the Infant Classes
By the time the child comes to school, he has learnt a good number of words in general use in his area, and he can put the words together in a fairly correct grammatical way. The home will have given the child his early language experience. Remember that young children only learn effective language from adults, first their parents and then their teachers. It is good and necessary for children to talk to each other, because in this way they practise using language. But the real **new** learning comes mainly from conversation with adults.

Every lesson is a language lesson, because in every lesson language is used. Some techniques, however, especially help the development of language.

Ways of Encouraging Language Development
The teacher's speech pattern: This is most important in language training, for the child will imitate the teacher.

Stories	Picture talks
Dramatization	Conversation
Poetry	News
Oral composition	Messages

Stories: These are very necessary in the language training of a young child, and should be on the timetable nearly every day. The teacher tells stories to introduce new words to the child, to give the child a wider experience of life through the characters in the story and to give the child a shared enjoyment with the teacher.

How to Choose a Story for a Young Child
1. It should widen his understanding yet should deal with things familiar to the child, e.g. home-life, shopping, working, playing, travelling in a way they understand, school, marriage and other celebrations.

2. It should be short and easily dramatized, so that the child can practise speaking.

3. Animal stories, which may deal with animals doing human things, are enjoyed, but right and justice must prevail.

4. When the child is a little older (about 7 to 10 years) stories can be chosen to give him experience of the wider world. There are many things

a child may not be able to do, but through a story, in his imagination, he can experience such things, e.g. the work of kings and chiefs, travelling to large, strange towns, helping the police to catch a thief, helping the doctor save someone who is very sick. He can also be taught simple history and geography through stories.

In all the stories it is essential that the people who do right should be successful and those who do wrong, though they may escape for a little while, are punished in the end. This is important moral training. We want the child to admire good people, and copy them.

At no time should young children be told stories where anyone is cruel or unjust to a child. The parents and teacher must always be shown as people who will protect the child whatever may happen. This helps to increase the child's feeling of security.

Telling the story: With Infants it is wise to group the class round the teacher in a semicircle. Little children like to be near the teacher, and they usually prefer a story to be told, not read.

Dramatizing the Story

The value of dramatizing the story:

1. It shows the teacher if the child has understood the language he has heard.

2. If the child is pretending to be a grown-up person, it gives him practice in using an adult form of language with words he would not normally use.

3. It helps him to understand other people's feelings, as he imagines himself as the character in the play.

4. It helps to develop the child's imagination.

5. It gives the child a chance to express himself, and enjoy himself.

As many children as possible in the class should take part in the dramatization. The teacher must make sure that those who do not get a part today, get one tomorrow. The shy child must be encouraged to take a small part, so that he can practise his language. If the story has been well told the teacher should be able to sit down and watch the dramatizing, only speaking very occasionally when a child has forgotten what he should do.

Poetry: This is the use of words in their most beautiful form. It is difficult to find many poems in the vernacular suitable for young children. The popular little jingles and short sayings cannot be called poems. These can be useful, however, for aiding articulation (clear pronunciation) and for introducing some new ideas. Poetry should increase the child's knowledge and use of words, especially descriptive words. Poems about children, family and village life, animals, birds and nature subjects are all suitable, but the poem must have high ideals to make it worth the child's time being spent learning it. Teachers should try to write good, interesting children's poems.

For young children the poem will not be written on the blackboard at all. The children will follow the teacher's speech pattern. When the children are learning to read, it will help their reading to put the poem on the blackboard **after** they nearly know it by copying the teacher's speech pattern. (Most of the notes on teaching English poetry can be applied to teaching vernacular poetry. See page 216-219.)

Oral Composition: Young children can build up a story in connection with familiar actions and objects, e.g. shopping, washing the baby, picking bananas, feeding the dog. Never say, 'Tell me a sentence about going shopping.' The child will not know what to say, or will give very uninteresting answers. The teacher's job is to awaken ideas in the child's mind. One good way is through questioning, but the questions must be prepared, so that the answers will follow a definite sequence or story. For example, a story about shopping. (A shopping bag, purse and money will add further interest and discussion.) 'What does Mother take when she goes shopping? Why does she take those things? How far does she walk to market? How do you know the distance? Which stall will she visit? Why does she go there first? Whom does she meet? What does Mother think when she meets her friend? What did her friend think? What did they say to each other?' and so on. Only expect a short story from young children. When the oral composition is finished the children can dramatize their own story.

Picture talks: If an interesting picture is used the children will be eager to talk about it. The picture should be big enough for all the class to see it easily. Pictures of African subjects must be used for young African children, as they will not understand foreign pictures. To help the children the teacher should ask questions. For example, the picture of a house and a family. 'Why is the father looking happy? What do you think the children have been doing? Where is the mother going next? What is she thinking? What are the children thinking? What do you think they are going to do?'

Conversations: The teacher and children talk about any subject that interests them. The teacher should bring various interesting things (e.g. things he has bought from another town: a weaving loom, fruit, eggs, pottery, etc.) to the classroom to interest the children and start them talking. Remember that a good teacher does not do all the talking, but encourages the children to talk.

News: This is a good way of giving the children practice in speaking. They can tell each other about anything interesting which happens to them. News can be taken for a short time each day.

Messages: It gives the children practice in speaking clearly if they are occasionally asked to take oral messages to other teachers in the school.

Increasing Intelligence through Language

Many modern psychologists think we can increase a child's intelligence by giving him a stimulating environment, plenty of concrete experiences, and by helping him to **understand** his environment and **express** his experiences through language. Intelligence and language are very closely connected. As teachers we should try to increase each child's effective intelligence. Increasing the child's ability to use language will help him to **reason,** to **consider,** to **compare** and to **predict** possibilities. The child will do this in the mother tongue for many years. The development of the intelligence through language is most successful in the vernacular.

Vocabulary: The words a person uses are called his vocabulary. We all understand more words (passive vocabulary) than we actually use (active vocabulary). In school we try to increase the number of words the child uses. Teaching naming words (nouns) and doing words (verbs) is fairly easy, but we must also try to include more difficult ones, e.g. adjectives and adverbs. Instead of saying, 'I see a man walking along the road', help the child to observe the man more carefully. 'What kind of man?' old, lame, rich, smiling. 'How does he walk?' fast, quietly, uncertainly. 'What kind of road?' rough, winding, narrow, etc. Prepositions need careful teaching, e.g. above, below, between, in front of, behind, by, on, under, in, outside, inside, to the right, and to the left. Right and left are especially important and rather difficult and will need much practice. Plurals and negatives need to be given the correct form. If the grammatical order is incorrect help needs to be given. With young children this is best done during conversation, by gentle correction (a set grammar lesson has not much value) and by the teacher's own speech pattern.

An intelligent person usually has a good vocabulary, but words alone are of little benefit. They must be used sensibly.

Questioning Technique: Asking **why, what, where, who** and **how** questions are very good, because the child has to **think** of reasons. Just naming objects when the children are taken on a visit, or to look at pictures is insufficient. When choosing a picture make sure it has plenty of action.

For example, the following are the types of question that could be asked about a picture of a man and woman walking along a bush path, with a goat.

1. Questions should require more than one-word answers.
2. Questions should encourage thought, by helping the child to describe what he sees and hears and feels.
   'What is this picture about?'
   'Why do you think that?'
   'What else is happening?'
   'Why do you like the picture?'
3. Questions should help the child to remember similar places and experiences, which he can relate to the present situation.
   'When did you see a goat like this?'
   'What did it smell like?'
   'What was it doing?'
4. Questions should help the child to think into the future.
   'What do you think will happen next?'
   'Where do you think the man is going?'
   'What will the woman say when she gets home?'
5. Questions should help the child to use his imagination.
   'What other places could the man be going to?'
   'How do you think he would get there?'
   'Why do you think that?'
   'Whom do you think he will meet?'
6. Questions should help the child consider how other people feel.
   'What is the man thinking?'
   'Why is he thinking that?'
   'How does he feel as he walks along?'
7. Questions should help the child to reason, and to give a number of possibilities.
   'If the goat runs into the bush what do you think the man might do? What might the woman do?'
   'If it starts to rain heavily what might the man and woman do?'
   'Can you tell how old the goat is? What are your reasons for thinking this?'

It will be obvious that children will not be able to use language like this in English for many years, but the techniques of thinking in this way are very important, so it is best to practise this type of questioning in the vernacular. Later the same kind of language experience can be given in the second language.

Chapter 14   Preparing for Reading

In primitive times men first communicated by signs and sounds, which developed into speech. Later, when they wanted to communicate with absent friends, they used picture writing.

Later still, symbols were used which began to be standardized, so that people could write to others who were too far away for speech.

A child follows the same sort of steps. First, he uses signs and cries, then words, and later drawings, which mean a lot to the child. He will in fact be pleased to explain the meaning of his drawings to the teacher. Learning the standard symbols of his country will follow when he is ready.

Reading Readiness
The age at which a child is ready to read depends on:

1. His intelligence.
2. How far the home environment has encouraged him to read.
3. How well he can speak and understand his own language.

Some children are ready to read at five years, others not until they are eight or nine years old. Most children will be ready by the time they are six and a half, but the slower ones must be treated sympathetically in a special group.

How the Home affects the Child's Language Skills
Language skills which are necessary before the child is ready to read.
   The ability to:

1. listen with concentration;
2. understand the sounds he hears;
3. use the words and phrases of the language in a recognized

sequence to express meaning;
4. be able to describe what he is doing or seeing;
5. be able to tell what has happened in the past (maybe only a few minutes ago);
6. use words to reason in a simple way,
    e.g. 'If I do that, this will happen.'
        'That happened because I did this';
7. be able to use words to express ideas about the future,
    e.g. 'This afternoon, I shall . . . .';
8. be able to express thoughts, one after the other in a sensible related sequence, e.g. a story;
9. have reached a certain maturation of motor skills and discrimination (see pre-reading activities);
10. be able to cope with the routine and social demands of home and school;
11. show that he is fairly secure emotionally.

All children can communicate, even if it is only by crying to show hunger. We need much more than that before a child is ready to read. A home where the parents talk freely and frequently to the child, allowing him to talk and discuss with them, will have developed his listening and speaking skills well before he comes to school.

If the parents read and have books around the home, the child will want to be like his parents. Illiterate parents who show a great interest in reading will encourage the child to read. But a child from a home where the parents do not look at books or newspapers, and who do not seem interested in reading, will think it is not important. He will not see any need to learn to read.

The teacher should remember that all children are different and all members of the class will not be ready to read at the same time. A certain amount of group work is always necessary in reading with Infants, and also in most classes of the Junior school.

Pre-Reading Activities
Before the child is ready to read, he needs help to experience and develop the following:

1. Spoken language.
2. Auditory discrimination.
3. Visual discrimination.
4. Tactile discrimination.
5. Left to right orientation.
6. Understanding of positions.
7. Motor control.

8. Hand and eye co-ordination.
9. The use of symbols for notices and labels.
10. Sentences on the blackboard about pictures and news.
11. The use and enjoyment of picture books.
12. The understanding that meaning comes from printed books.

1. *Spoken language:* Activities and exercises as described on pages 138 to 142.

2. *Auditory discrimination:* The child should be helped to notice small differences between sounds, because there are only small differences between many of the sounds of his language. (Auditory – of the ear.)

Listen to:
  simple clapped rhythms and repeat them;
  simple rhythms on drums, bells, shakers, etc., and repeat them;
  different pitches of sound: notice which are high, which are low;
  different strengths of sound: notice which are loud, which are soft;
  music: move the whole body to the rhythm;
  poems, songs, stories.

3. *Visual discrimination:* If the child cannot discriminate between small differences, he is not ready to be introduced to letters b d p n u m. There is not much difference between these shapes. (Visual – of the eye.) Start with large differences and progress to small differences.

Games to help train the child's eyes to notice different shapes

Picture dominoes: These are played in the same way as number dominoes (page 77). They help the child to observe different shapes. This prepares him for noticing the difference between the shapes of words and letters later.

These should be very simple shapes

Fitting shapes into a box: The top of the box has various shapes cut out of it. The child is given the pieces to fit into the correct spaces.

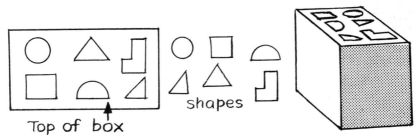

Top of box   shapes

A cheap way of making this apparatus is with a calabash. The shapes can be cut out fairly easily with a sharp knife.

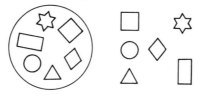

Jig-saws: Keep each jig-saw in an envelope or the pieces will get lost.

A clear picture should be chosen, and stuck on to cardboard. The picture is then cut into pieces, five or six simple pieces for the first jig-saws, though more difficult ones can be tried later.

Colours: Give the children beads, material, flowers, etc., of many colours, and let the children put them into groups of the same colour.

4. *Tactile discrimination:* (Tactile – of the sense of touch.) Give out different materials to feel: smooth, rough, silky, uneven, etc. Let the children feel without looking, with their hands under the table, or behind their backs. Put an object in a bag and let them guess what it is without looking, e.g. a ground-nut, a matchbox, 'What is it? How does it feel?'

5. *Left to right orientation:* To read we must start on the left, move to the right and then make a big sweep back to the left again. Let children draw paths from left to right. For example, a dog running home, a man walking to the town. If these are drawn big in mud or sand, the **big** movements should help the children to learn more quickly. Always make sure they start on the left, and draw a path or road to the right.

Picture stories:

These stories, in picture form, train the child to move his eyes from left to right as he will when reading. A teacher can draw the pictures himself using stick men.

6. *Understanding positions:* To read a child needs to understand a number of positional words. 'Top' and 'bottom'. We start at the top of the page. 'Beginning', 'middle' and 'end'. Which letter is at the beginning? Which letter comes in the middle? 'Up' and 'down'. See the b has a line going up and the p has a line going down. First, second, third, etc. Which sound comes first?

All these can be taught with simple game activities. 'Put the picture on the top of the cupboard. Put the book at the bottom of the cupboard.'

7. *Motor control:* To read the child must be able to control his book, that is, balance it in his hands or keep it on his desk and turn the pages. All P.E. activities and Art and Craft activities help the child to control his large and fine motor movements.

8. *Hand and eye co-ordination:* As writing goes 'hand in hand' with reading, the child needs to be able to 'draw' the letters he can see. Big brush painting, big crayon drawing, drawing in the sand, clay work, carefully filling tins with water, all help control.

9. *The use of symbols for notices and labels:* All these words would of course be in the vernacular, though the same idea can be used later to introduce the children to written English.

book corner	nature table	weather chart

The teacher hangs the labels on the objects in the room, and tells the children what they say. A game is played by taking the labels off and asking who can remember where to hang them, e.g. 'Who can remember where this should be hung. Musa. Good. Hang it up then. Is he right? Uwa. Yes. What does the word say? The window. Good.' The children are not really reading the words at this stage, and if they forget where to hang the labels, the teacher should tell them again. At this stage the teacher is trying to show the children that meaning can be had from the written word, and in this way he is preparing them for the teaching of reading later.

Aina has a new baby brother.

These notices will also help the child to realize that meaning can be obtained from the written word. The teacher should tell the children what the notices say, and often refer to them.

10. *Sentences on the blackboard about pictures and news:* At the end of a picture or news talk, the teacher writes one of the children's sentences on the blackboard. When the children have 'read' it they can draw a picture. Remember this is not real reading, but is showing the children the usefulness of reading and writing.

Another way of introducing a child to written sentences is for the teacher to write one under each child's picture in the drawing lesson.

11. *The use and enjoyment of picture books.* These are fairly easily made and each Infant class should have as many as possible. They are the child's first introduction to books, and should be interesting. The pictures should be of the part of Africa the child knows and should deal with familiar subjects, e.g. home and village life, school, animals, farms.

 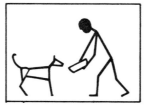 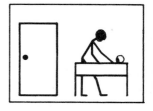

  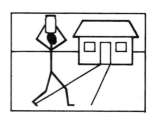

If possible get coloured pictures, or colour the most important parts of the picture with crayon for further interest. The class should be told that the books must be treated carefully, and that anyone disobeying this rule will not be allowed to use them for a day or two.

To make the books, cut a large sheet of sugar paper or brown paper in half. Fold and stitch the two pieces together to make a book with eight pages.

12. *The understanding that meaning comes from printed books:* Although I said that children prefer to be **told** a story, they should occasionally be read one to introduce them to books and show them the pleasure of being able to read. Read letters from people the children know. Perhaps if a teacher moves to another town he will write, so that the children can hear the letter and realize how useful it will be to be able to read and write.

Once the children have been prepared and when the teacher feels that most of the class is ready, the children can be taught to read.

Chapter 15 Reading in the Infant Classes
1. The Phonic Method
2. The Look and Say Method

Reading in the Infant Classes
The most generally used methods for teaching reading are the Phonic method and the Look and Say (word or sentence) method.

The Phonic Method of Teaching Reading
This is based on the sounds of the alphabet being sounded together to form words, e.g. 'a' 'n' 'd' and 'k' 'a' 't' cat. The sounds, **not** the names of the letters, are taught.

Advantage: In most African languages each symbol stands for one sound, and once the child has learnt the sounds he can **help himself to read,** as he sounds out the words.

Disadvantages: 1. The child may lose the meaning and sense of the sentence because he is so concerned with sounding the letters.

2. He may manage to read quite difficult words after some time, but perhaps will not be able to understand them.

These reasons will make reading rather puzzling to the child, especially the slow child, as he wonders what all these sounds are about.

How to Teach the Sounds
Usually the sounds are taught in connection with the first sound of a word, and a picture of that word. If the picture can be made to look something like the shape of the letter so much the better. These English examples will help you to think up suitable vernacular ones:

(a snake)

(a feather)
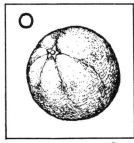
(an orange)

These pictures and sounds are drawn on cardboard and hung as a frieze on the wall. Do not introduce more than one sound a day, and continually revise them. Let the children draw the letter and the picture on their blackboards or in sand and let them make them in clay. Gradually introduce other words with the same sound at the beginning, e.g. write 's' on the blackboard, and tell the children to listen to the 'sss' sound in snake, sand, sugar, sit and soap. Ask the children to tell the class words with the 's' sound. The sound can be at the beginning, middle or end of the word, though it is easier for the children to hear it if it is at the beginning.

Building up Words
When the children know some sounds build them up into words. This is done in three stages. The teacher progresses slowly when he feels the children are ready. English examples are:

(1) Two-letter words.		(2) Three-letter words.			(3) Bigger words and double sounds.	
a	**i**	**a**	**o**	**t**	**sh**	**ch**
an	in	cat	dog	tap	shut	catch
at	is	bat	hot	hat	shop	church
am	it	fan	pot	ten	share	chair
		has	lot	let	ship	match

The teacher and children build up lists of vernacular words on the blackboard. The children are encouraged to give as many suggestions as possible. In Stages 2 and 3 the children need examples with the sound at the beginning, in the middle and at the end if possible.

Simple Sentences
These sentences are made with simple words, which the child can sound. Easy English examples could be:

I am a cat.

I am a dog.

A fat cat sat on a wall.

A dog sat on a mat.

The teacher, again, will make up his own simple vernacular sentences.

Apparatus to help the Children Learn the Sounds
Wall frieze as described on page 149.

Individual Matching Cards based on the Wall Frieze

a caterpillar   a girl   a lamp

The child is given an envelope with six pictures and six letters, which he matches on his desk. If he cannot do any of them he can look at the frieze on the wall to help himself. The child draws the pictures and letters on his board, puts the cards back in the envelope and gets another. The teacher should go round to hear each child say the sounds he is drawing.

Word Building Cards

Stage 1. Two-letter words.

Stage 2. Three-letter words

Stage 3. Longer words

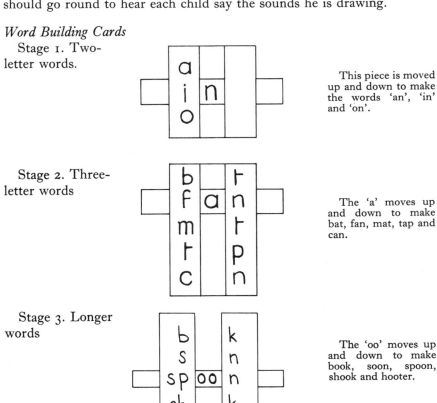

This piece is moved up and down to make the words 'an', 'in' and 'on'.

The 'a' moves up and down to make bat, fan, mat, tap and can.

The 'oo' moves up and down to make book, soon, spoon, shook and hooter.

Again,* note that I have used English examples. The teacher will adopt similar methods in vernacular reading.

The child makes the words and writes them on his blackboard. If he can he draws a picture of the word.

How to Make the Cards

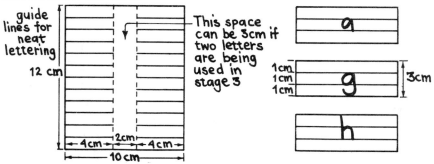

Cut the dotted lines with a razor. Leave 1 cm uncut at the top and bottom. Draw guide lines 1 cm apart, and write the letters as near the dotted line as possible, because when the horizontal strip is put in position the letters need to be close together. Do not write on the centre strip. Write the moving letter on the horizontal strip.

Jig-saws

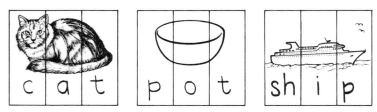

These give practice in making words and are self corrective (i.e. if the word is wrong the picture will be wrong).

Word and Picture Matching

* This applies throughout this Section (i.e. Chapters 15 to 22).

A reading book is usually introduced at this stage. It will be carefully graded, and new sounds and bigger words will be introduced very gradually. Such reading books are a great help, but the thoughtful teacher will introduce his own ideas to add variety and interest to the children's learning.

The Look and Say Method of Teaching Reading

In this method each word (or short phrase or sentence) is taught as a whole. The teacher reads the word (or phrase or sentence). The children listen, look and say. They learn and remember the whole printed shape, so the more varied the shape and size of the words the better. The words must be introduced gradually and systematically, with plenty of revision. This grading of the vocabulary is really a job for an expert, and a good series of graded reading books is needed for proper teaching.

The following examples will give you an idea of how the words are introduced. On each page would be an interesting picture with the sentences underneath or alongside (as shown below).

1st Lesson (The capital 'D' and the small 'd' will look different to the child, so both must be taught.)
Words to be taught—Do, do, the, work, Chinua.

Do the work.
Chinua, do the work.
Do the work, Chinua.

2nd Lesson New words to be taught—Father, I, hard.
I do the work.
Father, do the work.
Do the hard work, Chinua.
I do the hard work.

153

3rd Lesson New word to
be taught—you.
I work hard.
Do you work hard?
You work hard, Father.
Chinua, you work hard.

Very gradually a reading vocabulary is built up. Each word is taught as a whole and then introduced into the reading matter.

Advantage
The child will get some reading skill quickly, if he reads only the special graded books from which he is learning.

Disadvantages
1. The child has no way of finding out a word for himself.
2. He must keep to the graded readers, as other books may contain words he has not been taught.
3. Because of the limited number of words the child knows at the beginning, the sentences are not very interesting.
4. If a child is absent for a few days and has missed the teaching of new words, he will be unable to follow the lesson the rest of his group is reading. The teacher must be careful to help any such child. Plenty of revision is necessary.

Apparatus to give Interesting Practice in Reading
All the sentences **must** be taken from the graded reading book, and must not be given until the child has read them in his book.

Matching Words and Sentences

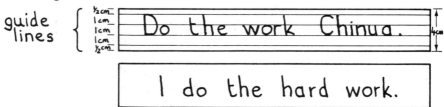

Three or four sentences like this are put in an envelope. The sentences are written again, and then cut up into separate words, which are also put in the envelope. The child matches the cut-up words with the sentences.

The child copies the sentences on to his board, and draws a picture. The teacher must hear each child read his sentences, or he may be matching the words successfully without remembering what they say.

Sentences cut in half:

About six sentences which the child has already learnt are cut in half, and put into an envelope. The child matches the pieces to make sentences and writes them on his board. Again the teacher must try to hear each child read his sentences.

Picture and Word Matching

These are made and used in the same way as on page 152, but only words the child has been taught can be used.

Remember that though these suggestions are in English, they are intended to give the teacher some ideas for teaching vernacular reading.

Chapter 16   Reading in the Infant Classes
3. The Eclectic Method

The Eclectic Method of Teaching Reading
This method tries to use the best of all methods. Phonic and Look-Say techniques are used, plus any others the teacher thinks will help individual children.

Advantages
1. Some children learn better by sight (Look and Say), others learn better by sound (Phonic), so most children will do better with a mixed method.
2. From the beginning reading makes sense, and is interesting.

Disadvantages
The teacher needs to adapt more to individual children, and this may mean more work.

The need for adaption
The experts who write reading books grade the vocabulary carefully and try to pick subjects which will interest children. But stories which are suitable for town children may not interest farm children. Books which are about places children in the North understand, may seem strange to children in the South. The teacher needs to use the books in an intelligent way, adapting them and adding extra apparatus, according to his special understanding of his class.

I shall explain how I should begin to teach reading, and then you, the teacher, will be able to pick out any ideas which will help your children to read in the vernacular.

Before the reading book is introduced, the children are taught some of the sentences (about twelve). Big class pictures, copies of those in the reader, are needed.

Stage 1. *Introducing the sentences*
Introduce the first picture (see overleaf). Ask the children questions and let them talk about it. Tell them the boy is called Sule. Show the children

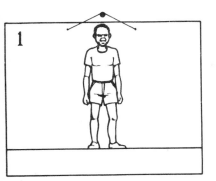 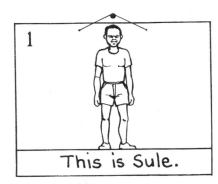

This is Sule.

the sentence and tell them what it says. Many children are given a turn reading the sentence. Hang the picture on the wall, and let the children draw it on their boards.

Next day introduce the second picture. Again cover the sentence, and have a picture talk, before reading. As many children as possible are given a turn at reading, and acting Sule going to school. Hang this picture on the wall and revise the first one.

Sule goes to school.

Next day introduce the next picture and revise the first two.

The teacher rings the bell.

Sule sits beside Aina.

Next day introduce the fourth picture and revise the first three.
Next day revise the four sentences.

157

The pictures should be hung on the wall and continually revised. How often the teacher introduces new pictures depends on how well the children are remembering the first ones. To add interest and help the children remember the sentences, let them draw for the last part of the lesson. They can also try copying sentences. The feel of the letter shapes in the muscles of the arms (use of the kinesthetic sense) helps discrimination and memory.

Stage 2. *Matching a flash card of the sentence*
When the children have learnt a few sentences, the teacher will introduce flash cards of the sentences.

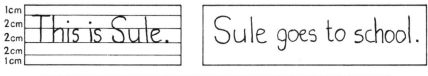

The teacher holds up one card and says, 'Who can match this to the right picture. Good. What does it say?' This stage can be started when the children have learned about six sentences.

Other pictures and sentences will still be introduced slowly.

Stage 3. *Recognition of the sentence without the help of the picture*
At this stage the teacher holds up the same cards as in Stage 2, but asks the children to read them without matching them to the pictures. Bright children will remember, but the slower ones should still be allowed to match the sentences to the pictures on the wall.

Stage 4. *Flash cards of words are matched to the sentences*
Each word is written on a separate card. The teacher pins up the sentence.

'Who can read the sentence?' When it has been read by a few children, the teacher holds up the first card. | This | 'Who can match this word to the same one in the sentence? Good. It says 'This'. **This** is Sule.' The teacher holds up | is | and a child matches it. 'Good. This says **is**. **This** (points to **This**) **is** (points to **is**). Who can come and point to **is**? Good. What does it say? Good. Who can point to **this**? Do you notice the shape of the last letter in each of these words? Yes, it is a curly shaped letter, and it makes the sound **sss**. **This, is,** listen to the sound at the end of the words. Draw the letter in the air. What is its sound? Good. Now look at the last word, **Sule**. Who can match it? Good. Can anyone see the curly letter, which makes the **s** sound? Good, it is at the beginning of the word, **Sule**. Can you hear it?' The three children with the words will stand in a row making the sentence.

Stage 5. *Recognition of the word without matching to the sentence*
The teacher holds up each flash card the children have learnt, and they put up their hands if they can read it. Children enjoy reading flash cards; play a little game by letting the children arrange themselves into the sentence, e.g. | The | teacher | rings | the | bell | Five children are given a card, and stand in the correct order so the class can read the sentence. Sometimes, let one child at a time pretend to be the teacher, and hold up the cards, asking other children to read them.

Stage 6. *The reading book is introduced*
The children will love to use the reading book, especially when they find they can read the first few sentences. They will feel successful and proud of reading. Success and interest give the child the will to work hard.

Stage 7. *New sentences in the reading book*
After a few days when the children have read and copied all the sentences they know, new sentences must be taught by writing them on the blackboard. Teach them much in the same way as before, but without the large class pictures, and the large sentence matching cards. Let the children look at the next picture in the book and talk about it. Read the sentence from the blackboard, then let various children read it. The children look at their books again and read the sentence, this time from their books. They will then copy the sentence and the picture. In the next lesson revise the sentence and introduce flash cards of the words. These will be matched with the sentence on the blackboard. Keep revising the flash cards of previous lessons. Occasionally draw attention to similar sounds, e.g. **t** in **t**eacher and in wa**t**er.

Individual Apparatus for these Stages
These are copies of the large class apparatus, but give the children the opportunity to work and be active on their own. They are especially useful to keep one group busily occupied while the teacher helps another group.
   Small picture and matching sentences.

Small picture and matching sentences.

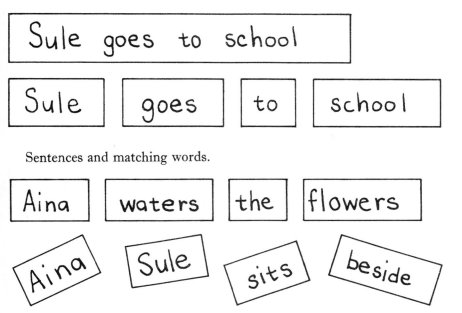

Sentences and matching words.

Cut up sentences to be placed in the correct order by the child. About four sentences should be in each envelope.

Stage 8. *Word likenesses*
The children will have learned to read a number of words, and will know a few sounds. Now phonics will be taught more systematically. The teacher writes on the blackboard lists of words children know. He draws the children's attention, as they read the words, to certain sounds in a group of words being alike, e.g. bell, book, bag, all start with the **b** sound, so the letter **b** makes this special sound. Similarly for **d**, **g**, and **f**:

desk	**g**o	**f**loor
do	**g**irl	**f**lower
dust	**g**et	
did	ba**g**	
ha**d**		

The Phonic apparatus can be used at this stage.

Some More Apparatus and Aids to help the Child to Read
Jig-saws: To add interest and variety the following type of self-corrective jig-saw can be introduced. About six words should be put in each envelope.

Jigsaws

Word and picture matching: The child can be introduced to words which are not in the reader through the four stages shown below.

Stage 1: Make a set of six envelopes, and put four pictures in each envelope. Each of the twenty-four pictures must be different, but they should all be drawn on the same coloured cardboard (e.g. white). My examples are for envelope 1.

Stage 2: Make six more envelopes. The same twenty-four pictures are drawn on cardboard of another colour (e.g. pink) and are cut in different ways, so that only the correct word will fit the picture.

Self-corrective word matched to picture

Stage 3: Six more envelopes are needed. The same twenty-four pictures are drawn on yet a different coloured cardboard (e.g. blue), and the letters of the words are cut.

Letters matched to words

Stage 4: The words and pictures are prepared on another coloured card (e.g. green) and the word is cut off by a straight line. The child has to decide which word goes with each picture.

Each child doing these exercises will be given each envelope in Stage 1 (though there is no need for them to be in the correct order, e.g. he can be given 6, 3, 2, 4, 1, 5) before he progresses to Stage 2. He will be given each envelope in Stage 2 before progressing to Stage 3. By the time he has completed each envelope in Stage 3, he should know the words, and should be able to match them in Stage 4, without help.

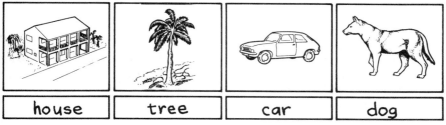

Word matched to picture

The teacher can make as many sets of this exercise as he wishes, all with different pictures, but a record must be kept, so that the child is led through each stage until he has learnt the words. He will not learn if he jumps about without guidance. He must be led step by step.

Each envelope should be clearly marked. The different coloured cardboards for each stage will help the teacher to recognize at a glance which stage a child is doing. If a card is dropped or misplaced, the teacher will know which stage to put it in, because of its colour.

Command Cards

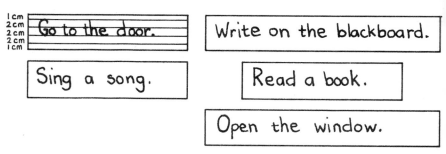

Children love reading these cards and obeying the command. The cards will be introduced one or two at a time, and the teacher will read them to the children. They will be continually revised; sometimes individual children can do the action and then read the card aloud; at other times individual children can read the card, then one or two can do the action.

A class picture dictionary. A large book is made by the teacher. When the children find a new word during the day, the teacher will write it in thick crayon in the dictionary, and either the teacher or a child will draw a picture of the word. Do not write the words from the reading book, but write any extra ones.

An individual picture dictionary. Each child has his own little dictionary and when he finds a new word the teacher tells him its meaning, and he writes it in his dictionary, drawing a picture beside it.

Both the above dictionaries can be used when the children have passed the first stages of reading, and are able to read a simple book. During the second year or even the third year, depending on the children's progress, the new words can be arranged in alphabetical order, either in a dictionary or as a wall frieze.

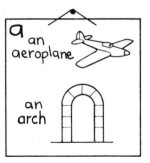
a
an aeroplane
an arch

b
bouncing
a boat
a bottle

c
a chair
catch

When a child wants to spell a word he can go to look at the dictionary for help.

A book corner. This should have a place in every class. The very small children will need picture books, and books with pictures, under which will be written a word or a short sentence. As the children learn to read their appetite for books must be fed, by giving them as many suitable books for their age and ability as possible. Often this is difficult and expensive, but a good teacher will find a way to get some books (he should make them if necessary) and will gradually add more books each year to his collection.

Reading cards. These are very useful, especially if there are not many books in the class.

This is Aina. She is working on the farm. She is digging the yams. She will take them to market.

More sentences about the picture can be written on the back of the card to give further practice.

1cm spacing and margins

The child reads and copies the sentences. The teacher must try to hear each child read part of his card. There should be sufficient cards for the child to change and get a new one when he needs it.

165

Reading and drawing cards

<u>Draw this picture</u>
Ali is playing with
his ball. It is a
big ball. He kicks
it in the playground

<u>Draw this picture</u>
Aina likes drawing
pictures. She draws
an old chief. She
paints his clothes
in bright colours.

The child reads the card, copies the sentences and draws the picture. The teacher can tell if the child has understood the reading by looking at the drawing. Use the names of children in the class, and when possible put something interesting about the children. They will think it is very exciting to read and write about themselves and their friends.

Missing words. For these cards be careful only to use words the children know. The missing words should be written on the back of the card to help the children get the spellings correct. (These will not be introduced until the second year at the earliest.)

<u>Missing Words</u>
Sule and Aina go to ____ .
They ____ a book.
Mary has a new ____ .
My little dog's name is ____ .
Our ____ helps us to write.

read
Brownie
dress
teacher
school

Reading cards with questions. When the children's reading ability has progressed further, write a story under the picture, as shown below, then write a few simple questions about the story. (This is only for bright Infant children, but is very useful for Juniors.)

This lady is making the
supper. Her name is
Mrs Taiwo. She has two
children, one boy and
one girl.

Questions

1. What is the lady doing?

2. What is her name?

3. How many children
   has she?

The back of the card

Chapter 17 Organisation of Reading Lessons

Class reading (i) by one child at a time. The main disadvantage of this method is that only a few children in a lesson get a chance to read. The rest may read silently, but they will more probably sit and dream.

If this method is used, a record must be kept of each child who reads, so that in the next lesson different children may have a turn. Questions must be asked to keep all the children attentive. Children get very bored if the same passage is read over and over again.

Class reading (ii) all together. This method can sometimes be useful for practising short passages on the blackboard, but it is very easy for a child to be lazy, when all the class is speaking together. Watch to see that all the children work, and only use this method for a few minutes, *never* for a whole lesson. Insist on very soft speech.

Silent reading. This can be useful **after** the teacher has taught the words and sentences. When the child is learning to read, he cannot read new words on his own unless he is being taught by the Phonic method, and even then he should not be left to do much on his own. After the child has a little reading skill, he will be able to read cards for himself, for the teacher will have written the sentences using words the child knows, with only a very occasional new word which he will be able to guess. An Infant child will never really read silently. There will be a small murmur as he says the words to himself.

Group reading. In this method the children are divided into groups according to their ability to read. Juniors can read to a leader because they have some reading skill, but Infants are only beginning and they must read to the teacher. Obviously the teacher cannot be with all the groups at once, and this is when individual apparatus is very useful.

The teacher plans his lesson so that he hears each group in turn. When they are not reading, the children use the apparatus suitable for the stage they have reached; the teacher must make sure that the apparatus is not too easy and not too hard for the group.

Before the lesson starts the teacher explains like this: 'While I am hearing Group 1 read, Group 2 will use this apparatus. Here are extra cards on my desk, and you may take another when you have finished the one the monitor is going to give you now. Amadu, please give one of these cards to everyone in your group. Group 3 will use this apparatus, and I have put extra apparatus for you in this box on the floor. Uwa, please give everyone in your group one of these envelopes. When Group 1 is ready, Sule can give out these cards in the box on top of the cupboard. I shall come to hear each group in turn and I want to see everyone being very busy.'

In this way all the children are active, and practising their knowledge, so making it firmer in their minds. The teacher will teach each group in turn. Three groups are usually sufficient, one for the quick children, one for the average children and one for the slow children. If a child plays about in a group, it may be because the work is too easy or too hard, and the teacher must arrange that the child has suitable work. Every child should have plenty of work to keep him working busily.

Suggested Patterns for Reading Lessons in the Vernacular
The following suggestions may help the young teacher when preparing his vernacular reading lesson notes. I give the lesson procedure but not the headings, such as Objectives and Apparatus, because colleges have different ways of arranging these. The lessons are planned step by step, 1, 2, 3, etc.

Always try to have any reading sentences, new words or questions on the blackboard before the lesson begins. It is very bad to keep children sitting doing nothing while the teacher gets ready for the lesson. Most of the work can be written during recess.

Pattern 1. Class method
1. Revise sentences under wall pictures, by matching with sentence

flash cards, e.g. | Sule plays with Chinua | 'Who can match this

to the right picture? Amadu. Good. What does it say? That's right. What does it say? Sule. Good. Uwa. Good.' The other sentences are revised in the same way.

2. The teacher asks the children to open their books at a certain page, e.g. page 13, and they discuss the picture. Ask questions to encourage children to talk.

3. (Before the lesson the sentences from page 13 are written on the blackboard.) The teacher reads the sentences while the children listen. The teacher reads them again while the children, all together, repeat them softly.

Sule collects wood.
He makes a fire for his mother.

4. Children act the sentences. 'Who can be Sule collecting the wood? Pick dry pieces of wood. Who will be Mother? Watch Sule make the fire. What do you think Mother will cook on the fire?' Some other children will be given a turn to act.

5. Read the sentences again from the blackboard. Individual children read the sentences, with help from the teacher if necessary. A number of children are given a turn.

6. Children look at the sentences in the reading book. The sentences are the same as the ones on the blackboard, but when they are taught from the blackboard first, the teacher can point to make sure all the children look at the right sentence.

If children are taught straight from the book at this stage, they may get muddled. Children and teacher read very softly all together from the book. Individual children read a sentence each. (Do not do this for long or the children will become restless.)

7. Children draw the picture and copy the sentences. The teacher goes round and hears as many children as possible read one of the sentences to him. Children who did not read in step 6 can be heard now.

As some of the children will learn more quickly than others, the class method will not be possible for long, and groups will be introduced. The following suggestions are for the group method. The lesson is planned step by step, and the teacher can only be with **one** group at a time. I underline the group the teacher is helping at each step.

Pattern 2. Class introduction followed by group method.

1. Class introduction: Vernacular poem, or command cards, or word building, or questions about a former lesson, or sentence making using words which will be useful to the whole class, or revising words in the picture dictionary.

Vary the introduction; do not use the same one for each lesson.

2. Divide the children into groups explaining what each will do.
Group A. Word and picture matching cards (or some other suitable apparatus).
Group B. Revise and copy, e.g., lesson 16, page 19, which they did not finish yesterday.
Group C. Teaching of the sentences from, e.g., lesson 10, page 14, from the blackboard. (The sentences will have been put on the blackboard during recess.) The teacher helps each child read.

3.
Group A. The teacher checks the work the children have been doing and then teaches the new words in, e.g., lesson 22, page 25. (The

words are written on the board before the lesson starts.) Each child then reads from lesson 22 in turn.

Group B. As the children finish copying lesson 16, they take a reading card (or any other suitable piece of apparatus).

Group C. Copy the sentences from the blackboard and draw a picture.

4.

Group A. Children copy lesson 22 to fix it in their minds, then take a reading card.

Group B. The teacher checks the work the children have been doing, and hears each child read part of his card. There will not be time in this lesson for the reading book to be used with this group, but the teacher will plan his next lesson, so that Group B will be helped to read their next lesson, which will be lesson 17.

Group C. Continue as in Step 3.

5. Monitors collect apparatus while the teacher has a quick look at the work done by Groups A and C since he helped them.

This is a simple lesson using just a small amount of apparatus, and also making good use of the reading book. All the children are kept busy and they all know that the teacher will look at the work they have been doing. The teacher will have heard each child read, either from the book or from a reading card.

The next lesson pattern has no class introduction, so more time can be spent with each group.

Pattern 3. Group method with no class introduction.

1. Divide the children into groups explaining what each will do.

Group A. (The new words from, e.g., lesson 23 are put on the blackboard before the lesson.) The teacher teaches each word. Children practise them by pointing and reading, e.g. 'Who can point to the word which says "pretty"? What does this word say?' Teacher hears and helps each child read from lesson 23.

Group B. Children use self-corrective word and picture matching cards (or any other suitable apparatus).

Group C. Children use 'Cut-up sentence' apparatus (or any other suitable cards).

2.

Group A. Silently read lesson 23, then copy the sentences.

Group B. (The sentences from, e.g., lesson 17 are put on the blackboard before the lesson.) The teacher helps the children to read the sentences and learn the new words, using flash cards; then hears each child read from lesson 17.

Group C. Copy the apparatus, and get another envelope when they have finished.

3.
Group A. Finish copying, then take a reading card.
Group B. Silently read lesson 17, then copy it to fix it in their minds.
Group C. The teacher marks each child's work and helps him with his apparatus. Each child reads the words on his apparatus to the teacher. If there is time, a new sentence can be introduced on the blackboard.

4. Monitors collect apparatus, while the teacher has a quick look at the work Groups A and B have done since he helped them.

Evaluation: After each lesson write notes about what happened. Did you prepare too much, or too little? Was the work too hard or too easy? Which children understood? Which children will need more help tomorrow? How could you have made the lesson more interesting? By evaluating *yourself,* the *children*, the *subject matter* and *your organisation*, you will improve your teaching and the children's learning.

Chapter 18 Vernacular Reading in the Junior Classes

This chapter deals with reading in the vernacular in the Junior classes. At the present time few vernacular books are available, and it may be impossible to carry out some of these ideas. They are included, however, because the information will be useful to the teacher if more vernacular books are published during the next few years, and also because many of these suggestions can be used when teaching reading in English to older children (of about 9 or 10 to 13 years of age), when they have a knowledge of a number of English sentences and phrases. The teaching of English to younger children is described in Chapters 21 and 22.

Reading in the Junior Classes
The work of the Infant classes must be continued, using the same graded reader, but also introducing others. Once the child has the ability to read, he must be encouraged to read as much as possible, for **information,** to **increase his reading ability** and for **enjoyment.**

Group reading will still be necessary in the first Junior class, and for slower children in the higher classes. The children are grouped according to reading ability, and use the graded readers. The group lesson can be taken as described on page 170, or all the groups can read at the same time to their respective leaders.

In each group a leader is chosen, and the group takes turns to read to him. The leader is not a better reader than the others in his group, but he is in charge and comes to the teacher to ask for an explanation of any word the group cannot understand. Change the leaders once a month, so that a number of children have a turn at leading.

There should not be more than six children in a group, or it may become noisy. If eleven children in a class have the ability, for example, to read Book 4, let them all read it, but instead of forming one group, say Group 1, make two groups, **1a** with six children, and **1b** with five children.

Tell all the children they must whisper, and not disturb each other. The teacher visits each group in turn, hearing each child read and asking questions to encourage intelligent thinking about the reading. For questioning technique see pp. 141-2. If the teacher does not wish the children to finish the book too quickly, he should give reading cards to each group in turn as they finish a lesson. It is not good for children to read and re-read the same lesson. Give them variety to keep them busy and learning.

Reading aloud (class lesson): In the Junior classes occasional class reading lessons will give the teacher opportunities to teach and correct pronunciation and expression. Help each child to vary his voice, so that all who listen are interested in the reading. Keep a record so that the children are given an equal number of turns, and after each paragraph ask questions to make sure that all the children are listening and have understood.

Sometimes choose a passage and give a written comprehension (i.e. understanding) exercise on it. Write questions about the passage on the blackboard, and let the children answer them orally before writing the answers.

Silent reading: There will be more silent reading in the Junior classes than in the Infant classes, because the children have some reading skill to practise and use.

The teacher must guide and test each child's silent reading. Give questions about the book on a card. Let the child discover the answers as he reads, or give the questions when he has finished and tell him to write the answers. Written questions should be varied like spoken questions. For ideas see questioning techniques, page 142. When children are reading silently, always tell them to put up their hands if they do not understand a word, or they will be wasting their time.

It often happens that in a large class, of say forty children, each child reads the same silent reading book, and when one is finished it is no good changing with his partner if he has the same book. Whether the school or the children buy the books, it is the ideal, for silent reading, that the books are all different; then when one book is finished and the questions answered, it can be changed for another, until each child has read and gained knowledge from forty books. The same amount of money is spent in buying forty different books as in buying forty copies of one book, but the educational value is vastly different.

The teacher must watch carefully to prevent children reading books which are too hard for their ability; he should go to the bookshop and advise each child what to buy. If the school is buying, of course the correct stage of reading books will be ordered.

A library is most important and every school should try to build up a good one. This may seem a big task, but even if only twenty books are bought each year, after five years there will be one hundred books. One hundred books are not nearly enough for a school library, so more must continually be bought. Even from a very small beginning a fairly large collection can be made.

In the library all the books should be different, and they should be

173

divided into sections, with easy ones for the first classes and gradually getting more difficult as the children's reading ability increases. The children from each class in turn should be allowed to change their reading books once or twice a week, the aim being to give the children opportunities to read as much as possible. Each child should keep his own record of the books he has read (page 49).

As I said at the beginning of this chapter, the general shortage of vernacular books hinders the making of a suitable library. My comments, however, apply also to books in English.

Dictionaries: Each child in the Junior classes should have his own dictionary. On each page he will put one letter of the alphabet. When the child has discovered a new word in his reading book, he gets an explanation of it from his teacher, then writes it in his dictionary.

The following patterns may help the teacher of young Juniors when planning his lesson.

Pattern 4. Class reading method. (All children must have enough reading skill to follow the lesson.) Pick out all the new words, or difficult words and put them on the blackboard before the lesson.

1. Teaching of the new words, by pointing to each in turn, using it in an oral sentence and by helping the children to use it in sentences of their own.

This makes sure that the children understand the meaning of the word.

2. Point to the words (not in order) and ask different children to read them or ask individual children to point to the words (e.g. Who can point to 'jumping').

3. Reading of the passage. Individual children read a sentence or two.

Pick children from different parts of the room to read; if they do not know whose turn it will be next, they are all more likely to pay attention.

4. The teacher asks questions after every few sentences, to make sure the children understand what they are reading.

This also helps to keep all the class attentive, because they do not know when they will be asked a question.

5. If the passage is short, it can be re-read in order to give more children a turn, and to fix the reading in their minds.

Do not read it more than twice, or the class will become bored.

6. Written activity for practice and to fix the words firmly in the children's minds.

Examples.

(*a*) Copying the passage (for slower children).

(*b*) Copying the words from the blackboard and putting them into sentences.

(*c*) Answering questions from the passage. Take this orally first.

(*d*) Drawing a picture of the story and writing a few sentences underneath.

(*e*) Writing the passage in the children's own words.

Pattern 5. Class introduction followed by group reading.

1. Introduction suitable for the whole class. (Not too easy for quick children and not too difficult for slow children.)

Examples.

(*a*) Word building.

(*b*) Finding 'doing words' (verbs). The teacher explains what they are, and the children read any page to find doing words, which they read and act to the class.

(*c*) Use of the full-stop. When reading we take a breath at the end of the sentence. Practise with sentences on the blackboard.

(*d*) Children tell the teacher of any new words they found in their reading books yesterday, and the teacher puts them on the blackboard to teach all the class.

2. Divide children into groups (not more than six in a group) and choose leaders. Change the leaders once a month.

3. Children read to their leaders. The teacher visits as many groups as possible to hear each child read a little, to ask questions and to make a record of those who have been heard, so that in the next lesson the other groups can be visited first. The teacher should hear each child read two or three times a week. Leaders come to the teacher if their group cannot read a word, and all the group will then write the word in their dictionaries.

4. Written activity: As each group finishes its lesson it will do some written work, e.g. (*a*) the leaders can get reading cards for their groups, or (*b*) the children can draw a picture of the story and write sentences, or (*c*) the children can do an exercise which the teacher has put on the blackboard. A library book can be read when the children finish their writing.

Pattern 6. Class introduction followed by group work.

1. Missing word exercise, using sentences from Group A's book. The sentences should be written on the blackboard before the lesson. Every fifth word is missed, in order to give practice in different parts of speech. Children tell the teacher which word to put in the spaces in coloured chalk. Individual children read the sentences. The teacher rubs out the words which were written in coloured chalk.

2.

Group A. The children do the missing word exercise in their books.

Group B. The children find all the words beginning with **o** in their last lesson, and write them in their books.

Group C. The teacher teaches the new words (written on the blackboard before the lesson). When the children know the words, each one reads a few sentences from the reading book.

3.

Group A. Continue with the missing word exercise. Children who finish take a reading card with questions.

Group B. The teacher asks different children to read the words they have found beginning with **o**. The new words for the group are taught, and individual children read from the new lesson.

Group C. Copy the sentences they have learnt with the teacher.

4.

Group A. The teacher marks the work the children have done, then teaches the new words for the group, and hears each child read from the new lesson.

Group B. Children read silently and copy the passage they read with the teacher.

Group C. Finish copying the sentences, then take a reading card.

5. Monitors collect the apparatus while the teacher has a quick look at Groups B and C.

Chapter 19 Writing.
(i) Handwriting

Writing (the Formation of Letters) in the Infant Classes
When writing is on the timetable it usually means the teaching and practice of the letter shapes. The Infant child is learning so many new things – counting, adding, reading and social behaviour – that we cannot also expect him to write neatly. This will, however, come in time, some children being slower than others.

A child learns big movements before he can learn small ones. For writing the child has to learn to make very small movements with his fingers. The teacher who understands the principle of big movements first will give the child chalk and a blackboard, and will only expect large letters. As the child gains more control between his eyes and hand (called hand and eye co-ordination) the teacher will notice that the child makes his letters smaller. The child is then ready to write on plain paper (no lines), with a crayon or thick pencil. When the teacher notices that the child's hand and eye co-ordination has progressed further, and the writing is improving, the child can be introduced to lined paper, but the lines should have at least 1·5 cm spacing.

In Number the same principle applies, big movements first on boards with chalks, then plain paper and a thick pencil, leading to lined paper if desired. The teacher should know what a child is capable of at a certain stage, and should not expect too high nor yet too low a standard of work.

Often because of the way our eyes are made, a child will write some letters or figures backwards (called mirror writing), e.g. 2 ᗡ Ƌ .

Just help the child, but make no fuss, for Nature will adjust the eye in time.

Teaching the letters: An Infant child is taught to print, because this form of writing is most like the printing in his reading book. At first with little interference the child will copy his reading sentences from the blackboard, but later when he has learnt to read a little, teach the shapes of the letters. Do not expect too much neatness or accuracy from the child. Choose a word the child knows, e.g. Mother , and show how the letters are made. Draw these very big, one at a time, with the side of the chalk on the blackboard, showing the children how your hand and arm move.

The Teacher writing in the air

Let the children draw the letters in the air with the teacher, remembering that the teacher must write from right to left, backwards, so that the letters look correct to the children facing him. The teacher must practise this beforehand. The children write the word on their boards, and draw Mother. Other words can be practised in the same way. Once the children start learning sounds (stage 8 of the Eclectic method) letters can be taught individually and more systematically.

Writing in the Junior Classes
When he can read simple books well, the child is usually introduced to a joined type of writing. If this is taught properly it will help the child to write quickly yet clearly as he grows older. There are many styles of joined writing, and a number of books are on the market explaining in detail how to teach them, so I shall only mention a few points.

   1. The same style should be taught throughout the school.

   2. The aim of joined writing is quicker yet legible writing. If the pencil is taken off the paper after each letter, the writing will be as slow as printing. The child must be shown how to join the letters without taking the pencil from the paper.

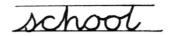

This can be written in one continuous movement, but going over and back for **c** and **o**, and up and down for **h** and **l**. If the **s** is written like this, $\int$ then the pencil must be lifted once, after the **s**.

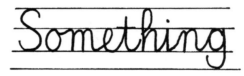

3. This kind of lined paper does not train the child to use his eyes and judge the size of the letters.

With two lines, at first 1·5 cm apart, the long letters can touch the top and bottom lines, with the little letters half the size.

As the writing of the class improves the letters need not touch the top line.

Usually the small **t** is a three-quarter size letter.

4. Pencil should be used until the child has really learnt the new style.

5. As ink can cause much trouble with all its blots, many teachers now encourage children to buy ball-point pens. Children can be taught to write legibly with these, instead of the old-fashioned pen.

6. Although the teacher will want the child to be as neat and tidy as possible, always remember that **how** a child writes is not nearly as important as **what** he writes.

Suggestions to help the teacher plan his writing formation lessons.

Objective: Formation of the letters **o**, **c** and **a** correctly. Before the lesson the teacher writes three sentences with words containing these letters, on the bottom half of the blackboard. The top half is left for the teaching of the letters. Lines are also drawn if the children are using lined paper.

1. The teacher writes the first letter **o** on the line.

2. He then shows the children how he moves his hand by drawing with the side of the chalk a large **o** at the side, telling the children that the join in the letter must not show.

3. Children and teacher write the letter in the air.

4. Children write the letter five times in their books. (Do not ask children to write a line of letters, because though they will start carefully, they will get careless if they have many to write.) As they write the teacher looks at a few children, helping and encouraging them. The teacher rubs off the very big **o**.

5. The teacher asks, 'Who can tell me a word with letter **o** in it? Orange. Good. Open. Good. Old. Good. I shall write orange on the board.'

6. Children write the word three times in their books, while the teacher helps a few more children. As soon as some of the children have finished the words, the teacher goes back to the blackboard, as no child must be allowed to sit doing nothing. 'Never mind if you have not all finished. You can finish in a minute. Now everyone must put down his pencil to watch how I do the next letter.'

7. Letters **c** and **a** are taught in the same way. (Letter on the line,

big letter, letter in the air, letter five times in the book and then a word with the letter.)

8. The teacher reads the sentences at the bottom of the board; individual children read them.

9. Children copy the sentences, and draw a picture when they have finished. The teacher helps and marks.

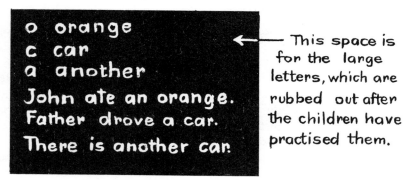

The same type of lesson can be taken when teaching children joined writing. Sometimes teach two letters and how they join.

For variety some writing lessons can be copying a passage from the blackboard, but the reading of the passage **must** be taught first. It is a waste of time for children to write something they cannot read.

Chapter 20 Writing. (ii) Sentences and Composition

Original Writing in the Infant School (i.e. The child writing his own ideas in sentences)
While the child is still learning to read he will only be able to copy sentences. He will not be able to write his own ideas, though he should be given plenty of opportunities to speak his thoughts. **Speaking** always comes before **writing**, and a child who can speak well should later write well.

Copying: After a child has read, the new words will be more firmly fixed in his mind if he copies them on to his board.

The writing of the children's own sentences: The small child should be encouraged to draw anything which interests him. The teacher will say, 'Tell me about your picture, Ali.' and will then write a sentence (using the exact words of the child) under the picture. The child will copy the words, which he **can** read, because they are his **own** words. It is a good idea to give each child a news book or a Diary, and every day he can write about any interesting happenings, and draw a picture. The child should also be encouraged to write a sentence or two after oral compositions and picture talks.

At this stage the teacher will not worry much about the actual shape and size of the letters. The child will be thinking about the sentence and he will not be able also to think about the shape of the letters, because he cannot concentrate on two things at once. In lessons when letter shapes are taught, all the child's attention will be on them, because he will be copying from the blackboard.

Spelling will also be difficult and the teacher must train the child to look in the picture dictionary, or hold up his hand to ask a spelling. If, however, he tries to write it on his own, correct and help him, but do not make a great fuss about spelling at this stage. In fact if there are a number of mistakes, only correct two or three of the simpler ones, **for it is very discouraging for a small child to have all his efforts covered with the teacher's marking pencil.** The aim is to encourage him to write his own thoughts and if he is worried about spelling or the shape and size of the letters, he will not be able to write freely.

Original Writing in the Junior Classes

Building on the foundation of the Infant work, the aim is to encourage the child to continue to express his thoughts in writing, at the same time helping him to use a larger number of words, and to make his sentences more varied and grammatical.

Exercises to Help the Child's Grammar

Grammar teaching must not be the learning of a number of rules, but the **use** of the rules. If a Junior is encouraged to read many books, he will be able to write fairly correctly, without formal grammar teaching, because the correct sentences and phrase patterns will be fixed in his mind through reading.

The Junior should, however, be taught to use capital letters, full-stops, commas, apostrophes, speech marks, singulars and plurals, past, present and future tenses correctly, what a noun is, and how to make it more interesting by using an adjective to describe it, e.g. a boy, a little boy, a good boy, and what a verb is, and how to make it more interesting by using an adverb, e.g. he ran, he ran quickly, he ran slowly. He should be given practice in finishing sentences, e.g.*

      Sule ran along......................

      We went to the house by......................

      Although it was raining......................

      The boy went to market because......................

This is really practice with phrases and clauses, but they are **never** called that to a Junior child. He is just asked to finish the sentences in an interesting way. In the same way a child can be asked to think of interesting beginnings to sentences, e.g.

      ....where the old man sat.

      ....when the sun was shining.

The best way to choose grammar exercises for a Junior class is to note common errors in the compositions and make up some exercises to teach the correction.

Missing word exercises can be used to give the child practice in using words. Missing every fifth word will (in time) give practice in all parts of speech.

Spelling should be systematically taught at this stage, as the child (when he is between seven and a half and eleven years) likes learning repetitive things. It is a good idea for the teacher to set twenty spellings a week (five each day for four days, with revision and testing on the fifth day). The spellings should be ones the child uses regularly, and should not be too difficult.

---

* As in previous chapters in Part 3, teachers will provide their own vernacular examples and exercises.

Dictation is a test of the child's ability to listen carefully, and then to spell correctly what he hears. It is bad to give hard dictations, as the child will be writing down a number of mistakes. Writing helps to fix things in the mind, and we do not want to fix mistakes. I would suggest that there is very little educational value in dictation. It should only be given very rarely. Young children, and children who find reading and writing difficult will only be discouraged and unhappy.

Composition. In the vernacular the child should write much more freely, and at a much earlier age than he will in English. Usually, oral preparation should be taken to avoid too many mistakes, and also to give the child some ideas, but sometimes each child can be allowed to make up a story, and as each subject will be different, oral preparation will not be much help. Always put difficult spellings on the blackboard, and tell the child to look in his dictionary, or hold up his hand if he cannot spell a word. The teacher should go round all the time helping and marking, while the compositions are being written.

Composition titles should be interesting to the child. The Junior loves rewriting stories the teacher has told him, and this is a good exercise; he likes describing something without mentioning its name. Later he will read his description to the class, to see if anyone can guess the object. He likes writing imaginative stories, which he has made up himself. He also needs practice in describing parts of the town, in writing clear directions about how to reach a certain place, and in letter writing. Stories, when the child pretends he is someone else, are interesting, e.g. I am a policeman. I am going to tell you something about my work, etc. I am a fisherman. Yesterday I went up the river in my boat, etc. If the child sees something beautiful, or feels very happy or sad, encourage him to write about what he sees and feels.

For this type of composition some reading and oral discussion will add to the child's general knowledge and understanding of the subject.

These ideas will, I hope, help you and you will be able to think of many more examples. Do, however, remember that original writing is most important in the vernacular. If the child cannot think and then express his ideas on paper in his own language, he will never do it well in a foreign one.

Part four   The Teaching of English

Chapter 21 English in the Primary School. The Early Stages

Why do children in Africa learn English? This may be a question in the mind of young teachers, and it is wise to consider the reasons why English is taught in the schools.

A Common Language
While there are many languages in Africa, each of which should be preserved and used at its best, a common language is necessary for contact in the fast-growing countries of Africa, between different peoples and between different countries. English has a number of advantages over any other common language.

The Advantages of English as a Common Language
1. In the countries for which this book is intended all educated people, and many uneducated people, already speak English. A new common language would mean a great deal of extra study and hard work for a number of people.

2. The wisdom of many ages can be read in English. It would take many years, and the books would be very expensive, if all books of knowledge were to be translated into each vernacular. To those who can read English, further studies can be aided by books, printed in English, which can be bought at reasonable prices.

3. For trading and business dealings with other countries, English is very useful, as so many people speak it; for example, people from other

parts of Africa, America, India, Australia, and many countries in Europe.

4. People who are interested in world affairs can study them easily through newspapers and magazines printed in English. Radio talks can be given in English to many people at the same time, and programmes from other African countries and from Europe can add to the understanding and general knowledge of those who speak English.

The Teaching of English in the Primary School

Having decided to teach the child English, let us consider how it should be taught.

Speaking and Listening

Speech comes first. It is the basis of all future language learning. The child must, therefore, be helped to lay a good foundation on which he can build later. Listening to the teacher's **speech pattern** is most important, as the child will imitate it; mistakes of speech must be immediately corrected and the child must not be allowed to get into bad habits.

Much time is wasted in Secondary schools and Colleges in correcting bad habits of speech. This could be avoided if the earliest classes in English were always taken by the best possible teachers. Teaching a foreign language needs a skilled, trained teacher, and if necessary the headteacher could take the English lessons himself. I have stressed this point because, in the same way that you cannot build a good house on bad foundations, so you cannot build good learning on bad early teaching.

As well as speaking, the child must be able to **understand** what he is saying and what is being said to him. It is quite easy for a child to learn English sentences parrot-fashion. (A parrot can be taught to speak words, but it does not understand what the words mean.) The teacher should use pictures and actions to make quite sure that the child **understands** what he is saying. A good vocabulary should be built up slowly. It is better for the child to know a few words and be able to use them well, than to be taught many words which he only half knows in a muddled way.

Reading and Writing

No English word should be seen by an African child, either in print or on the blackboard, until the teacher has taught it orally. The reasons for this are obvious: speech naturally comes first in the child's development, many English words do not sound in a regular phonetic way, and to see them written before he can speak them only confuses the child. **When** the teacher actually decides to start English reading will depend largely on **how** the child is progressing with his vernacular reading; to introduce a young child to English reading before he can read fairly well in his own language leads to confusion.

When reading is taken the teacher must remember the importance of **speaking first.** For at least the first four years of teaching English, the first half of any English lesson should be speaking. Even when the time-table says English Reading, the first part of the lesson must be oral preparation. The sentences or new words should be written on the blackboard before the children use the reading books. Reading and writing go hand in hand, as the child will copy the sentences he has read; at first the child will only copy, but he will gradually be led to write on his own. This is dealt with later.

After a time a child can often read fairly well, but when questioned he has no idea what he has been reading about. This shows bad teaching in the early years, and means that the child has been hurried through the reading book, without understanding the lessons. **'Slow and sure'** should be the motto when teaching English. One lesson well understood is better than four lessons only vaguely understood. It does not matter if it takes four weeks to teach one lesson, if in the end the child can read it well and can tell the teacher clearly and in good English what it is about. **A good teacher does not push the child to fit in with the syllabus, but changes the syllabus to suit the child.**

The aims of teaching English can therefore be written down like this:
To help the child
1. To understand spoken English.
2. To speak English correctly.
3. To read in English with understanding.
4. To write in English in an interesting way.

Teaching of New Words in English

Why the Translation Method should not be used
When words and sentences are spoken in the vernacular and then translated into English, the teacher is using the translation method in which the child continues to think in his own language, and before speaking has to change all the sentences in his mind into English. This will not only make the child slow in speaking, but also the forms of the sentences and the arrangement of the words (or as they are called: sentence and phrase patterns) will be vernacular in style. English sentence patterns are usually very different from vernacular sentence patterns, so that it is obviously better to teach English sentence patterns from the beginning in the English lesson, using the direct method with no translation.

After the child has been learning English for two or three years, there may be odd occasions when the translation method can be used, for words which cannot be explained with objects, actions, pictures or a short story. Remember that the translation method is an easy method for the lazy teacher, who cannot be bothered to prepare interesting ways to teach the new words, but it will make the learning of English more difficult for the child.

The Direct Method

When a child is young he learns his own language by hearing his family speak as they go about their daily work. The child finds that by making certain sounds his mother pays attention to him, is pleased with him for trying to talk and gives him what he wants. Gradually he imitates more of the words he hears, and he learns to speak by the direct method of hearing words used in sentences and then repeating the words when he wants something. This method is therefore considered the best for teaching a foreign language to a young child: he is learning English sentences and phrase patterns from the beginning.

The direct method does need very careful preparation, and the beginning stages have to be taken rather slowly, but it is worth while in the end. An important rule to remember is that only English should be spoken in the English lesson.

Introducing the New Words

Usually three or four new words are sufficient for one lesson. They should be introduced with as much variety and action as possible. As it is natural to speak in sentences, so the new words should be introduced in sentences. The teacher must give each child opportunities to speak as much as possible, for it is only through practice that the child will learn. If a child makes a mistake the teacher must correct it immediately, or the mistake will be fixed in the child's mind.

In the early stages of teaching English it is better to have two fifteen-minute lessons each day, than one thirty-minute lesson. A short discussion with the headteacher should be enough for the timetable to be arranged to make this possible.

The Early Stages of Teaching English

It is helpful, and indeed practically essential, for the teacher, to use a good teacher's textbook, written in conjunction with a reading scheme. This textbook will tell which words to teach in preparation for the reading book.

Such teachers' textbooks are written by experts and the words are chosen carefully for each set of lessons. They nearly all begin in the same way, by teaching the names of things found in the classroom, the reason for this being that the baby learning to speak the language of his parents first learns the names of objects he can see around him in the home. It is most natural therefore for the child, when he is learning English, first to learn the names of things he uses every day in the classroom.

If you have no textbook to help you, you cannot go wrong if you teach the names of things commonly found and used in the classroom, a book, a pencil, a chair, a desk, a table, the floor, the window, the door, the cupboard, the blackboard (but **a piece of chalk**). Lead on to things often seen in the school and at home—a case, a bowl, a plate, a basket, a ball, an orange, a flower, a dress, a shirt (but **a pair of trousers**). Lead on then to commonly used **verbs,** sitting, standing, running, carrying, pointing, showing, writing, drawing, shutting. Parts of the body are also interesting to little children. We do not talk very often about **the** leg or **a** head—we say my leg or your leg, my head or his head; so **my, your, his** and **her** will have to be introduced.

These examples should give you a good idea of the type of word you should introduce in the earliest stages. Once children start reading you will get help, because the reading book will plan which new words should be introduced. A trained teacher will, however, introduce other new words which are not in the reading book, if he feels they are necessary and helpful to the children.

I shall give two patterns of English lessons, which I have found simple yet effective for little children who are just starting to learn English. For the first few weeks the children will not say much in English, and do not worry if they say nothing at all. Each child knows that by speaking his own language he can tell others what he is thinking about and planning, or he can tell other people what he wants. Your aim in these early lessons is to help the child to realize that he can tell his thoughts to other people by speaking English. In other words your aim is to help the child to realize that English is not just a jumble of strange sounds, but that meaning can be expressed through English. In the first few lessons, too, you are letting the child's ear become accustomed to the sound of English being spoken.

A First English Lesson
   Time: 9.30–9.45.
   Objectives: Understand that meaning can be expressed by speaking in English. Respond to English sentences and especially the words **Good morning, a book** and **a pencil.**
   Apparatus: a book and a pencil.
   Procedure:
   1. The teacher greets the children. 'Good morning, children. Good morning, children. This is our first English lesson. Good morning, children. Say "Good morning, Mr Jimoh." Good morning.' (The children will probably not respond to this, but do not worry. They are getting used to the sound of English words.)
   2. The teacher shows the children a book, and does various actions with it. 'This is a **book**. I am putting the **book** on the table. I am pointing to the

book. I am holding up the **book**. It's a **book**. I am putting the **book** on Ali's desk. I am putting the **book** on the table. It's a **book**.' (The word 'book' should be slightly stressed.)

3. 'It's a **book**. Hold up your **book**. (Help one or two children to hold up their books and the rest will copy them.) Good. It's a **book**. Put the **book** on the desk. (Again help one or two children and the rest will copy.) Good. Point to the **book**. (Do the action and the children will copy.) Come here, Chinua. (Help Chinua by beckoning to him.) Give me the **book**. (Point to the book, and hold out your hand for it.) Thank you. It's a **book**.' (Call out other children to do the same action.)

4. 'It's a **pencil**. I put the **pencil** on the table. I hold up the **pencil**. I put the **pencil** on Aina's desk. I put the **pencil** on the table. It's a **pencil**.' (In these sentences the word 'pencil' will be slightly stressed.)

5. 'Hold up a **pencil**. (Help one child and the rest will copy.) It's a **pencil**. Put the **pencil** on the desk. (Again help one child and the others will copy.) Ifi, come here. (Beckon to Ifi.) Good. Give me the **pencil**, Ifi. (Help her by pointing and holding out your hand for the pencil.) Thank you. I give the **pencil** to Sule. Put the **pencil** on the table, Sule.' (Help him by pointing.) Call out other children to do the same actions.

6. 'Good morning children. Say "Good morning, Mr Jimoh." Good morning.'

Points to Note about the Lesson

1. The success of this lesson depends on the teacher's voice and actions. He must really appear interested and happy to teach these words, and this will be shown by the variety in his voice and manner.

2. We speak in sentences, therefore we should teach the words in sentences. The special words we have chosen should be slightly stressed. The meaning of 'good' and 'thank you' should be clear to the children because of the teacher's expression and smile.

3. The children do not just sit and listen. They take a part in the lesson and are given something to do even though they do not speak.

4. Although I said on page 42 that when asking a question a teacher should not name a child until all the class have thought of the answer, and a number of children have put up their hands, this is not possible with the first few English lessons. The teacher must call the child's name first before asking the question. It is surprising, however, to notice how quickly the children learn the questions, 'Who can touch . . .?' or 'Who can point to . . .?' and put up their hands because they want to do the action.

5. As we are not introducing reading for some time, the shortened form 'It's' may seem more natural than 'It is'.

6. The first English lesson is bound to be a little puzzling to the children and they will not be able to attend for long. It should be a short lesson,

lasting only ten or fifteen minutes. The aim is fulfilled by helping the children to realize that meaning can be expressed by using English words.

The Following Lessons

For three or perhaps four weeks, depending on the ability of the children, the same pattern of lesson should be followed, except that of course revision must be taken each lesson. Probably only four or five words will be introduced in one week, but again each teacher will have to judge for himself whether the children are responding and learning quickly or slowly. Remember that no two classes are alike, and so the teacher must plan his work according to the ability of the class. To put it briefly the lessons will follow this pattern:

    1. Revision of words already learnt.

    2. Introduction of a new word (or words). Children listen while the teacher does the actions.

    3. Teacher tells a number of children in turn to do an action using the new word. Point to .... Show me .... Touch ....

    4. To add variety the teacher can draw the object on the blackboard. The children can do actions pointing to and touching the drawing.

    5. Revise the words the children know or let the children draw the object they have learnt in this lesson.

The children are not speaking yet. They are hearing English and doing actions. If, however, any of the children do try to speak, encourage them.

The Second Type of English Lesson

The children have been **hearing** English, and **doing** actions when commanded in English, now they are going to **speak** in English.

    Time: 8.45–9.00.

    Objectives: Revising of words learnt in previous lessons. Practise the sentences, 'It's a table.' 'It's a chair.'

    Apparatus: Various objects in the classroom, a table and a chair.

    Lesson procedure:

    1. Revision: 'Who can show me a book? Hassan. Good. It's a book. Point to a pencil. Data, Ifi, Umoh. Good. It's a pencil.' (Continue in this way revising all the words the children have learned. The children will not speak. They will only do the actions. The class has had a number of English lessons now, so do not call anyone's name until they put their hands up.)

    2. The teacher will encourage the children to say, 'It's a table.'

'Who can point to a table? Sule. Good. What is it? It's a table.' (As you say the sentence encourage the child to say it with you. Then turn to the class and encourage them to say the sentence altogether. It may be difficult to get the children to speak at first, but do not be disappointed if the result

193

is poor. The teacher needs a great deal of patience to teach these little children English. Praise and encourage any small effort, and the children will try hard to please you.) Continue to practise 'It's a table.'

'Who can touch the table? Okeke. Good. It's a table. Okeke say it, "It is a table." Everyone say, "It's a table".' (Give a number of children a turn.)

3. Teach, 'It's a chair,' in the same way. (Give a number of children a turn, but remember to share the turns as equally as possible among the children.)

4. Draw a table on the blackboard. 'It's a table. Point to the table. Aina. Good. Say, "It's a table." Class, what is it? It's a table.' Draw a chair on the blackboard. 'It's a chair. Who can point to the chair? Pius. Good. What is it, Pius ?It's a chair. Class, what is it? It's a chair.' (Again give a number of children a turn in this way.)

5. The children draw a table and a chair, while the teacher goes round the class asking, 'What is this?' as he points to each child's drawing. Be careful not to leave the quick children doing nothing when they have finished the drawings. Tell them to draw some of the things they heard about in other lessons, while the teacher quickly goes round to hear each child speak.

Variety when Teaching New Words
One of the main troubles when teaching a foreign language to small children is the dullness of the lessons. We cannot expect children to learn and remember well unless they are interested, and a good teacher will do all he can to give variety to his teaching and to present it in interesting ways.

Objects are essential for teaching the names of things, and pictures are not nearly so good. A small child often finds a drawing puzzling, and he has to learn to understand a picture just as he has to learn to understand other things. If the object cannot be taken into the school, the children can often be taken to see it, e.g. a tree, a house, a river, the church, a goat, a car. Only teach small children words of objects which can be found in or near the school.

Actions should be used as much as possible. With a little preparation the teacher will be able to think of many interesting actions, which will add variety to the lesson. Always give as many children as possible opportunities to do the actions. It is better to give each child a small turn than a few children a long turn. Often the class can do the actions all together.

Blackboard drawings are most useful **after** the objects and the actions have been used, for they give variety to the lesson and a child loves to watch his teacher drawing. The drawings should be as simple as possible and quickly finished. Some time spent on practising blackboard drawing is time well spent. The children will understand the drawings, because they have just seen the concrete object or the action shown.

Examples of simple blackboard illustrations. The words in brackets are what the teacher says. Nothing is written in the early stages.

(This is a table.) (I am pointing to the chair.)

(This is a book.) (This is a pencil.)

(This is a house.) (This is a tree.)

(I am pointing to the door.) (I am pointing to the window.)

(I am running.)   (Ali is sitting.)

Pictures will be used frequently for older children (children who have been learning English for some time) when new words are taught. For smaller children they can be introduced **after** using the actual objects and seeing the blackboard drawings. They will then add variety to the lesson.

Children's drawings add more variety, and even before English reading and writing are introduced, the lessons can be concluded by allowing the children to draw the objects which have been used. As they draw the teacher can go round and ask individual children, 'What is this? Point to the book? Show me the desk?', etc.

Songs and poems which are very simple and use words the children have been learning add variety. If you look through English poetry books you may find a few suitable poems, but they must be very simple. The ones teachers make up to suit their own classes are often much more useful. The first one, which can be sung to any suitable tune, was composed by my students and proved quite helpful. The underlined words can be changed to suit the lesson, and it provides some action, standing up and clapping.

This is a book.	This is a desk.
I am holding up the book.	I am pointing to the desk.
This is a pencil.	This is a chair.
I am pointing to the pencil.	I am sitting on the chair.
We all stand up	We all stand up
And clap our hands	And clap our hands
One, two, three.	One, two, three.

For this song the children stand in a circle and dance round the teacher's desk.

We are dancing round the desk,
Round the desk, round the desk,
We are dancing round the desk,
Boys and girls together.

This is the way we brush our hair, (Children pretend to brush their hair.)
Brush our hair, brush our hair,
This is the way we brush our hair,
Boys and girls together.

A number of verses can be sung, putting in different actions for the underlined words.

Chapter 22   Introducing Reading in English

In my opinion reading in English should not be introduced until:

1. The child can use and understand orally a number of simple English sentences. (Speaking must come before reading.)
2. The child can read simple vernacular books. (It may confuse the child if he is introduced to reading in a foreign language, before he has mastered it in his own language.)

How to introduce English Reading
Command cards are probably the best and most interesting way of introducing reading in English to small children.

Example of a Lesson introducing a Command Card
   Objectives: Revision of sentences about objects in the classroom. Response to the written command, **Open the door.**
   Apparatus: Objects in the classroom for revision and the command card, **Open the door.**

   Procedure:
   1. Revision of words the children know, e.g. a book, a pencil, the table, the cupboard, the blackboard, a window, standing, sitting, pointing, shutting, opening, touching. The teacher gives the commands, and individual children do the actions, saying what they are doing, e.g. 'Point to a pencil. What are you doing? Open the door. What are you doing? Touch the window. What are you doing?'
   2. The teacher says, 'Who can open the door? Ali. Good. What are you doing? Good. Look at this card, children. It says, **"Open the door."** What does it say? Chinua. Good. What does it say? Aina. Good. Open the door, Aina. What are you doing?' Other children will also read the card, and open the door.
   3. 'Now I shall write the words on the blackboard. Watch while I write. **Open** (pause and write), **the** (pause and write). Who can tell me the last word? Chinua. Good, the **door.** Now who will read the sentence from the blackboard?' After a few children have read it, ask another child to do the action. 'Now I shall draw Toyin opening the door.'
   4. The children will copy the sentence and the drawing. Quick children

can draw some of the other actions which were revised at the beginning of the lesson.

Blackboard work

Open the door.

Points to Note about the Lesson

1. The reading is new, but the sentence is already well known as a spoken sentence.

2. The children may not yet follow each word the teacher says as he explains what he is writing and drawing, but they can follow the general meaning of his words.

3. The teacher must remember to turn round and look at the children when he speaks, then turn back to the board to write the next word.

4. In the next lesson, after the oral introduction, this command will be revised and another introduced.

Introducing the Reading Book

Usually there are a number of sentences on each page in the reading book. The teacher cannot be sure that each child is looking at the right one, so I would suggest that, at first, the sentences are taught from the blackboard.

Pattern of a Reading Lesson using Sentences from the Reading Book
  Procedure:

1. Revision of sentences the children have been learning during the past week, using objects and actions. Children say what they are doing.

2. Revise especially words which will later be written on the blackboard, 'the boy, the girl, reading, writing, the class', e.g. 'Come here, Yisau. Yisau is a boy. Come here, Toyin. Toyin is a girl. Are you a boy, Yisau? Are you a girl, Toyin? Is Yisau a boy or a girl? Is Toyin a boy or a girl? We are in the class. This is Class 2. What is our class called? Is this our class? Is this Class 2?' Various questions are asked to give a number of children a turn at speaking.

3. 'Hold a pencil, Amadu. What is he doing? Write, Amadu. What is he doing? What is the boy doing? Good. The boy is writing. I am going to put that on the blackboard. The ... boy ... is ... What is the boy doing?

199

The boy is **writing**. Good . . . writing. Who can read the sentence? (A few children will read.) Now I shall draw the boy writing. I am drawing.'

The boy is writing.

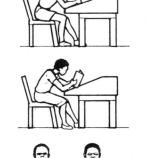

The girl is reading.

The boy and girl
are in the class.

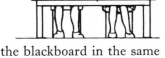

(The next two sentences will be written on the blackboard in the same way, speaking the sentence before writing it.)

4. Practise reading the sentences. 'Who can point to the sentence which says, **The girl is reading?** What does this sentence say?, etc. Who can point to the word which says, **writing?** the words which say, **the class?'** etc.

5. Read the sentences all together softly from the blackboard. Children copy the sentences. Quick children are asked to draw some other things in the class, because they have not yet learned sufficient sentences to be given reading cards. The teacher goes round to hear individual children read.

Points to Note about the Lesson

1. Speaking comes before anything is written on the blackboard.

2. The reading is new but the children understand the spoken words. They are being helped step by step.

3. The teacher keeps the children's attention by talking about what he will write on the blackboard, then turning to write, then turning back and speaking to the children again. No child will play about, because he knows the teacher will quickly turn round, and he will expect everyone to be watching.

4. The children do not only listen. They are given plenty of opportunities to speak, act, read and write.

5. As much **variety** as possible is introduced, yet the lesson is very simple, and could be taught successfully by a student.

The same pattern can be used for a series of lessons.

1. Revision.
2. Making sure the children can speak and understand the words which are to be read in a few moments.
3. Writing the sentences on the blackboard and drawing pictures.
4. Practising the reading of the sentences, and pointing to some of the words.
5. Copying the sentences to fix them in the children's minds, while the teacher hears some of the children read as he goes round.

When all the sentences from one page of the reading book have been taught, they can then be read from the book, to give further practice.

Apparatus

Flash cards can be introduced to add variety, and they are very useful for revising reading words. The children enjoy the exercise, and are eager to read the words. At this stage do not teach new words with flash cards, only **revise.** Teach new reading words as in the lesson pattern on page 199.

As the children learn to read a number of English sentences individual apparatus can add variety to the lessons, and it is especially useful for quick children who soon finish copying the sentences on the blackboard.

Picture and Sentence Matching Cards

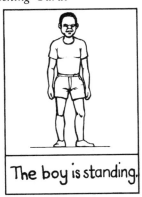

Cut-up sentences. (These must only be sentences the children have learnt to read from their reading book.)

| The boy | is writing. |

| The boy and the girl | are in the class. |

About six of these sentences should be put in each envelope. The children can look in their reading books to match the sentences.

Questions and Answers

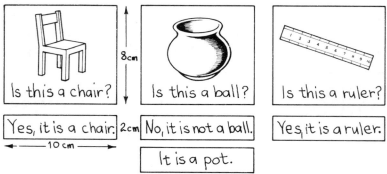

Is this a chair? | Is this a ball? | Is this a ruler?

Yes, it is a chair. 2cm No, it is not a ball. Yes, it is a ruler.

It is a pot.

8cm

10 cm

Card 1

reads   market   brushes
teacher   chair   man

1 Ali is going to the _____.

2 Mary _____ her book.

3 Mr Jimoh is the _____.

4 The _____ works on the farm.

5 Chinua _____ his dog.

6 Mother sits on the _____.

Missing word cards (Only use words which the children have learnt from their reading book.)

202

Reading Cards (Only use words which the children have learnt.)

|15cm

Mrs Taiwo is going to the market. She is carrying a pot on her head. There is some oil in the pot. She is going to sell it in the market.

Drawing Cards

Card 1
Draw a dog.
Draw a boy giving the dog some food and water.
Draw a girl helping her mother.

When the teacher is making individual apparatus for English lessons, he must only use words which the children have been taught to read. When reading a foreign language, the child must be helped much more **carefully** and slowly than when reading in his own language. A child must never be left to guess at English pronunciation: if only words the child knows are used, this danger will be avoided.

Class reading: This is usually the best method for English reading. English is not a phonetic language, and the words often do not sound as we might expect from the spelling. The words **must be taught** by the teacher. The first ten or fifteen minutes of every English lesson (even one which is called a reading lesson) should be spent in oral preparation and pronunciation.

When the children read, do not let one child read more than a couple of sentences, because as many children as possible must be given a chance to read aloud and receive the teacher's help and corrections. If a child cannot read a word, tell him it quickly, and let him finish the sentence. Then

203

return to the word he did not know, write it on the blackboard, teach it and make sure that the child can pronounce it correctly. Stopping to teach in the middle of a sentence breaks the sense of the words and hinders the child's understanding.

If the words are well prepared at the beginning of the lesson there will be very few mistakes. After each child has read his small part, the teacher must ask questions to make sure that the rest of the class have been listening, and have understood. If some of the children are puzzled the teacher must explain the sentences, and they must be read again by another child. Keep a record, and those children who do not read in one lesson must be called first in the next.

Group reading: The children must not be left to read on their own in English. With group work, only children working with the teacher should read aloud. The other children must practice and revise from individual cards.

Reading for comprehension: Oral questions will always be asked to make sure the children understand the reading. When the children have had about three or four years' practice with English, they may be helped to do written comprehension. The questions must always be answered orally first, to prevent the children writing mistakes.

Reading for information: This type of reading will be left to the higher classes of the Primary school or even the Secondary school, but it should be mentioned as it is one of the aims of teaching English reading. Once the child has gained sufficient mastery of the English language to read for information, there is no end to the knowledge he can learn from books. The teacher can help to train the child to read for information, by setting questions for the older Junior, who will find the answer by reading.

Chapter 23 Writing in English

The child writes much more slowly than he speaks or reads. As he writes a deep impression is made on his mind, for he breaks the sentence into words, and the words into letters. All that is written in English should be as perfect as possible, because the child will remember what he writes.

A good teacher will try to avoid written mistakes in the vernacular, but they are not as dangerous as English written mistakes, because the child has a long period of correct spoken vernacular fixed in his mind.

Oral preparation is essential before any kind of written English, to ensure that the child understands what he is writing, and that the sentence and phrase patterns are correct. All written work must be carefully corrected, and the sentences re-written if any mistakes are made.

Copying: In the first two years of reading, copying helps to fix the sentence patterns in the child's mind.

Missing word exercises have already been mentioned. They give the child practice in writing sentence patterns, but they require a little more thought than just straight copying. The missing words should be written at the side of the blackboard in coloured chalk, to prevent spelling mistakes.

Sentence patterns: The child will of course not be able to write English sentences on his own for some time, but he can be helped to make guided sentences in the following stages. The methods discussed have been tried and found by experience to be successful. Teachers' textbooks which accompany English courses do not always follow exactly the methods described here.

Stage 1. *Using a table:* A number of these can be obtained from textbooks, but the teacher can also make up ones he thinks are suitable for the class. In any case they are best copied on to the blackboard at first.

The man		going to the market.
The old woman	is	walking to the church.
Mr Blank		hurrying to the farm.

The teacher can point to make sure that all the children can understand how the sentences are made.

From even a small table like this, the child can make nine sentences. The oral preparation helps him to speak correctly, and when writing it is hardly possible for him to make a mistake, yet he is not just copying, but is having to think for himself.

Stage 2. *Changing one word*, e.g. The boy is <u>running</u> to the market.

The child will think of a different word (orally at first) to put in the place of the underlined word.

    e.g. The boy is going to the market.
        The boy is walking to the market.
        The boy is riding to the market.

The child has to think of his own word, and he is making his own sentence, even if it is not very different from the teacher's pattern. In my example the verb is changed, but practice can be given changing other words, though at this stage only **one** word is changed at a time.

Stage 3. *Changing a phrase*, e.g. The boy is running <u>to the market.</u>

In this stage the whole underlined phrase is changed.

    e.g. The boy is running from the school.
        The boy is running to meet his friend.
        The boy is running to see the chief.

The child has to think and makes his new sentence, yet only one phrase is changed, and with good oral preparation there should not be any mistakes.

Stage 4. *Changing the whole sentence step by step*, e.g. The boy is running to the market.

Step by step the teacher leads the child to make an entirely new sentence.

    e.g. The boy is running to the market.
        The girl is running to the market.
        The girl is hurrying to the market.
        The girl is hurrying to the school.
        The girl is hurrying from the school.

Every word has been changed except **the** and **is,** yet the sentence pattern remains correct because the exercise was done step by step. The changing of **is** involves the changing of the verb tense, which must also be taught very carefully and step by step.

Verbs

The first column headed 'Tense' is not to be written on the blackboard.

Tense	Guiding word	Sentence
(Present continuous)	now	Now he is coming to school.
		He is coming to school now.
(Simple present)	every day	Every day he comes to school.
		He comes to school every day.

(Simple past)	yesterday	Yesterday he came to school.
		He came to school yesterday.
(Simple future)	tomorrow	Tomorrow he will come to school.
		He will come to school to-morrow.

I consider that at first the present continuous tense should be used. **The teacher must see that the child is actually doing the action when he is speaking,** e.g. 'I am putting the book on the table.' It is wrong if the child puts down the book, and then says the sentence. This needs a present perfect tense and comes much later. He must be doing the action – the book must be in the child's hand moving through the air – as he says the sentence. When the child has progressed with his speaking and reading, then the other tenses are gradually introduced, using the guiding words, 'now', 'every day', 'yesterday' and 'tomorrow'. The child is **not** told the names of the tenses, as that would only muddle him. The guiding words should be used sometimes at the beginning of a sentence, when a capital letter is used, and sometimes at the end of the sentence.

A table can be built up on the blackboard, e.g.

Now	I am walking	I am writing	I am singing
Everyday	I walk	I write	I sing
Yesterday	I walked	I wrote	I sang
Tomorrow	I shall walk	I shall write	I shall sing

He is jumping	He is running	He is reading	now
He jumps	He runs	He reads	everyday
He jumped	He ran	He read	yesterday
He will jump	He will run	He will read	tomorrow

Use coloured chalk for the lines. Parts of the table can be rubbed out, and the children copy the table, filling in the missing parts.

Later, the present perfect and past continuous will be introduced.

(Present perfect)	just	He has just come to school.
	already	He has come to school already.
		He has already come to school.
(Past continuous)	while	While he was coming to school he met Aina.

207

when   When he was coming to school he met Aina.

The guiding word 'just' must be put between the two parts of the verb, 'has' and 'come'. The guiding word 'already' can be put at the end of the sentence, but it is better English if it is also put between the two parts of the verb, 'He **has** already **come**.'

Pronouns and Verbs

The verb sometimes changes according to the pronoun that is being used. The best way to introduce this is to give practice in the above tables using the different pronouns at different times.

Singular . . . I, you, he, she and it.
Plural . . . we, you, they.

In most verbs the third person 'he', 'she' and 'it' are the only ones that change the verb, e.g.

Simple present

I come	I sing	I look	I go
you come	you sing	you look	you go
he ⎫	he ⎫	he ⎫	he ⎫
she ⎬ comes	she ⎬ sings	she ⎬ looks	she ⎬ goes
it ⎭	it ⎭	it ⎭	it ⎭
we come	we sing	we look	we go
you come	you sing	you look	you go
they come	they sing	they look	they go

The verb 'to be' is used in the present continuous tense and there are words to learn: 'am', 'are' and 'is'.

I am	I am working	I am washing
you are	you are working	you are washing
he ⎫	he ⎫	he ⎫
she ⎬ is	she ⎬ is working	she ⎬ is washing
it ⎭	it ⎭	it ⎭
we are	we are working	we are washing
you are	you are working	you are washing
they are	they are working	they are washing

Care must also be taken when the verb 'to be' is used in the future.

I shall	I shall draw	I shall lie down
you will	you will draw	you will lie down
he ⎫	he ⎫	he ⎫
she ⎬ will	she ⎬ will draw	she ⎬ will lie down
it ⎭	it ⎭	it ⎭

we shall	we shall draw	we shall lie down
you will	you will draw	you will lie down
they will	they will draw	they will lie down

Notice that we say, 'I shall' and 'we shall', and all the other pronouns use 'will'. This verb tense is very often misused. 'I will' is not simple future, but shows determination in the future. 'I will go to the market (I am determined to go to the market) whatever happens.' 'Even if it rains, we will come (we are determined to come) to see you.' If 'shall' is used with the other pronouns instead of 'will' this also means determination. 'You shall clear up this mess,' said Mother. (Mother is determined the child will clear up the mess.) This use of the future tense to show determination should **not** be introduced until the secondary stage (or the very end of the primary stage), but I mention it because the teacher must make sure that his own speech pattern is correct.

These examples will give a foundation from which to start, but more detailed help will be found in a good teacher's reference book, dealing with the actual lessons in the children's reading books.

Note: Although I have used 'shall' and 'will' for future tenses, 'I shall, you will, he will' etc., and they are still given in many textbooks, modern English usage often prefers the present continuous of the verb 'to go' with a *future time word*. Examples: **Tomorrow** he is going to school. She is going to walk to the market on **Tuesday**. Mother is going to visit her sister **next week**.

Look at modern books, listen to educated people on the radio and television, and decide which 'future' pattern of speech will be most useful for the children in your area. When you have decided, teach only *one* pattern or the children may be confused.

Dictation must be very well prepared, but it is better to leave dictation until the child is older; let the child copy instead.

Completing the Sentences

At first only let the child write one or two words on his own, e.g.

................is going to school.

Sule................to the market

The farmer works in................

The old lady walks................up the hill.

Later the child can add phrases and clauses as suggested in the vernacular notes on page 182, but this is quite difficult and should not be attempted until the child is able to speak and read well.

Composition

Although the final aim of written English is to help the child to express his own ideas through writing, he will certainly not have sufficient command of a foreign language to do much original writing in the Primary school. He can, however, be greatly helped towards achieving this aim. One good way is by changing and finishing sentences in the way already described.

Finishing Sentences to make a Composition

If the teacher plans the sentences carefully, then, when the child has finished them, the results will be a connected passage like a composition, e.g.

> I met Yisau by ———. We went to ———. ——— sold us some bananas. On our way home———. It began to rain ———. ——— pleased with the bananas.

The child finishing the sentences might write the following short composition.

> I met Yisau by the old church. We went to the market. Our friend Laide sold us some bananas. On our way home we played a game. It began to rain so we ran quickly to our houses. Our mothers were pleased with the bananas.

The exercise would be taken orally first, and the teacher would write suggested phrases on the blackboard to finish the sentences. He would rub them out afterwards, and each child would write the composition. The slower children would probably try to write the same as the teacher, but the brighter children would make an attempt to finish the sentences in a different way. The teacher must put any spellings the children need on the blackboard. Each child would benefit by making his own English dictionary at this stage. When the child needs help with a word, he raises his hand, the teacher writes the word on the blackboard and the child copies it into the dictionary.

Questions and Answers

Another useful way of helping a child to write sentences in a connected passage is through questions and answers

What is your name?	My name is Abe Blank.
Where do you live?	I live at 33 Guinea Street, Newtown.
How many brothers and sisters have you?	I have three brothers and two sisters.
Which school do you go to?	I go to Newtown School.
Which is your favourite lesson?	My favourite lesson is Science.

The teacher will prepare by dividing the blackboard in half, and writing the questions before the lesson starts. The children will answer the questions orally, and the teacher will write the best answers opposite the questions.

After reading the sentences on the board, the answers are rubbed out, and the children write their own. The questions are **not** written by the children, as this is just a waste of time. If the teacher has planned the questions well, the answers will make a connected composition, e.g.

> My name is Abe Blank. I live at 33 Guinea Street, Newtown. I have three brothers and two sisters. I go to Newtown School. My favourite lesson is Science.

By this time, the children will have learnt in their vernacular composition that a new line is only started when we start a new paragraph. As the children will only be writing one paragraph in English at this stage, encourage them to write to the ends of the lines. Each sentence does **not** need a new line.

Let the children choose a title for the composition, e.g. Myself. Each word in a title usually has a capital letter. The teacher will write any words the children cannot spell on the blackboard.

Descriptions and retelling stories can be taken with this question and answer method, which guides the children and prevents mistakes.

Chapter 24 Some Teaching Points

The articles 'a' and 'the': The teacher must take special care when introducing something which has no equivalent in the vernacular. The article in front of the noun will be something quite new in the experience of the child, so every common noun should **always** be taught with the article in front of it, e.g. a book, a window, a tree, or when referring to one particular object, the book, the window, the tree. If teachers would remember **never** to say or write an English common noun in the singular without an article, the children's English would greatly improve.

Sounds: When a child has difficulty with a sound the teacher must show him how to shape his mouth and where to put his tongue. For example the **th** sound is difficult: show the child how to put his tongue right out between his teeth, and then blow his breath out along the top of his tongue. To make the **h** sound let the child hold his hand about 15 cm from his mouth and blow on to his hand while his mouth is fairly wide open. When practising the sounds in words, use words which have the sound at the beginning, or in the middle or at the end, e.g. for **th** use **th**ank, **th**ose, mo**th**er, bro**th**er, bo**th**, wi**th**, tee**th**.

Nouns must always be taught with the object if at all possible. The teacher must be particular about capital letters at the beginning of nouns. Proper nouns begin with a capital, and the children will find it quite difficult to remember this, so never confuse them by writing common nouns with anything but a small letter. Some teachers start words with capitals when they write lists on the board, but this is not wise. Always help the children; never confuse them. A singular common noun should not begin a sentence; it should have the article in front. (A common noun may start with a capital letter only in the title of a composition.)

Verbs must be taught with actions.

Adjectives describe nouns, so they must be taught while showing an object. Try to remember, when you were learning English in your own childhood, how strange and muddling it all sounded. Do everything possible to make your teaching clear.

For example, when you teach the colours, a blue book, a red pencil and a green leaf will not help the children. They will think that 'blue' and book must always go together, and 'red' and pencil, etc.

Instead, have ready a number of objects the children know, all of a 'red' colour. The only new word will be 'red', and they will see that it can be used with any object of that colour, a red book, a red pencil, a red dress, a red shoe, a red ball, a red mat.

If the children are being taught the difference between colours, only introduce two at a time, e.g. blue and green. Show the children a blue book and a green book, a blue ball and a green ball, a blue piece of chalk and a green piece of chalk, a blue pencil and a green pencil, a blue stick and a green stick. Have plenty of examples, two of each, one blue and the other green. In this way the two colours are clearly taught. (Note: A few children are colour-blind and they cannot see colours. Everything looks grey. Some children can see some colours, but not others. Be careful when teaching colours that these children are not blamed for being lazy, if they cannot tell the colours.)

Often a good way to teach adjectives is to teach opposites, e.g. a fat boy, a thin boy; a big man, a small man; a long stick, a short stick. Use objects when possible, but do **not** use children. If a fat boy is called to the front of the class, all the children may laugh at him and he will feel miserable. If 'ugly' and 'pretty' are being taught **never** say, 'This is a pretty girl and this is an ugly girl.' It is very wicked to make a child unhappy in this way. Use blackboard drawings to illustrate things like this.

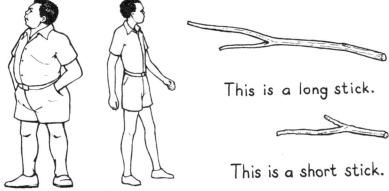

This is a long stick.

This is a short stick.

This is a fat boy.　This is a thin boy.

Prepositions are quite easy to teach with actions, and are usually best taught in pairs, e.g.

I am putting the book **on** the table	I am putting the book **under** the table.
I am standing **in front of** the desk.	I am standing **behind** the desk.
I am standing **outside** the classroom.	I am standing **inside** the classroom.
I am putting the pencil **in** the box.	I am taking the pencil **out of** the box.

Pronouns must be taught carefully with actions. **I** is used from the very beginning of English teaching, and can be best emphasized by pointing to yourself while speaking. 'I am sitting on the chair', 'I am pointing to the door', etc.

You can be used for one person or for a number of people, e.g. 'Mary, brush the floor' (point to her), 'You are brushing the floor. Ifi and Yakubu, stand by the blackboard. You are standing by the blackboard.'

Show the children that we use **he** for a boy, **she** for a girl and **it** for an animal or an object, but in the plural all of them are **they,** e.g. 'Ali is putting the pen on the table. He is putting the pen on the table. Mary is putting the pen on the table. She is putting the pen on the table. Ali and Mary are putting the pens on the table. They are putting the pens on the table. The pen is on the table. It is on the table. The pens are on the table. They are on the table.'

We use **we** when the person speaking is doing the action with someone else, e.g. 'I am going to the door. Ifi and I are going to the door. We are going to the door.'

They is used for two or more people or things, e.g. 'Ali, Ifi and Yakubu are going to the door. They are going to the door.'

This and **that** are best taught together, **this** being something near the speaker, **that** being further away, e.g. 'This is my pencil. Please bring me that pencil' (pointing to a pencil on the other side of the room). 'This is my book. That is your book' (pointing to it).

Here and **there** should also be taught together. 'Here' is near at hand. 'There' is some distance away, e.g. 'Here is a flower' (holding it up). 'There is another flower' (pointing to one further away). 'Here is my chair' (holding it). 'There is your chair' (pointing to it).

Who *and* **which**: Remember, **who** refers to a person, and **which** to a thing. 'Ali is writing on the blackboard. Who is writing on the blackboard? Who spilt the ink? Yakubu is the boy who spilt the ink.'

'That is my book. Which is your book? The book which Ifi gave me is an Arithmetic book.'

Adverbs add to the verb, so must be taught with the verb, e.g. 'I am walking to the door. I am walking slowly to the door. I am walking quickly to the door. I am speaking. I am speaking softly. I am speaking loudly.' (The adverbs are underlined.)

In conclusion we shall consider some of the causes of common mistakes and how they can be prevented.

The Causes of Common Mistakes

1. The teacher makes mistakes in his speech pattern.
2. The children are not carefully corrected, and they fall into bad habits of speech.

3. Reading is introduced before the spoken work has been thoroughly practised and understood.
4. Mistakes are written because of insufficient oral preparation.
5. Written mistakes are not carefully corrected.
6. The teacher does not make sure the children understand the work.
7. The lessons are uninteresting and the children do not attend.
8. The teacher's discipline is weak and the children play about.

How to Prevent Mistakes
1. The teacher's speech pattern must be perfect, and all the sentences well prepared.
2. If a child makes a mistake he must be corrected and helped to develop a good speech habit.
3. Reading must not be introduced until the children are able to say a number of simple sentences. When reading is taken, oral work should always be planned for the first part of the lesson, to make sure the children can understand and say any new or difficult words.
4. Careful oral preparation must always be taken before the children do any written work. Often the work should be written on the blackboard and read, before it is rubbed off and the children write. Difficult spellings should always be left on the board.
5. Corrections must always be written out carefully to fix the correct pattern or spelling in the mind.
6. Whether speaking, reading or writing the teacher must make sure that all the children understand the work. If some children understand while others do not, groups may have to be formed.
7. The lessons must be well prepared and interesting.
8. The teacher's discipline must be good, so that all the children are working and none is wasting his time.

Chapter 25 English Poetry

This subject should be very carefully taught. There are many beautiful poems for the child to enjoy when he is older, and the teacher of small children must be careful not to spoil their pleasure through bad teaching while they are young. Most English children's poems are, of course, written for English children, and describe things or use words which the African child will find very strange. The teacher must hunt through as many books as he can, to find suitable poems. Often jingles and rhymes, which are not real poetry, can be used, as they are easily understood, and give practice in clear speaking.

If simple poems cannot be found, it is better to leave poetry until the child is older than to let him think poetry is a miserable exercise as he struggles with words he cannot understand.

How to Choose an English Poem
1. The children must already know most of the words.
2. The subject of the poem must be something which could easily happen in Africa.
3. The poem should tell a story and be suitable for acting. (Descriptive poems are difficult to understand and should be left until the children are older.)

How to Teach an English Poem
Probably the easiest way to explain how to teach a poem is through a lesson pattern. For this pattern I have chosen a rhyme which would be suitable for children who have been learning English for two or three years.

Objectives: Understand a short rhyme called 'The Beggar'. Learn the poem through drama.

Apparatus: A beggar's stick, a beggar's bowl, some ragged clothes such as might be worn by a beggar, and a kobo.

Lesson procedure:
1. Explanation of difficult words. The teacher will judge which words will need special teaching or revision. The sentences below will give some idea of how to revise them with actions. Be sure to give the children plenty of opportunities to repeat the sentences and to answer the questions.

216

'Who can knock at the door? What are you doing? I am knocking at the door. Who can put on these old clothes? Chinua. Good. Take the bowl. Beg from the children. What are you doing? I am begging. What do we call a man who begs? He is a beggar. Is he happy? No, he is not happy. He is sad. He is a beggar. Is he young? No, he is not young. He is old. Are you young? Yes, I am a child. I am young. Is your grandmother young? No, my grandmother is not young. She is old. Is the beggar old? Yes, he is old. Who has a kobo? Show me a kobo. This is a kobo. Put the kobo in the beggar's bowl. What are you doing? I am putting the kobo in the beggar's bowl. Is the beggar sad to have the kobo? No, he is glad. He smiles. He is glad. What does the beggar say? He says, "Thank you." Here is a stick. The stick goes tap, tap, tap on the ground. Chinua, you are the old beggar. Make the stick go tap, tap, tap. Who can make the stick go tap, tap, tap?'

2. Tell the children a story. 'A woman was working in her house when she heard "Tap, tap, tap" outside her door. (The teacher can tap on the door with the beggar's stick.) She said, "Who's that knocking at my door?"

'An old man answered, "I'm a beggar".' (The teacher should put on the rags and use the begging bowl to demonstrate 'a beggar'.) 'The beggar held out his bowl to the woman. She was poor and she only had a kobo. She was sorry for the sad, old man and gave him the kobo. The beggar was happy and smiled.

'"Thank you," he said. "You have made me glad." He walked off, and the woman could hear his stick going tap, tap, tap down the road.'

3. To make quite sure the children have understood the story ask a few questions, e.g.

Who was outside the woman's door?
What noise did the stick make on the door?
Was the woman sorry for the beggar?
How much money did the woman have?
What did the beggar say?

4. The teacher says the poem.
'Now I am going to tell you a poem about the beggar. Listen carefully to hear when the woman is talking, and when the beggar is talking.' The teacher must vary his voice a little, to sound like a beggar. His voice should not be altered too much or he will spoil the clear speech necessary for the correct teacher's pattern.

'Who's that knocking at my door?' Tap, tap, tap.
'I'm a beggar, old and sad.' Tap, tap, tap.
'I've a kobo, nothing more.' Tap, tap, tap.
'Thank you. You have made me glad.' Tap, tap, tap.

5. The teacher says the poem again.

'I shall say the poem again, and you can all tap very softly with one finger on the desk, when I say, "Tap, tap, tap".' If the children do not do it softly, do not let them tap at all.

6. Questions about the poem.

Who is knocking at the door?

Is the beggar sad?

How much did the woman give him?

What did the beggar say?

7. The teacher says the poem again and the children join in where they can. As the poem has been discussed and explained, the children will already nearly know it. They must be told to speak very softly when they join in with the teacher, as his voice must be easily heard above the children's voices.

8. The teacher divides the class into two. One side is the beggar and the other is the woman. The teacher helps both sides to say their part. Again the children must speak softly.

9. Two children are chosen to act (the beggar will wear the rags) while the other children say the poem. Other children can act the poem, but do not say it too often or the children will get bored with it.

10. Revise other poems which the children have learnt before, or draw a picture of the story.

Points to Note about the Lesson

1. The children are familiar with a beggar and his ways.

2. The children know most of the words. Any new ones are taught with actions, and other difficult words are revised.

3. The children are told the story of the poem before the teacher says the poem.

4. The poem is learnt by listening to the teacher's speech pattern.

5. The teacher thinks of many interesting ways of repeating the poem. The children learn it through interest and almost without realizing they are learning. This is much better than learning it through dull repetition.

6. The children are given plenty of opportunities to speak and to take an active part in the lesson.

7. The children will enjoy the poem and it will improve their English.

The Following Lessons

A short poem like this is very quickly learnt, but it needs to be practised and revised in the following lessons. A longer poem will of course need more revision before it is learnt by heart, but do not bore the children by spending too long a time on it in one lesson. It is better to stop while they are still interested, leaving further learning until the next lesson.

English poems must **always** be taught through the teacher's speech pattern. They must **never** be taught through reading. *It is a great mistake,* unfortunately made by many teachers, *to put the poem on the blackboard and to read it to the children.* Reading is always more difficult than speaking, and the children have to struggle to understand the words on the blackboard. Because of this difficulty their concentration will be on the reading and not on the poem, and their speaking of the poem will then be poor and dull. The lesson then becomes a misery, and instead of enjoying poetry the children begin to dislike it.

On the other hand, the children will enjoy the lesson and will say the poem well if they learn it through listening and copying the teacher's speech pattern.

After the children have learnt it through speaking, the poem can be written on the blackboard for the next lesson. It will give the children confidence to read it, and because they know it, they will read it well. The children can then copy the poem as a writing exercise, which helps to fix the words in their minds.

The lines of poems all have a rhythm, and the teacher must guard against the children bringing out the rhythm too strongly, by saying the words in a voice which goes up and down. This is bad poetry speaking. Whoever is saying a poem must think of the **meaning** of the words and should say them in as interesting a way as possible. When reading a passage from a book, a breath is taken at a comma or a full stop, and the same rule applies to poetry. The end of a line is not always the end of a sentence or idea. The teacher must pay attention to the punctuation when he learns the poem, so that his pattern brings out the sense of the words.

Question and answer poems, as in the lesson pattern on pp. 217-18 are useful, as the class can be divided and the poem said in parts. This adds variety to the lesson and also helps the children to put expression into their voices as they ask the question or answer it.

Poetry can form very interesting and useful lessons but such lessons do need careful preparation.

Part five   Some More Subjects

Chapter 26   Art and Craft

Art and Craft form a very big subject which really needs a book to itself, but I mention here a few items which can be quite easily taught on teaching practice. Further suggestions can be obtained from the helpful books on the subject.

When people talk of Art they usually mean drawing and painting pictures, while by Craft they mean the making and shaping of something with the hands. The two are, however, very closely linked, for often a piece of craft is painted and decorated with designs, while pictures can be mounted which introduces craft. Here I consider the two together.

The Aims of Art and Craft
1. To let the child express himself and enjoy himself.

It is natural to enjoy making things, and we get satisfaction from doing so.

2. To help the child to take care and to persevere.

A good piece of art or craft must be done carefully, and often we have to try again and again before it is right.

3. To help the child to think and decide things for himself.

In so many lessons the child has to do just as the teacher tells him, but in art and craft lessons he can often make his own decisions when he chooses the colour to paint something, or decides what he will make or draw.

4. To train observation and hand and eye co-ordination.

We cannot draw well if we do not look carefully at the things around us before we try to put them on paper. We cannot make things well until we look carefully at finished articles. When we have observed carefully, our eye and hand must co-ordinate to produce the finished result.

5. To help the child to see and appreciate beautiful and well-made things.

If we do not try to do these things ourselves, we shall never realize how much practice and work are needed to do them well.

Art and Craft Equipment

Most schools can supply a little equipment, but in order to do sufficient work, scrap materials should be used when possible.

Chalks and boards: Though other things should also be used, the teacher should not neglect the chalks and boards which many Infants use. Each child can have a great deal of pleasure and practice in drawing on his board. If coloured chalks are used they add to the value of the lesson and they train the child in the use of colour.

Charcoal: This is cheap to buy. It can be made from dry sticks, which are first burned between heaps of grass and cold water is then poured over them.

Brushes: Real ones are expensive to buy, but last for years with careful treatment. Chewing sticks can successfully be chewed until the fibres form a brush-like end. String or raffia can be tied to sticks to make quite suitable cheap brushes.

Paint: This is expensive, but market dyes make a very good cheap substitute. Local dyes cost nothing if the teacher makes his own from leaves and roots.

Paper: Old newspaper should be collected from the teacher's friends and from all the parents. You cannot have too much old newspaper. Painting is successful on newspaper, and there are some other uses for it which I shall describe later. Any other scrap paper should also be saved and used, e.g. old exercise or examination papers, or cement bags. If paper is to be bought, the cheapest is plain newsprint paper. It is better to give the child a big sheet of cheap paper than a small sheet of expensive paper.

Old matchboxes and cardboard boxes: These should be saved and collected, as a number of things can be made with them.

Clay: Quite good clay can usually be dug somewhere in the town, and many interesting things can be modelled from it.

Sticks and match-sticks: A collection of these should be kept, as they are useful when the children are making things with clay.

Tins and glass jars: These are useful for holding paint or water. The sharp edges of the tins should be smoothed so that the children do not get hurt. Tins are really better than glass jars because they cannot break.

Paste: A cheap, fairly useful paste can be made with maize flour.

Drawing and Painting Pictures

An Infant is allowed to express himself in the art lesson, and he is taught to use his materials properly. An Infant is **not** taught to draw, and he should never be asked to copy a picture or the teacher's blackboard drawing. (This does not apply to reading or writing lessons when he copies drawings to add interest to the lessons. In art lessons he must not copy.)

An Infant is taught to hold the paint brush gently. A pencil has to be pressed on the paper, but a brush is not like a pencil, and it has only to touch the paper lightly. He has to be shown how to wash his brush before he uses another colour, or the paints will get mixed and spoilt.

It is often better when using dyes to let the children work in groups. Have two brushes for each colour. The children share the brushes and, so that the dyes do not get mixed, each brush stays in the same tin. All the brushes must be carefully washed at the end of the lesson, and they should last a long time.

An Infant should be given as many colours as possible, so that he can experiment with the various colours and make his picture as bright and attractive as possible. Encourage him to use **all** his paper and to draw big, bold pictures. If paints and brushes cannot be used, coloured crayons and chalks are good. Remember (page 177) a child needs big crayons, big brushes and big paper. A pencil is not good for Infant art, as the lead makes such a small mark, and the child tries to draw a small picture. Charcoal is much better as bigger pictures can be drawn, but of course it is not so interesting for the child to draw his picture in one colour. Plain paper must be used for charcoal, as it does not show up on newspaper.

An Infant is usually quite happy with his picture, and the teacher's job is to encourage and praise him. If the teacher cannot understand the picture he should say, 'Please tell me all about your picture.' It is good practice in oral composition for the child to do this, and when the picture has been explained the teacher may be able to give a few suggestions.

Never say, 'What is this?' The child will be disappointed as his picture is very clear to him. One of the needs of the child is to do something on his own and express his individuality. Painting and drawing make this possible and a sympathetic teacher helps the child to develop properly if he uses this means of letting him express such individuality.

A little help in the form of suggestions can be given to the Infant, e.g. Could you draw a few hens here? Some trees would look interesting in this space. Are you going to give that lady a striped dress? Are you going to give those ducks bright yellow beaks?

A Junior, especially an older Junior, becomes more critical of his own work and sometimes says, 'I can't draw it', or 'This does not look right.' This is when the teacher can help the child through suggestions and by training him to observe things, e.g. if the child thinks his house is not correct, take him outside to look at a building, at the windows and doors, and then go back and try again. If he cannot draw a person sitting, ask one of the other children to sit in front of the class for a few minutes, and ask the child to notice how the legs bend and how the arms are placed. Then the child can try again.

Encourage all the children to use their eyes as they go through the town, and to notice the different shapes of houses, trees, flowers, cars, people, animals, and so on. Help them to notice that things which are near us look bigger than things which are further away. Help each child to look at his picture as a whole, and to notice if it is all connected and is making a pleasing whole. Encourage the child to cover all the paper, so that none of the newspaper (or white paper) shows. **All the paper should have been used to make the finished picture.**

Let the children sometimes hold up their pictures, while the rest of the class talk about them. Children can be quite hard and sometimes unkind about each other's pictures, so the teacher should always try to find something to praise in each one, e.g. 'Udoh has used some very bright colours. Ali has made his hills small and they seem far away. Good. Mary's tree is a very interesting shape. I like the way Aina has put bright colours against dark colours, so they both show up well. That is a fine pattern Chinua has put on the lady's dress.' Decorate the classroom after each lesson by hanging the best pictures on the wall.

On the whole Juniors are fairly content with their pictures. **Always help and encourage them.** Never say anything is wrong, because art depends on individual taste, and pictures which some adults like and pay for, may look uninteresting to other people. What may seem bad painting to one person, may seem good to another. Discuss the children's pictures and make suggestions, but always encourage, never condemn. None of the children may grow up to be a famous artist, but all of them should grow up at least to enjoy painting and looking at pictures.

Choosing a Subject
The children must be given an interesting subject. A chair, a tree, a sheep, etc., are all uninteresting to a child. If the teacher wishes to include these objects choose a much larger subject, e.g.

The parlour with father entertaining his friends. (A chair will be included in this.)

The compound with the children playing. (A tree will probably be included here.)

A farm with the farmer and his animals. (A sheep can be included here.)

All these subjects require thought and will take some time to finish. It is not a good picture if the child is finished in a couple of minutes, as he generally is when asked to draw something simple like a chair.

Other Suitable Subjects

1. A street in the town showing houses, cars, bicycles and people.
2. The market with all the shoppers and stalls.
3. People carrying their loads to market.
4. Mother sewing and the children playing around her.
5. Labourers cutting down a tree.
6. The farmer and his family picking the cocoa.
7. Fishing by the river.
8. Any story can be illustrated.
9. Some part of the town which the children know well.
10. Often let each child draw anything he likes.

Lesson Pattern for an Art Lesson

Objective: Draw a picture of the school with the teacher ringing the bell and some of the children running across the compound.

Apparatus: Brushes, dyes, tins, water, newspaper.

Lesson procedure:

(Before the lesson, the monitors will give out the papers, the brushes, the dyes in tins and water in tins for washing the brushes.)

1. Discuss the subject with the children through questioning, e.g.

How many doors are there in our school?

How many windows can you see as you come to school?

What colour are the walls?

What is the roof made of?

What can you see in the compound? (Trees, flowers, a well, etc.)

Where does the teacher stand when he rings the bell?

What do the children do when they hear the bell?

2. Take the children outside to refresh their memories of the outside of the school and the compound.

3. Ask the children to shut their eyes and think of the school and compound. 'In a few minutes I want you to draw a picture of the school. Now shut your eyes and see the picture of the school in your minds. Can you see the yellow walls, the grey roof? Can you see our blue-painted

doors and shutters? Keep your eyes shut and see in your mind a picture of a teacher ringing the bell. What is he wearing? Some children come running across the compound. How many are there? Are they boys or girls? What are they wearing? Can you see in your mind the palm trees at the side of the compound, and the mango tree on the other side? When you are quite sure of your picture you may start painting.'

4. Children paint while the teacher goes round to give individual suggestions when necessary, and to see that the children are treating their materials properly.

5. The children wash their brushes and the pictures are put in a safe place to dry. Monitors are chosen to collect the tins and brushes. The teacher chooses the best pictures to hang on the wall, and tells the children why he likes them.

Points to Notice about the Lesson

This is a simple lesson pattern, yet effective. All the children are busy and should have plenty to do; they have to think and use their memories. The teacher guided them before they started. Of course, the children cannot always be taken to see subjects, and then they have to use more imagination.

If some are very quick and have really done their best, they can be given another paper, and asked to draw anything they wish.

Patterns

For a child of any age, patterns form a useful exercise, as they can be simple for a small child, and more complicated for an older child. They teach the child about shape, design and colour, all of which are necessary in both art and craft.

A pattern can be likened to a dance, with rhythm and movement which is repeated over and over again. Young children will do very 'free' patterns. Later more guidance can be given.

Colours: Always let the child choose his own colours. Help him to use colours which look interesting together. Let him experiment with colours and mix his own. Red and yellow make orange; red and blue make purple; blue and yellow make green; red, blue and yellow make brown. Different shades can be obtained by using more of one colour and less of another. Help the child to see that two dark colours together do not show up as clearly as a dark one and a light one side by side.

Lesson Suggestions

Here is a simple series of formal patterns. Either paints, dyes, crayons or chalks can be used on newspaper or plain paper. The children must be taught how to fold the paper carefully.

1. Two colours are used, and the aim is to give the children practice in using the brush or chalks.
Encourage them to put the paint evenly on the paper by using straight even strokes from side to side.

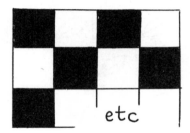

2. Diagonal lines and two colours.

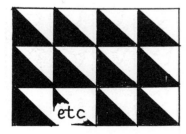

3. A and B diagonal lines and two colours.

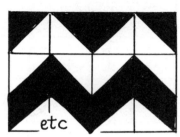

4. Pattern using the letter shape and two colours. The letter is in one colour and the area around it is another.

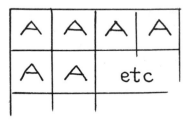

5. Pattern using a figure shape and three colours. The figure is painted thickly in one colour and the spaces on either side in different colours.

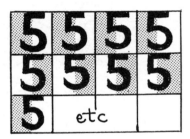

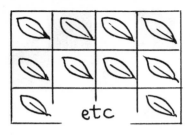

6. Pattern using shapes, e.g. leaves, flowers, houses, trees, jars.

Also paint a leaf. Press it on the paper. Paint it again. Press it on the paper again.

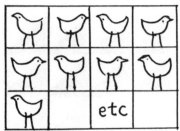

7. A and B pattern using shapes as in No. 6, but the B pattern faces a different way from the A pattern.

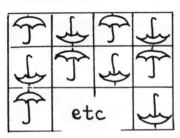

8. A and B pattern with the B pattern upside down. The second and fourth lines start with the B pattern.

9. The children should now have a fairly good idea of simple patterns and can be allowed to design their own. Ask them to think of a pattern which could be used on cloth to make a dress or curtains, or a pattern for the cover of a book. If the pattern is good let them cover a book to make it attractive.

Other Patterns

Patterns can be made in clay using sticks to draw shapes, or leaves and seeds can be stuck in the clay.

Writing Patterns

These give the children practice in continuous arm movement, which is necessary for good joined writing in the Junior classes. They can be drawn in paint or chalk in the art lesson on clay and in sand. They can also be drawn with pencil in the writing books as an introduction to a writing lesson.

Yam Patterns or any hard root or stem

A yam is cut into pieces about two inches thick. A piece of yam is cut with a knife from one of the flat edges (or if the children are small, and might cut themselves, it is better to scratch a deep mark with a stick). The paper is folded carefully. Paint or dye is put on the yam with a brush and the design is pressed on the paper.

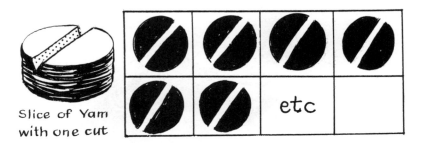

Slice of Yam
with one cut

The yam must be re-painted for each print, or the colour will not be even. Be careful not to use too much paint, or the print will smudge. The same colour should be used all the time, though, if another design is made, another colour can be used. As the children have experience of these patterns they can make more than one cut in the yam to make complicated patterns. Tell the children to cut a small mark in the side of the yam, so that they will know which is the top of their design. Then they can always place it correctly on the paper.

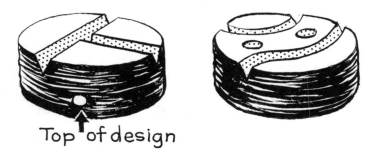

Top of design

Paste and Comb Patterns
Mix dye with thick paste. Give each child a cardboard comb.

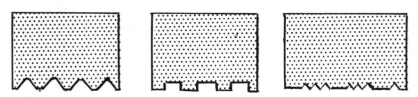

The child will paint the paste on to the paper with long straight brush strokes, moving the brush from left to right. Then with the comb he will make patterns in the coloured paste.

Matchbox and String Patterns
A piece of string (or button, leaf, cloth etc) is stuck on a matchbox, and left to dry thoroughly. The design is then printed on paper in much the same way as the yam pattern.

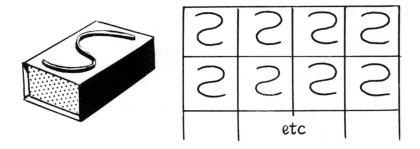

etc

Cut or Torn Patterns

Fold a square or circular piece of paper into eighths. Tear or cut out shapes. Open out and use paint or crayon to decorate it.

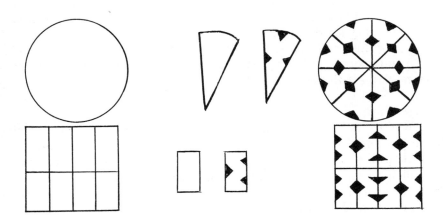

Use of Patterns

Whenever possible use the patterns which the children have made as covers for books, as mats on which to stand jars of flowers or to decorate the classroom with a border of patterns.

Paper Tearing

Newspaper can be torn into a number of interesting shapes, such as trees, flowers, houses, people, cars, etc. Each child can arrange the shapes into a picture on his desk, or big shapes can be torn, painted and then stuck on a long piece of paper to make a class frieze. Train the children to tear as neatly as possible. It is good for children to learn how to use scissors and to cut out with them, but it is often difficult to collect enough pairs for all the children, and tearing is the next best thing.

Clay Modelling

The clay should not be too wet. Show the children how to use their fingers and especially their thumbs to help them model. Suitable subjects for small children are oranges, bananas, paw-paws, cocoa pods, yams, beans, plates, bowls, cups, jugs, etc. The models can be used in the class shop when they are dry. Older children can work in groups to make little scenes, e.g. hills and valleys with streams running through, houses and compounds, streets, markets, churches with the people walking to the service, farms with the crops and animals.

Papier Mâché

If a newspaper is torn up into small pieces and soaked in a bucket of water for a few weeks, it becomes very soft. The water is squeezed out and the papier mâché (mashed-up paper) is mixed with paste. This grey modelling material can be used much in the same way as clay. When the models are dry they can be painted. Fruit and vegetables can be made for the class shop. Things made of papier mâché are very light and do not break if they are dropped.

Local Crafts

Any of the simpler local crafts make good, interesting lessons. **Teachers should try to encourage an interest and pride in local crafts, many of which produce things which are most beautiful,** but fewer young men and women are now willing to spend the time to learn them, probably because cheap factory-made articles are replacing locally produced goods. Unfortunately, such cheap goods are often ugly.

A lesson pattern for a craft lesson or a lesson where a demonstration is needed.

Objective: Model jugs out of clay.

Apparatus: Clay, a bucket of water, big leaves, newspaper.

Procedure: During recess, the monitors help the teacher to divide the clay so that each child will get a fairly big lump. The clay is wrapped in the leaves and put on the desks. If the lesson is taken outside each child can carry out his own clay in the leaf. If the lesson is to be taken inside, the desks must all be covered with newspaper.

1. The teacher shows the children the finished article. 'We are going to make a jug like this today. You made some good bowls last week, but a jug is a little more difficult, so I want you all to listen carefully while I show you how to make it.'

2. The teacher's demonstration. 'Who can remember how we prepare the clay? Uwa. Good, we beat it and knead it until all of it is smooth. If it is too dry we can get a little water from the' bucket, but be careful not to make it **too** wet.' The teacher continues in this way, questioning and reminding the children of what they already know about modelling. They must especially be shown how to fix on the handle. It must be well worked into the main part of the jug, or it will fall off when the clay is dry.

3. The children make their jugs while the teacher goes round helping and giving suggestions.

4. Any quick children can scratch a pattern with a stick on the jug, and then fetch more clay to make anything they like.

5. The jugs are put somewhere safe to dry, and the children help to clear the room. Some monitors will collect any clay which is left, others will collect the leaves and newspapers. All the children will take turns to wash their hands, and then each child should see that his own desk is clean. Children who have tidied up should read a book quietly, while the teacher and the monitors finish their jobs.

Points about the Lesson

1. The teacher shows the finished article. It is important that the children know what they are trying to make.

2. The teacher gives a clear demonstration. He must make sure that all the children can see.

3. The quick children are given some extra work, so they do not waste their time.

4. Some of the children are given jobs of responsibility, but all the class must help to clear up.

Chapter 27 Hygiene and Health Education

A number of books giving detailed information on this subject are on the market, so I only mention a few principles and aims which the teacher should keep in mind.

Hygiene leads to health, and we, as teachers, should aim to help the children to lead healthy lives. Hygiene, therefore, is a very important part of our lives and should not only be confined to one or two lessons each week, but should be taught at any suitable time when the need arises. Two important points to remember when considering hygiene training are:

1. The hygiene lessons and all health education should be as practical as possible, with the teacher helping the children to obey the rules of hygiene at all times of the day.

2. All the staff in the school should be very good examples of healthy living, not only while they are working, but also at home. **The children will soon find out if the teacher at home does not 'practise what he preaches' at school.**

In the classroom, every day, the teacher has many opportunities to teach hygiene. During the daily sweeping and dusting of the room, he can help the children to realize how necessary it is to keep the place clean. It is quite a good idea to have weekly monitors who are responsible for keeping the classroom clean and tidy. The teacher will have to supervise and help the children, but it is important that these monitors are thanked.

'Mary, Uwa, Udoh and Chume have kept our classroom very clean and tidy this week. We should all be very grateful to them, because, as you know, germs, which give us sickness, love to live in dirt; but no germs have found a home in our room this week. I have also noticed that the whole class has been helping the monitors by putting rubbish in the wastepaper basket, and no one has thrown anything on the floor. Now we shall see if the monitors for next week can be just as good, and we shall all try to help them by being very tidy.'

In this way the teacher helps the children to realize that the hygiene of the class is the concern of everyone in it. It is easier to be interested in keeping the room clean if it is attractive, so pin the best paintings, the best pieces of writing, the best compositions on the walls and have flowers wherever possible to improve the appearance of the room. Remember to change the paintings and writing at least every fortnight.

To keep the compound tidy the whole school must play its part. Perhaps one class each week can be responsible for sweeping the paths and generally keeping the compound clean. Special baskets or tins need to be provided for collecting rubbish.

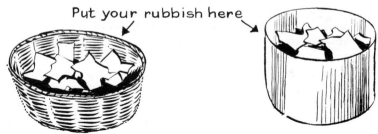

Put your rubbish here

Again it is easier to be interested in keeping a place tidy if it is attractive, so here hygiene can be linked to gardening and the growing of flowers. All the children should be encouraged to feel a pride in their school, and help to keep it in order, so that people passing by will stop to admire their efforts. Through this type of practical work the children learn to appreciate beautiful things, and also to realize that disease germs live and increase in dirt; that flies and other insects which carry disease live and feed in dirt; and that mosquitoes love bits of rubbish or old tins which hold water where they can lay their eggs. By keeping the classrooms and the compound clean, the children have a much better chance of living healthy lives.

The correct use of the latrines is a very important part of hygiene. Careful early training to help the children to form good habits is necessary.

In the first class the teacher should have time, at least once a day, to go to the latrines and urinals with the children to see that they obey the rules they have been taught. It is essential that lids are put on the latrines to prevent flies spreading disease, and that every child washes his hands after using the latrine, but little children often forget and need a great deal of patient reminding. Remember that it is always easier for children to remember rules if they are given reasons for doing so, but do not give small children long explanations. Keep all hygiene teaching as simple and practical as possible.

In the second and third classes it will not be necessary for the teacher to look at the latrines so often, but it will probably still be advisable to supervise their use once a week, as well as giving further training in how to disinfect and clean latrines. Even older children forget these lessons and need reminding and further teaching.

In the classroom a great deal can be done to help the children to keep themselves and their clothes clean. A short daily inspection is useful in the first two classes, and a weekly inspection with the older children.

At these times it is better to pick out good points and praise them, than to criticize bad things. 'Laide has on a lovely clean dress. You do look pretty, Laide. Musa looks very smart today. All the buttons on his shirt have been carefully sewn on, and his shirt is clean. Etim's finger and toe nails are clean and short. Good. He will not carry about any dirt.'

In this way, by spending only a few minutes each day on hygiene, the teacher can encourage the children to be clean and tidy. Remember to praise even a small improvement in a child, as this will lead to greater efforts. This praise will do far more good than grumbling at dirty, untidy children. With small children it is important to remember that frequently it is the fault of the parents if a child comes to school in a dirty condition. A teacher must **never** make a child ashamed of his family, even if they do seem to be rather dirty. Parents can be given advice through the Parent-Teacher Association, where they should be told that cleanliness helps to prevent disease.

It is also necessary through the parents to try to ensure that each child has sufficient sleep in a well-ventilated room, and that he is given a balanced diet. Small children can be told simply about the foods which help to make them grow strong, while older children can be taught in more detail about diet. Where it is provided, the school meal should be prepared under clean conditions, and should be supervised by the headteacher in order that it is made as nourishing as possible. Sleep and diet are most important for fighting disease, and, therefore, lead to healthy living and should be dealt with in the hygiene or health education lessons.

Often it is the incidental teaching of hygiene which makes it seem necessary and sensible to a child. It is rather a waste of time to give a lesson to small children on germs and how they spread. Instead, when a child comes to school with a bad cold, and coughs and sneezes all over the class, explain how the germs will spread and give other children colds too. Explain that he can prevent this happening if he uses a handkerchief and catches the germs. A clean rag is just as good as a bought handkerchief, and every child should be able to get a clean rag. The short time spent teaching this at a time when all the children are interested, because no one wants to catch a cold, will do far more good than a long lesson when no one has a cold and none of the children sees much reason for listening.

Small children cannot remember very well what happened during the last rainy season, nor can they really imagine ahead to the next cold season. Do plan your lessons to fit the needs of the children at a time when they can see the sense of your teaching.

Following a short explanation such as this, the next hygiene lesson could be used to revise the need to prevent the spread of germs, and, depending on the age of the children, some discussion might follow on infectious diseases. The teacher can tell the children how important it is for sick and ill people to stay at home and keep warm, firstly to prevent the spread of the disease, and secondly to save the sick person from getting worse, which is what happens when illness is neglected.

Another lesson could be given by visiting the local hospital or dispensary, where a doctor or nurse can explain to the children about the benefits they will receive if they ask for help before an illness gets too bad. It should also be pointed out to children how unwise it is to buy medicines in the market. Some of them can be very dangerous, and it is far safer to pay a visit to the hospital.

The children should also be told about the need for vaccination against smallpox, as a preventative against that disease. The teacher may be able to arrange with the hospital for those who need it to be vaccinated, as it could be too late if the children wait until an epidemic starts. From one child with a cold a very interesting series of practical lessons can be taken. No matter what is on the syllabus, if the children need this kind of knowledge give it to them. Remember the syllabus can be changed to fit the needs of the children.

Hygiene will be very closely connected with physical education, and the children should be encouraged to remove their top clothes or change into special clothes for their P.E. lesson. This will not only make their movements freer, but will also prevent perspiration making their clothes smelly and dirty. After the lesson they should wash before going back to the classroom.

A good water supply is very necessary if hygiene is to be taught properly, and the teachers should do all they can to have a good well dug, or to get a pipe from the town water supply laid in the school compound. Obviously, it is not much good telling children they should wash their hands before eating, and after going to the latrine to prevent carrying disease, unless the children have water with which to wash. Even if some school time must be spent in carrying water, it is time well spent, because there is little sense in teaching children to read and write if they are going to be very sick, or even die young, because they have not obeyed the laws of hygiene and health.

Note well: Drinking water must be boiled, and allowed to cool, unless it comes from a safe piped water supply.

When a definite hygiene lesson must be taken, the teacher of small children should read the facts for himself in a good textbook, then make up a simple story using these facts. Often it is a good idea to have two families in the story; one which obeys the rules of hygiene and one which does not. The children will be very interested to notice the difference between the families; the sensible one which is happy and healthy and the other which suffers because the people in it will not bother to obey the laws of hygiene. With small children, however, give the story a happy ending by showing how the unwise family learn to correct their mistakes and copy the good family. The story can be followed by practical work or dramatization. More formal lessons can be taken with older children to give them further reasons for observing the laws of hygiene and health; but still try to be as practical as possible.

It will be seen from these suggestions that hygiene teaching is very closely linked with social and good citizen training. The teacher should help the children to realize that hygiene is not only very necessary if they are to lead healthy lives, but it is also essential for them as good citizens to obey the rules of hygiene in order that they do not spread disease and hurt their neighbours. Hygiene is one of the most important lessons the children have to learn, but let me stress, it should not be restricted to just one or two periods on the timetable, but should be taught as a way of living, of healthy living, when necessary every day and at any time of the day.

Chapter 28   Science

In many schools Science has replaced Nature Study on the timetable. This means that the subject has been enlarged, but still includes the study of the natural things to be found in the school environment. Science should train children to be observant, and help them to answer their own questions. **How** did this happen? **Why** does this happen? **What** will happen **if** certain conditions are changed? It is better if the teacher does not give the children the answers. Do not try to teach facts. Instead try to teach a way of careful observation, of experimentation.

Remember that an educated adult does not believe everything he sees and hears. He asks questions and tries to **understand** what he sees and hears. In the Science lesson we try to develop this attitude.

1. Listen and look. (Keep notes, make graphs, charts, drawings, etc.)
2. Ask questions.
3. Try to find the **true** answer. (Set up experiments, reason things out carefully, study the observation notes and drawings, observe in other places, ask more questions, think carefully about the answer and decide if it is the best answer possible, considering all the facts which have been discovered.)

Often the answer will not be perfect, but the child will have **thought it out himself.** He will need help from the teacher, but he will have done much, **much** more than just listen to the teacher talk. (Remember that often scientists do not know the correct answer to questions. New facts about the world are continually being discovered, and what may seem true today may be only **partly** true, because all the facts have not yet been found.) Teaching facts has limited value. But teaching an **attitude** to learning and study, a **method** of observing and thinking, an **appreciation** of each man's need to understand for himself – these things will be useful all through a child's life.

Much of the Science taken with younger children is connected with the natural world around us. It is such a big subject, I can only give you a few suggestions to help you prepare your lessons, but for more detail read books written for Science lessons.

A child has a wonder and an appreciation of natural things, an appreciation which is often lost by adults, who become too interested in man-made articles and machines. This is a great pity and should never happen to a truly educated person, who realizes that we rely on Nature for our lives, for our food (seeds growing in the soil, animals for meat), for water (from clouds blown over our country by the wind), for our clothes (seeds growing into cotton, cattle giving us leather, sheep giving us wool), for our homes (clay bricks from the earth, wood from the trees and iron from under the ground); all we have, even our most complicated machines, come in the first place from the world of Nature.

If a man does not honour our world and treat it well he will suffer. For example, in some parts of the world people have used the soil so badly that it will no longer grow good crops, and the land is practically a desert inhabited by very poor families; in other places hunters have been greedy, killing too many female and young animals at all times of the year, so now the forests are practically empty and the people are short of meat, while in other places people have used the rivers badly and now there are no fish left in them to catch. The teacher will be able to find more examples where man has misused the world's resources, and he or his children have suffered for it. In a civilized community we must learn to understand and work with Nature, if we are to make the best use of our world. Even creatures which may seem useless to us may feed a useful animal or make the soil rich for the crops; so the dead leaves and the humble worm help to fertilize the soil; the white ant helps to feed the hen which gives us nourishing eggs; the bee pollinates the flowers to make the seeds fertile, and birds catch harmful insects or help to disperse seeds.

A teacher who has never thought about the marvels of our world himself will not be able to teach well, so he should go out into the compound or bush, and quietly observe the busy, well-planned environment. Notice how one small seed planted in the soil can grow into a plant and produce brightly coloured flowers, while another will grow in time into a tree under which many people will sit. Watch a trail of ants carrying food to the ant hill, and see how they communicate with each other as they pass, and how they care for their eggs and larvae. We sometimes think ants are a nuisance, but we cannot but admire and learn a lesson from their wonderful planning and hard work. Sit still and watch the different birds; the males with their beautiful plumage dancing to the females; the parents collecting food for their hungry youngsters. In the farm watch the goats and sheep with their young. If they are well-fed and treated properly they will grow fat and strong, to give the farmer and his family good meat when they need it. Observations such as these will give the teacher knowledge which he can share with his class.

The teacher will give the children as many opportunities as possible to observe and appreciate the world around them. Every class should have a Nature table, and the children should be encouraged to collect specimens to show to the class, e.g. flowers, leaves, stones, various kinds of soil, fruits and other seeds, roots and twigs, but **never** a living nor a dead creature.

Children do not know how to catch the creatures without hurting or frightening them, and as we are training these children to behave in a civilized manner we must never allow a weak creature to be hurt or frightened. Young children gradually learn about death, but they often find it very difficult to understand, and though they probably will say nothing, they will find it rather worrying to see dead creatures, even if they have been killed in a civilized manner. Do not, therefore, have them on the Nature table.

If the children are encouraged they will soon bring along many interesting leaves, flowers and seeds, etc. The children can say where they found the specimen, the teacher can ask questions and then add to the children's knowledge. It is no disgrace if the teacher does not know the name of a specimen; but he must be ready to find out as soon as possible. Just say something like this to the children, 'This is a most interesting seed which Yakubu has found. I don't know its name, but I shall lend Yakubu my science book, and together we shall try to find out about it. Where did you find it, Yakubu, because it will help us to know if it grows by a river, on flat land or on a hill? Could you bring some of the leaves from the tree tomorrow?' A teacher cannot be expected to know everything, but he is expected to be able to find out about things in which his class is interested. This is one reason why good teachers' textbooks are necessary. The head-teacher should keep a number of good reference books to help the staff find information. Older children, of course, will be able to read the books for themselves, but younger children will need more help.

The teacher should make labels for all the specimens, as this helps the children's reading as well as their Nature study. A simple way to make a label is to fold in half a piece of cardboard measuring about 8 cm by 12 cm, and print on it the name of the specimen.

Monitors need to be chosen to keep the table tidy and dusted. If possible keep some growing seeds, maize or beans, in a glass jar. Put the seeds between the glass and the soil so the children can see how the shoots and roots grow. Each day the children can measure the growth, as this will

243

help their Maths as well as their Science study. Pick some buds so that the children can watch the flowers unfold.

If the lesson is about animals or birds take the children out into the compound, farm or bush where they can see the living creatures. They will learn a great deal, by observation and careful questioning by the teacher, about how these creatures live, what they eat, how they walk or fly and perhaps even where the home is made. The teacher may have one particular creature he wants to show the children, but he should also be able to point out many other creatures, flowers, trees, birds, etc., which may be seen on any walk.

Sometimes a teacher may take insects or other small creatures into the classroom, but he should **never** take a four-legged animal, or a bird. The insect should be caught very carefully in a net and then placed in a clean glass jar.

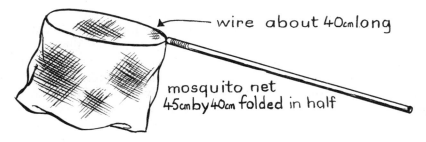

The jar must be as big as possible and quite dry, for water will hurt the insect's wings. Put in the jar a few leaves or flowers, which the insect likes, so that the children can watch it feed, and cover with paper in which small holes have been pierced, as the creature must be able to breathe. If the creature comes from the earth, e.g. a worm or an ant, put a little soil in the jar.

The children will observe the creature in small groups, so for a class of forty children six or seven examples will be needed. Help the children to observe the creature by carefully questioning them about what they can see. As soon as the lesson is over the creatures must be set free in the kind of soil or bush where they were found. The children should see the teacher do this and he should explain that as they have helped us to learn something, now we must treat these weaker creatures with consideration and set them free.

A class diary is useful for encouraging the children to be observant, and also helps their reading. Anything interesting which a child has seen can be written on a large calendar. At first the teacher can write the sentence, and the child can draw a picture, but as soon as possible the children will be encouraged to do their own writing (in the vernacular of course).

	70 cm			
OCTOBER				
1 Today Mary saw a wagtail	2 John brought an hibiscus flower to school	3	4	5
8	9	10	11	12
15	16	17	18	19

Older children can keep their own diaries.

A weather chart of some kind is also useful, as it helps the children to take an interest in the weather and to see how the climate affects the growth of plants and how animals behave in the different seasons. A record of the weather can be kept in the same way as the Nature calendar, but for small children probably a few pictures representing the main types of weather

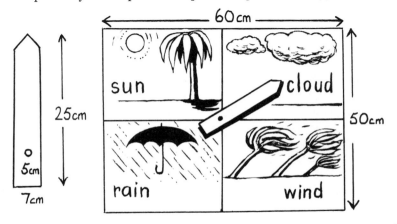

will be most useful. Each day the children can move the arrow to point to the kind of weather they are having that day.

In the higher primary classes a weather cock, to show the direction of the wind, should be made and observed. A thermometer should be hung in the classroom and a record kept of the temperature.

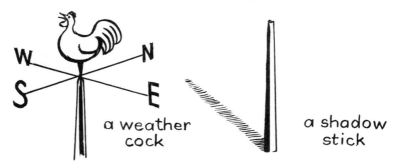

a weather cock

a shadow stick

If a stick about 1·5 m long is put in the compound the children can learn, by watching the shadows, about the movement of the earth in relation to the sun. Measuring the shadows at different times of the day will also help the children's Maths.

As with Hygiene, Science should not be confined to only one or two periods each week. Some discussion should be taken each day about what is happening to the weather, the animals or the plants. Gardening and Science should be closely linked. Help the children to take a real interest in the world, and lead them to appreciate it and to treat it with respect.

Index